GINO'S ITALY

Like Mamma Used to Make

GINO'S ITALY

Like Mamma Used to Make

PHOTOGRAPHY BY HAARALA HAMILTON

BLOOMSBURY PUBLISHING

LONDON · OXFORD · NEW YORK · NEW DELHI · SYDNEY

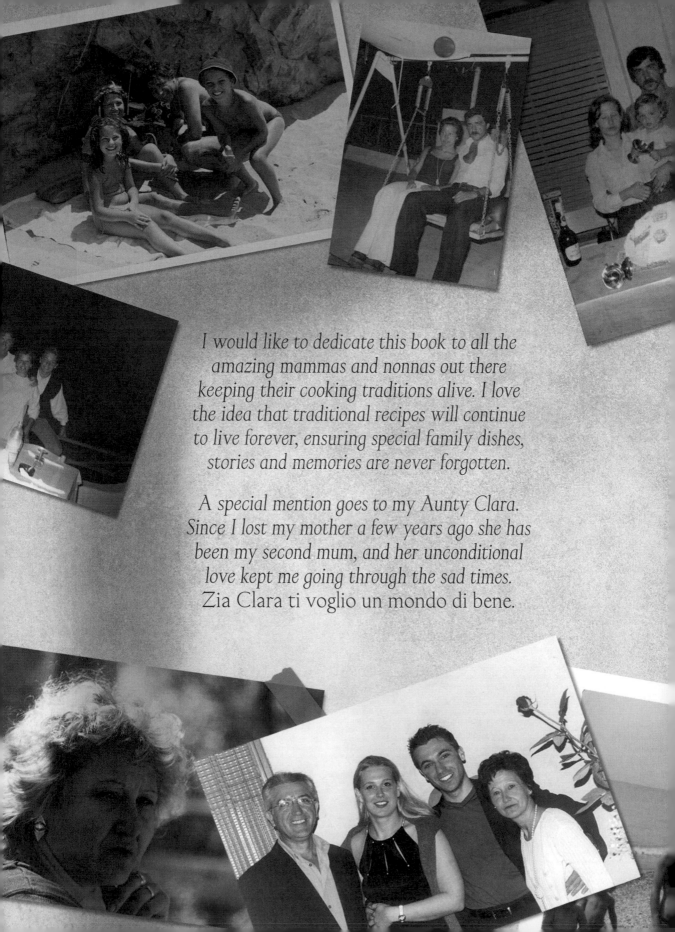

I would like to dedicate this book to all the amazing mammas and nonnas out there keeping their cooking traditions alive. I love the idea that traditional recipes will continue to live forever, ensuring special family dishes, stories and memories are never forgotten.

A special mention goes to my Aunty Clara. Since I lost my mother a few years ago she has been my second mum, and her unconditional love kept me going through the sad times. Zia Clara ti voglio un mondo di bene.

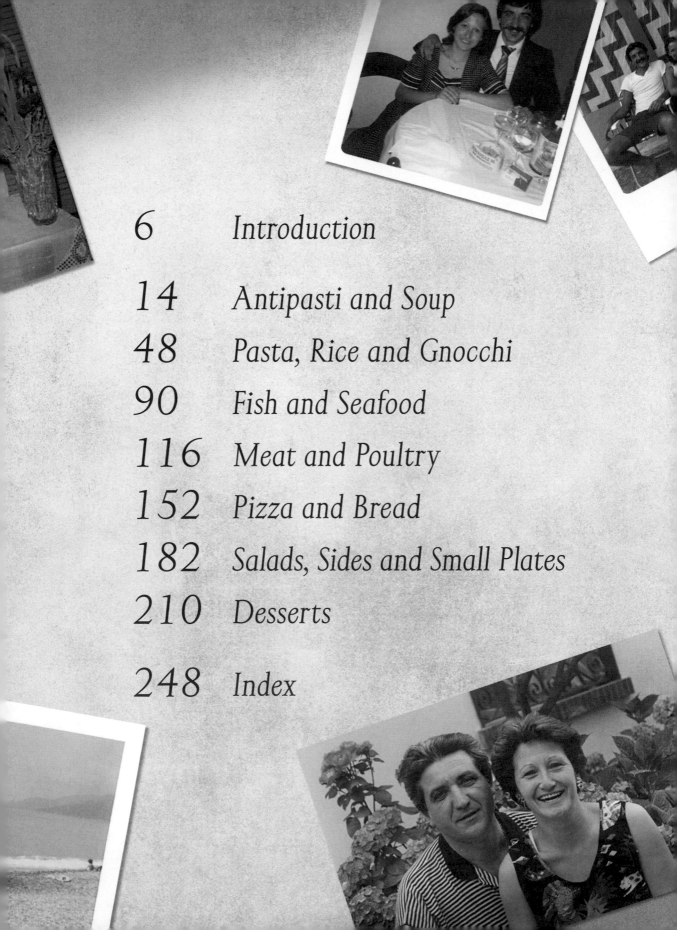

Like Mamma Used to Make

Celebrating All the Amazing Women

I've always been surrounded by lots of very strong women. My grandmother had nine daughters – and one son – so growing up, our house was always full of women! I owe so much to their influence. Between them and my grandmothers, they taught me all about food and cooking, and also about life.

I want this book to be a way of celebrating the amazing women in my family, and in all our families. Through the recipes I have learned from them, alongside my own recipes, and those shared with me by the wonderful families I've been fortunate to meet around Italy, I want to show my love and appreciation for everything they have done for me. But most of all, this book is to honour my incredible mamma, who I miss every day.

In Italian families, it may look from the outside as though the man is at the head of the household, but any man who believes that is an idiot. Everyone knows it is the women who run the show. They are the bosses. And at the head of our family is my Aunty Clara.

Aunty Clara is now 87 and is as formidable as ever. We call her the Godmother. But she is no Fairy Godmother, she is our very own Don Corleone. In fact, I think Don Corleone would actually be scared to speak to Aunty Clara! If there are big family decisions to be made or issues that need discussing, you will be sent to Aunty Clara for advice or for her approval. She is an amazing woman who has lived a truly exceptional life, and has had a huge impact on me since I was a child. Aunty Clara has been like a second mum to me, and since sadly losing my own mum a few years ago, she is my mum. She has shown me what it means to live with honesty, integrity and respect, and how you can have a good life, whether you have £1 in your pocket or £1,000. Aunty Clara is resourceful, tough, and, to her, family always comes first.

Watching the women in my family and how they do things, I realised early on that it should be women running the world. I am not joking! The quicker men realise this, the better for the world and for everyone in it.

Food from the Heart

I owe my lifelong obsession with food to the women in my family. When I think back to my childhood, I remember seeing my aunties, grandmothers and my mum cooking in the kitchen together. Watching how they made the recipes their own, how they worked with the ingredients available to them to put their own spin on dishes and produce something truly delicious – and the joy it brought to those who ate it – is what sparked my own career in food. I have a lot to thank them for.

It may sound old-fashioned but, until quite recently, in Italian families the kitchen was the women's domain. Men never really got involved in cooking. My dad couldn't even fry an egg, and neither could any of my uncles. It wasn't that they necessarily didn't want to get involved, they simply weren't allowed in the kitchen!

Even my grandfather, who was a professional chef, rarely set foot in the kitchen at home, and only then if my grandmother gave him permission. You could have all the Michelin stars in the world, but if you want to enter the kitchen in an Italian home, you need to ask the woman of the house first.

The only thing I ever remember my father doing when it came to cooking was grating cheese. My mum would buy huge blocks of Parmesan and dad would sit in the corner of the kitchen, grating away. It suited him fine. He was very happy to take a back seat and be the cheese-grater of the family while mum cooked for us.

My mum was the youngest of her sisters and she went to work as a nurse, whereas her sisters stayed in the home. Like any working parent knows, it can be tough balancing feeding your family with working life, so her approach to cooking in those early years was definitely more on the practical side. I remember when she turned 50, though, her attitude completely changed and she would go into the kitchen to relax, to sing, to discover new flavours.

But even though she maybe didn't love cooking as much when she was younger, she still made sure we all ate well and had proper home-cooked meals. She would also make an amazing vanilla breakfast cake, and, even now, the smell of it baking takes me right back to those days. Now you can try it yourself, as the recipe is in this book.

I truly believe that cooking is a way of showing your love for other people, and that sometimes it can be the only way. If you have a busy family, or a very large family, you can have a cuddle or a quick chat, but the ultimate way to show that you care is through the stomach! Italian families place a lot of importance on food, and I'm sure this is one of the main reasons.

For example, I love making steak Florentine-style, another recipe you'll find here, purely because I know how much my son Luciano loves it. I enjoy eating it too, and so does the rest of the family, but really, inside my heart I am making it for him to remind him that I love him. And there is nothing better for me than seeing the expression on people's faces when I know they are really enjoying something I have made for them.

Sharing the Family Secrets

People have this idea that in every Italian family there are these secret recipes that get passed down the generations, often for centuries. And it's 100 per cent true! For us, it's just a normal everyday thing that we do without even thinking about it. When I was a boy, my mum used to cook loads of great recipes that we all loved eating. They were packed with flavour and, as we got older, we wanted to recreate that flavour for ourselves. You naturally want to share that experience with your partner, or your children, or your friends.

I remember going to my mum and saying, 'I need to learn how to make spaghetti with crab exactly the way you do it because, for the rest of my life, I want to be able to cook it for myself.' And then, not long ago, my son Rocco came to me and said, 'Dad, please teach me how to make spaghetti with crab, so when I go to a friend's house, I can cook it there.' It was only afterwards that I realised that same recipe has now passed down through four generations: from my grandmother to my mother, to me and now to my son. And it has happened entirely organically. You can learn it as well, from this book.

There are so many other recipes I want to share with my children too: the way I do my carbonara, my cheesy leek and sausage baked risotto, my roast lamb stuffed with rosemary and mushrooms, or my Nutella calzone. These are the recipes which I love, and which I know my children love to eat, and they're all in these pages. My daughter Mia is only ten, but has been helping me to make authentic Neapolitan pizza for years!

Sharing recipes is also a way of passing something precious along to the next generation. Italians are very passionate about food, and if we don't have diamonds or gold, then our legacy can carry on through the recipes we make and the food we eat. We all want to be remembered when we die, and one way to do this is through a really unforgettable recipe. Even in conversation we might say, 'I made that beautiful chocolate cake that Aunty Anna used to make,' and that's how people can still feel part of your family after they are gone.

I feel this way when I'm cooking one of my mamma's recipes or an old family recipe. I enter the kitchen for two reasons: first, if I'm feeling creative and want to come up with something new, or second, when I've had a bad day and want to forget all about it. That's when I'll immerse myself in a comfort recipe. After a long day, the last thing I want to do is be creative; I need someone to give me a cuddle, and for me, that cuddle is a recipe from my mum. It reminds me of the flavours when she cooked it, of mum and dad, and everything that goes along with that. And all of a sudden, my day just got a whole lot better.

Crowded into the kitchen, I'd watch my aunties, grandmother and mum adding their own touches to a recipe, trying out this or that. Soon, a bit of competition would get going: who would make the best spaghetti with clams? Whose cake would people ask for on their birthday? I am grateful for that competitive streak, as it has vastly improved our family recipes! More than half the recipes I cook today don't belong to me: they belong to the women in my family. And I have a huge family. That's a lot of recipes honed and perfected over the years. I am just a vehicle to bring them to you, so you can share them with your families.

But there are, of course, some recipes that aren't for sharing. Aunty Clara is famous for her doughnuts made with potatoes, but has never revealed her recipe, not to her own daughter and definitely not to me. She wants to keep it for herself, and that's fair enough. It means that every year when she announces that she has made her special doughnuts, everyone visits and tells her how amazing they are and she enjoys all the glory!

What Makes the Best Family Recipes?

At the grand feast we held in honour of our Aunty Clara, I wanted to be shown again how to make some family classics, and also to share a few of my own recipes. Some of my dishes are updates on family recipes and it's part of the process to tweak them to make them our own. You know I love to put a Gino twist on things! It's just like my mum and aunties and grandmothers used to do.

Travelling around Italy for the TV series that goes with this book, I met some fantastic people and experienced incredible family recipes. Every region in Italy is like a different nation when it comes to its style of cooking, from the busy streets of Rome to Tuscan vineyards to the beautiful Bay of Naples, where I spent many summers as a boy. I can't thank all the families enough for welcoming me into their homes and teaching me their recipes.

The main lesson I learned was that the best family recipes are created when there's a little bit of everyone involved. It's to do with surroundings, people and ingredients all mixed together. Seeing people cook using seasonal local ingredients – often produced or prepared by members of their family – reminded me of my own childhood and my mum cooking the fish my dad and I had caught. It feels like a real collaboration and a true demonstration of love and appreciation for each other, where everyone's role matters. Even the person in the corner grating a big block of Parmesan cheese to sprinkle on at the end.

These are recipes from my family to yours, with some fantastic dishes I've learned along the way. I hope you enjoy them as much as we do and they quickly become your family recipes too.

ANTI PASTI

AND SOUP

1972-74

Grandparents are
everything

Antipasti in Italian cuisine is hugely important and is, to many, the best part of a meal. Antipasto, which is the singular form of antipasti, actually means 'before the meal' and is derived from the ancient Latin *ante* (before) and *pastus* (meal). The history of antipasto as a course is rooted in medieval Italy, when finger foods such as sliced meats or cheeses, or even sugared nuts, got diners in the mood for the traditional Italian meal to follow, which was normally pasta of some kind. Many poorer people would live off these antipasti dishes alone. In rural Italy years ago, every family had a pig which was killed each autumn, so different cuts of cured meat could be served all year round. The families would also make numerous jars of preserved seasonal vegetables and their own cheeses. I personally think there is something really magical about that way of living.

As with all food in Italy, antipasti options vary a lot between regions. Central Italy is known for rich sauces and punchy cheeses such as Gorgonzola. Southern Italy likes to serve fresh seasonal vegetables such as artichokes, and fish features a lot as well, such as anchovy fillets, or cold seafood platters like the grilled octopus and potato salad in this chapter. Northern Italy, closer to the Alps, offers slightly more substantial dishes such as tuna and bean salads or fried polenta. I like to combine them all and have a little bit of everything. Nowadays, the colours and flavours of antipasti are important considerations when pairing them with the meal that follows. I often have to tell my guests to slow down when tucking in, as antipasti dishes are only supposed to get your appetite going and prepare your taste buds for the main event... but often people just love the varied dishes offered and, when paired with a good glass of wine and some crusty bread, who could blame them? In fact, our family have a selection of antipasti for lunch during the summer pretty much every day. When you see antipasti on an Italian menu in the UK, it will normally mean starters or small plates. You can of course still get a selection, but many people just choose one antipasto and then go for a main course.

Over the years I have created many variations of antipasti, but in this book I'm sticking to the more traditional versions with maybe just a little twist here and there. The artichoke antipasto here was my nonna's recipe and the stuffed sardines, my mother's. The other recipes were taught to me along my journey to becoming a chef. I think my favourite in this chapter has to be the stuffed courgette flowers: a must-try and much easier to make than you might think.

SPICY FISH SOUP WITH TOMATOES + ORANGE ZEST

Zuppa di pesce piccante con pomodori e scorzetta di arance

SERVES 4

There are many variations of fish soup in the South of Italy, but this has to be my favourite because the flavour of the red mullet makes it unique. Ask your fishmonger to prepare the fish for you, but do rinse it under cold water when you come to make the dish and run your fingers along each chunk, as red mullet in particular does have a lot of bones. If you prefer, you can substitute the haddock with cod. Serve with my Focaccia with Rosemary + Sea Salt Flakes (see page 178).

4 tbsp olive oil
1 tsp chilli flakes
1 large red onion, *peeled and finely chopped*
200ml white wine
600ml hot fish stock
400g can of chopped tomatoes
16 large raw prawns, *completely peeled*
300g skinless red mullet fillet, *cut in 3cm chunks (see recipe introduction)*
300g skinless haddock fillet, *cut in 3cm chunks*
10 red cherry tomatoes, *halved*
4 tbsp chopped flat leaf parsley leaves
1 unwaxed orange
salt

Pour the oil into a medium-sized saucepan and place over a medium heat. Add the chilli flakes and the onion and fry for 6 minutes, stirring occasionally with a wooden spoon.

Increase the heat to high and pour in the wine, then bring to the boil and let it bubble for 2 minutes, allowing the alcohol to evaporate. Stir in the stock and canned tomatoes, season with 2 tsp salt and return to the boil once more. Reduce the heat to medium and simmer for 15 minutes, stirring occasionally.

Meanwhile, devein the prawns with the point of a knife, skewer or even a toothpick. The vein runs right along the back. Insert the point about 1cm down from the head of the prawn and pull it back up towards you. This will lift up the vein and you can pull it off with the knife or with your hand.

Add all the fish and the prawns to the saucepan, then stir very gently so you don't break up the fish. Bring to the boil, then reduce the heat and simmer for 10 minutes, stirring very gently after about 5 minutes.

Stir in the cherry tomatoes and parsley and continue to simmer for 1 minute.

Remove from the heat and divide equally between 4 warmed bowls. Grate orange zest over each bowl and serve immediately.

DEEP-FRIED COURGETTE FLOWERS FILLED WITH RICOTTA, LEMON ZEST + PARMESAN

Fiori di zucchine fritti ripieni di ricotta, scorzetta di limone e Parmigiano Reggiano

<u>SERVES 4</u>

This recipe is so pretty and a real wow for your guests and family. You can prep the courgette flowers beforehand, so you only need minutes to fry them when you're ready to serve. Courgette flowers are available from spring to summer, and they can vary in size. If yours are not large, you may need 10. If you prefer, you can substitute basil with parsley and Parmesan cheese with Grana Padano or pecorino. You will need a piping bag for this recipe, to fill the flowers.

8 large courgette
   flowers (*or see recipe introduction*)
1.5 litres vegetable oil

FOR THE FILLING
250g ricotta
30g fresh breadcrumbs
35g Parmesan cheese,
   finely grated
handful of basil leaves,
   finely chopped
finely grated zest
   and juice of 1 large
   unwaxed lemon
salt and freshly ground
   black pepper

FOR THE BATTER
3 eggs, *separated*
2 tsp lemon juice
3 tbsp plain flour

Place all the filling ingredients into a medium-sized bowl, mix well and season generously. Spoon the mixture into a piping bag.

Very carefully, open up the courgette flowers from the tips, remove the stamens in the centre and fill each with the ricotta mixture. Close the flowers by gently twisting the ends of the petals, sealing in the filling (see photos, overleaf). Gently place on a plate while you make the batter.

Pour the oil into a medium, deep saucepan and place over a high heat.

Beat the egg whites in a medium-sized bowl with the lemon juice and a pinch of salt until stiff.

In a separate medium-sized bowl, beat the egg yolks. Use a flexible spatula to fold the egg whites gently into the egg yolks. Sprinkle over the flour and again gently fold to combine.

Make sure the oil is hot (180–190°C) and that it remains at this temperature. If you don't have a thermometer, drop in a tiny bit of batter: if it puffs up and sizzles, the oil is ready. Carefully lift the courgette flowers by the stems and dip the flower heads into the batter, coating the whole thing. Place in the hot oil and fry for 3–4 minutes until golden brown. I would recommend only frying 3 at a time, so as not to crowd the pan. Turn them during frying, ensuring they are golden on all sides.

With the help of 2 forks, gently lift out the flowers and place on a flat tray lined with kitchen paper to allow any excess oil to drain. Repeat the process until all the flowers are fried.

Place 2 courgette flowers on each plate, sprinkle with a pinch of salt and serve immediately.

GRILLED ASPARAGUS WITH CRISPY PARMA HAM + POACHED EGG

Asparagi alla griglia con prosciutto crudo croccante e uova in camicia

SERVES 4

This recipe used to be one of my father's favourite dishes. Mainly because my mother did not really like asparagus and therefore she would never cook it for him. I've always enjoyed this dish as a starter and, if you prefer, you can substitute the asparagus with long-stemmed purple-sprouting broccoli. If you prepare the poached eggs in advance, dip them in ice-cold water so they stop cooking and retain their runny yolks, then simply warm them up briefly in boiling water before serving.

3 tbsp white wine
　vinegar
300g thin asparagus
　spears, *woody
　ends removed*
extra virgin olive oil
8 Parma ham slices
4 very fresh large eggs
salt and freshly ground
　black pepper

Preheat a large, ridged griddle pan over a high heat for 5 minutes.

Fill a medium-sized saucepan with 2.5 litres water and pour in the white wine vinegar, place over a medium-high heat and bring to the boil.

Meanwhile, put the asparagus spears on a flat plate and drizzle over 2 tbsp extra virgin olive oil. Sprinkle over ½ tsp salt and use your hands to coat the spears in the oil and salt. Set aside.

Place 4 Parma ham slices into the hot griddle and cook for 2 minutes. Use tongs to gently turn them over and cook for a further 2 minutes until crispy. Remove and place on kitchen paper. Repeat the process with the remaining Parma ham slices.

Put the asparagus spears into the same hot griddle pan and cook them for 5–6 minutes, turning occasionally. Equally divide the spears between 4 plates. Place 2 slices of Parma ham crossed over each other at the base of the spears on each plate and set aside.

Reduce the heat under the boiling vinegar water until it is at a gentle simmer. Poach the eggs in 2 batches: break 1 egg into a small cup, then slowly slide it into the water. Repeat the process with the second egg. Poach gently for 3 minutes until the whites have set. Use a slotted spoon to lift out the eggs and transfer to a plate lined with kitchen paper to drain any excess water. Repeat the process with the remaining eggs.

Use a tablespoon to gently place 1 egg on top of the crispy Parma ham on each plate, season with a pinch of salt and pepper and drizzle over ½ tbsp extra virgin olive oil. Serve immediately.

STUFFED MUSHROOMS WITH PANCETTA, COURGETTES + GORGONZOLA

Funghi ripieni con pancetta, zucchine e Gorgonzola piccante

SERVES 6

*as an antipasto, or
2 as a main course*

6 large Portobello
   mushrooms, *total
   weight about 500g*
5 tbsp olive oil
1 large onion, *peeled and
   finely chopped*
200g diced pancetta
1 courgette, *trimmed and
   finely chopped*
50g creamy Gorgonzola
   piccante, *chopped*
20g toasted
   breadcrumbs,
   shop-bought is fine
20g Parmesan cheese,
   finely grated
salt and freshly ground
   black pepper

I absolutely love mushrooms and really feel we don't use them enough in this country. People say they can be a bit boring or too earthy in taste and, for those of you who agree, I strongly recommend you try this recipe, as it will definitely change your mind. The combination of flavours is incredible and, if you have a guest coming who is vegetarian, just eliminate the pancetta and use a vegetarian Parmesan and the dish still works really well. You can substitute the Gorgonzola cheese with milder Dolcelatte if you prefer, and the best part of this recipe is that you can stuff the mushrooms in the morning and cook them later that day, when you are ready.

Preheat the oven to 200°C/fan 180°C/Gas 6. Place a sheet of baking parchment, or a cooking liner, on a small baking tray.

Remove the mushroom stems, roughly chop them up and set aside.

Place each mushroom on the baking parchment or liner, stem side down. Brush 1 tbsp of olive oil equally between the 6 mushrooms and season with a pinch of salt and pepper. Bake in the middle of the oven for 12 minutes. Remove from the oven, turn it off and carefully place the mushrooms on a plate lined with kitchen paper, allowing any excess liquid to be absorbed. Dry the baking tray and replace the baking parchment, if using, with a clean sheet. Put the mushrooms back on the tray, stem side up this time.

Pour the remaining 4 tbsp oil into a shallow saucepan and place over a medium heat. Fry the onion for 8 minutes, stirring after 4 minutes. Add the pancetta, courgette and mushroom stems and fry for a further 15 minutes, stirring occasionally. Add the Gorgonzola with ½ tsp pepper and stir continuously, melting the cheese and combining all the ingredients together for 2 minutes. Remove from the heat and, using a tablespoon, equally divide the mixture between the mushrooms, using about 1 heaped tbsp each.

In a small bowl, mix the breadcrumbs and Parmesan together. Put 1 tbsp of the cheesy breadcrumb mixture on top of each mushroom and place in the fridge for 20 minutes. Preheat the oven to 200°C/fan 180°C/Gas 6 once more.

Place in the preheated oven and cook for 20 minutes. If serving this recipe as a starter, put 1 mushroom on each plate and serve immediately. If this is a dinner for 2 people, serve 3 mushrooms on each plate with a crispy salad. I hope I have renewed your faith in the mushroom: enjoy!

MY GRANDMOTHER FLORA'S ROMANESCO ARTICHOKES

Carciofi di Nonna Flora

SERVES 4

Every single time I cook or eat artichokes, it reminds me of my Nonna Flora. I can still see her in her kitchen, cleaning and prepping them for my grandfather Giovanni: he loved artichokes.

Artichokes are in season between March and June, but you may need to go to a greengrocer rather than a supermarket to get the large round artichokes needed for this recipe. In Italy we pick them when the buds are still closed, so that the hearts are tender when cooked.

The garlic butter sauce here is also fantastic drizzled over any kind of fish or vegetables cooked on the barbecue.

4 large Romanesco
  artichokes, *stalks intact,*
  about 400g each
2 tbsp finely chopped
  mint leaves
1 garlic clove, *crushed*
2 tbsp finely chopped
  flat leaf parsley leaves
4 tbsp olive oil
100ml water
salt and freshly ground
  black pepper

FOR THE BUTTER SAUCE
150g salted butter
30ml olive oil
1 garlic clove, *peeled*
  and crushed
1 tbsp finely chopped
  flat leaf parsley leaves
2 tbsp lemon juice

Cut off and discard the artichoke stalks 3–4cm from the heart. Tear off 20–25 outer leaves, by pulling them down towards the stem, until you reach the paler leaves inside. With a sharp knife, trim away the bases of the torn leaves. Using your thumbs, prise open the remaining artichoke leaves and, with the help of a teaspoon, remove and discard the choke (the white and feathery part in the middle). Season the cavity with a pinch of salt and pepper.

Mix the mint, garlic and parsley together. Place 2 tsp herbs into the middle of each artichoke, leaving 2 tsp in the bowl for later.

Drizzle 2 tbsp oil into a large saucepan and add the artichokes, with their stalks pointing up; they should fit snugly. Drizzle over the remaining 2 tbsp oil, then sprinkle over the remaining herbs and a pinch of salt and pepper. Pour in the measured water. Lightly scrunch up a large piece of baking parchment and use it to loosely cover the artichokes, so they steam in the oil and water. Cook over a low heat for 20 minutes.

Remove and discard the baking parchment. Cover the artichokes with boiling water and add 1½ tbsp salt. Ensure the stalks are still pointing upwards, then put the lid on. Place the saucepan back over the heat and bring to the boil. Reduce the heat and gently simmer for 45 minutes.

Meanwhile, put all the butter sauce ingredients into a small saucepan, season well and gently cook over a medium heat until the butter has melted. Stir with a tablespoon, switch off the heat and set aside.

Very gently lift the artichokes from the cooking water and place on a serving plate, stem side down, so you can pull the leaves off. Reheat the sauce if needed and divide between 4 small bowls. Serve immediately.

If you never had artichokes before, peel each leaf off and dip it into the butter sauce. Eat the soft base of each leaf and discard the rest. You will eventually get to the best bit – the heart of the artichoke – which will be super-soft and delicious.

MUSSELS + CLAMS COOKED IN WHITE WINE WITH OREGANO BRUSCHETTA

Cozze e vongole al vino bianco con bruschetta all'origano

SERVES 4

This recipe always reminds me of my little princess Mia. Every time we are holidaying on the island of Sardinia, it is the first thing she asks me to cook, and not just a normal portion, she literally eats the lot! This is a very cool starter for sharing and a must to serve with my oregano bruschetta, so you can dunky-dunky the bread into the sauce. If you prefer, you can substitute the basil for parsley or chives and the white wine for a rosé.

4 tbsp olive oil
4 garlic cloves, *peeled and finely sliced*
600g fresh mussels, *rinsed, beards and any barnacles removed and discarded*
600g fresh clams, *rinsed*
120ml white wine
20 red or yellow cherry tomatoes, *halved*
10 large basil leaves
3 tbsp good-quality shop-bought red pesto

FOR THE BRUSCHETTA
8 slices of ciabatta bread, *about 1cm thick*
8 tsp extra virgin olive oil
dried oregano
salt and freshly ground black pepper

To prepare the bruschetta, lay a sheet of foil on a medium-sized baking tray and place the ciabatta slices on top. Drizzle 1 tsp extra virgin olive oil over each slice, along with a pinch of oregano, a pinch of salt and a pinch of pepper. Set aside.

Preheat the oven grill to high.

Heat the regular olive oil in a large saucepan over a medium heat. Add the garlic and fry until it starts to sizzle. Place in the mussels and clams and cook for 2 minutes, stirring continuously with a wooden spoon. Increase the heat to high and pour in the wine. Simmer for 3 minutes, stirring occasionally. Cover the saucepan with a lid and continue to cook for a further 3 minutes, shaking the saucepan occasionally.

Add the tomatoes, basil, red pesto and 1 tsp each salt and pepper. Stir and continue to cook for 3 minutes, uncovered, stirring occasionally.

While the mussels and clams are cooking, place the bread under the hot grill for 4–5 minutes until golden and toasted. Remove and set aside. You only need to toast one side of the bread.

To serve, discard any mussels or clams that have not opened. Pour the seafood and their juices into a large warmed serving bowl, or 4 smaller individual warmed bowls, and serve immediately with the toasted oregano bruschetta.

NONNA STEFANIA'S HOMEMADE TOMATO SOUP WITH BREAD

Nonna Stefania's pappa al pomodoro

SERVES 4

Meeting people on my culinary travels in Italy is always amazing, but meeting nonnas is a real treat. They always greet you with love and wisdom and I never come away without learning something new. I could sit for hours listening to their stories. This is a really traditional Tuscan recipe which I'm sure you will love. For the bread part of this recipe, Nonna Stefania would use *pane sciocco* (Tuscan salt-free bread), but I have substituted that with a country loaf, which is more easily available here in the UK. You will need 400g of the lovely fluffy inside, so make sure it's a big one!

1 large (600–800g) white
  country loaf
4 tbsp extra virgin olive
  oil, *plus more to serve*
1 red pepper, *deseeded and
  finely chopped*
½ leek, *trimmed, washed
  well (see page 63) and
  finely chopped*
½ red onion, *peeled and
  finely chopped*
1 garlic clove, *peeled and
  finely chopped*
handful of basil leaves,
  plus more to serve
2 bay leaves
500g tomato passata
500ml vegetable stock,
  plus a little more if needed
salt and freshly ground
  black pepper

Preheat the oven to 180°C/fan 160°C/Gas 4.

Cut the bread into 2cm-wide slices, remove the crusts, then cut it into cubes (you need 400g trimmed bread cubes). Place on a baking sheet lined with baking parchment, then put into the middle of the oven for 12 minutes, or until toasted, lightly golden and dried out well. Set aside.

Meanwhile, pour the oil into a large non-stick saucepan for which you have a lid, add the red pepper, leek, red onion and garlic and fry for 5 minutes over a medium heat. Stir occasionally. Tear in the basil leaves and add the bay leaves. Cook for 10 minutes, or until the vegetables have softened but not browned, stirring occasionally with a wooden spoon.

Pour in the tomato passata and cook for another 5 minutes. Add the bread, stir and let it cook for 5 minutes, then pour in the stock, reduce the heat to a minimum and cover the pan.

Cook for 1 hour, stirring occasionally.

Towards the end, if needed, add some more stock. Using a hand-held whisk or fork, beat well to squish the last chunks of bread, creating a really thick soup. Right at the end, season with salt and pepper.

Equally divide the *pappa* between 4 bowls and drizzle a little extra virgin olive oil on top. Grind over some pepper, decorate each bowl with a basil leaf and serve immediately.

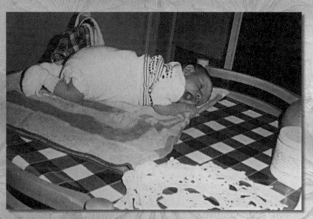

1976-77

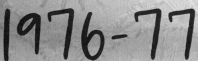

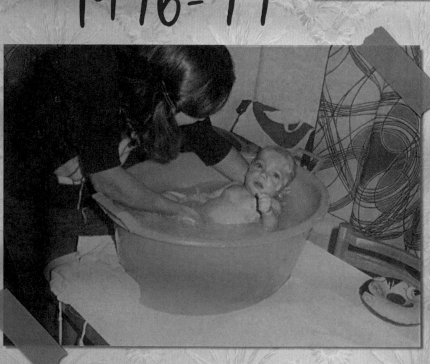

And so it begins...

BROCCOLI + GORGONZOLA SOUP

Zuppa di broccoli e Gorgonzola piccante

SERVES 6

There is nothing nicer than a warm bowl of soup and this recipe is perfect all year round. I love the combination of flavours. If you prefer, you can substitute the Gorgonzola cheese with Stilton, and the vegetable stock with chicken stock. This can be prepared a day ahead and reheated when needed, and is the perfect dish to make everybody jealous at the office. Serve with warm crusty bread, or my delicious Soft Bread Rolls with Extra Virgin Olive Oil (see page 177).

80g salted butter,
  cut into cubes
1 large onion, *peeled and
  roughly chopped*
350g floury potatoes,
  *peeled and cut into
  4cm cubes*
1.5 litres vegetable stock
350g head of broccoli,
  cut into small florets
100g Gorgonzola
  piccante, *roughly cut
  into 2cm cubes*
olive oil, to serve
  (optional)
freshly ground black
  pepper

Place the butter into a large saucepan and melt over a high heat. Add the onion and fry for 4 minutes, stirring occasionally with a wooden spoon. Stir in the potatoes, then pour in the stock and add ½ tsp pepper. Stir well, cover with a lid and bring to the boil, then reduce the heat to medium and simmer for 15 minutes.

Increase the heat to high and add the broccoli, then cover and reduce the heat to a gentle simmer. Cook for 6 minutes with the lid on.

Remove from the heat and blitz, using a hand-held blender, until you have a smooth consistency.

Place the saucepan back over a medium heat and add the Gorgonzola. Stir continuously until the cheese has melted, about 2 minutes.

Serve in warmed bowls with a little sprinkle of black pepper on top, along with a swirl of olive oil, if you like.

OCTOPUS + POTATO SALAD WITH OLIVES

Insalata di polpo e patate con olive

SERVES 4

as an antipasto, or 2 as a main course

I could eat this dish every other day: I love the fresh flavours, it is so easy to prepare and a real wow to serve. If using fresh octopus, ask your fishmonger to prepare it by cutting off the beak, cleaning out the body and removing any scales stuck in the suckers. If using frozen, all that has usually already been done for you. You can prepare this dish and place it in the fridge until needed, but do take it out at least 1 hour before eating, as it should be served at room temperature.

FOR THE OCTOPUS

750g octopus, *rinsed under cold water*

1 red onion, *peeled*

2 celery sticks, *each cut into 4–5 pieces*

1 red chilli

stalks and leaves from 8 flat leaf parsley sprigs, *kept separate*

1 unwaxed lemon, *plus more to serve*

FOR THE SALAD

600g small waxy potatoes, *such as Charlotte, peeled*

8 tbsp extra virgin olive oil

2 tbsp capers in salt, *rinsed under cold water and drained*

75g pitted Leccino olives, or other good-quality pitted black olives such as Kalamata, *drained*

salt and freshly ground black pepper

Put the octopus into a large saucepan. Add the whole onion, celery, whole chilli and parsley stalks. Peel off the lemon zest with a vegetable peeler and add it to the pan, cover with cold water, place over a medium heat and bring to the boil. Reduce the heat to a minimum, half-cover the saucepan with a lid and gently simmer for 1 hour. Switch off the heat and allow the octopus to cool in the water for 2 hours.

Meanwhile, pour 2 litres water and 1 tbsp salt into a medium-sized saucepan and bring to the boil. Add the peeled whole potatoes and boil for 20 minutes. Drain and cut into 2cm pieces. Put them into a medium bowl and add the chopped parsley leaves, 4 tbsp extra virgin olive oil, 8 twists of black pepper and ½ tsp salt. Gently toss together using 2 tablespoons. If not serving the dish straight away, cover with clingfilm and place in the fridge until needed. Remember to take it out 1 hour before serving to bring it back to room temperature.

Drain the octopus, place on a chopping board and cut it into 2cm pieces. Place the pieces in a medium-sized bowl and add ½ tsp salt, 6 twists of black pepper, the juice of the peeled lemon, the capers, olives and the remaining 4 tbsp extra virgin olive oil. Mix the ingredients together using 2 tablespoons. (Again, if not serving the dish straight away, cover with clingfilm and place in the fridge until needed; remember to take it out 1 hour before serving, to bring it back to room temperature.)

Gently fold the octopus pieces into the prepared potatoes and transfer to a large oval serving dish. Place a few lemon wedges around the dish and *buon appetito*! Perfect for a starter, a lunch or a light dinner.

FRIED SARDINES STUFFED WITH RICOTTA + LEMON

Sardine fritte ripiene di ricotta e limone

SERVES 4

When making this recipe, I just think back to summer holidays when I was a boy. I first ate something very similar when I visited the Amalfi coast. I remember my mother and father sitting down at a little café restaurant and ordering us some stuffed sardines... and it was love at first sight. I always serve my sardines with a fresh crispy salad, as nothing else is needed in my opinion. When filling the sardines, you will still feel some tiny bones. Take out as many as possible; it will be impossible to get them all, but don't worry too much, as you won't really feel them once fried. If you are prepping the sardines for later, loosely cover with clingfilm and place in the fridge, keeping back any unused breadcrumbs. Take the sardines out of the fridge half an hour before cooking and re-coat them in breadcrumbs before frying.

3 eggs
120g fine toasted
   breadcrumbs
12 large sardines,
   butterflied, heads, tails and
   backbones removed (ask
   your fishmonger to do this)
300ml sunflower oil
1 lemon, *quartered*
salt and freshly ground
   black pepper

FOR THE STUFFING
70g ricotta
150g can of tuna in oil,
   drained
3 anchovy fillets in oil,
   drained and finely chopped
10g capers in salt, *rinsed*
   under cold water, drained
   and finely chopped
2 tsp finely chopped chives
15g pecorino Romano
   cheese, *finely grated*
finely grated zest of
   1 unwaxed lemon,
   plus the juice of ½

Place all the stuffing ingredients in a medium bowl, mix and set aside.

Lightly beat the eggs and 1 tsp salt in a medium-sized bowl. Pour the breadcrumbs on to a plate.

Pat the sardines dry with kitchen paper and lay them on a chopping board, skin sides down. Spoon about 1 heaped tsp filling mixture into a sardine cavity and with the back of the teaspoon smooth it out to fill the whole length of half of the fish. Close the sardine as best as you can, but don't worry if the filling is showing. Repeat to fill all the fish.

Gently dip the stuffed sardines into the beaten eggs, then place in the breadcrumbs. Coat well on all sides and place on a tray ready to fry.

Pour the oil into a large frying pan and place over a medium heat until hot. To test the oil, take a small pinch of breadcrumbs and sprinkle over the oil: if they sizzle straight away, the oil is ready.

Gently place 6 sardines into the hot oil and fry them for 1½ minutes. Use 2 forks to turn them over and fry for another 1½ minutes until golden and crispy all over. Remove from the heat with a slotted spoon and drain on a plate lined with kitchen paper. Repeat with the remaining sardines.

Place on a large serving platter, or put 3 sardines per person on each of 4 plates. Sprinkle a pinch of salt and couple of twists of black pepper over each sardine and place the lemon quarters on the side. Serve immediately with a simple crispy salad.

STEAK TARTARE WITH OLIVES, GHERKINS + SHALLOTS

Tartara di manzo con olive, cetriolini sottaceto e scalogno

SERVES 4

This is the ultimate starter for a dinner party. It looks fantastic, tastes amazing and because you prep the sauce and cut up the meat in the morning, it will literally take you minutes to serve, leaving you more time to spend with your guests. Don't combine the meat and sauce until 10 minutes before serving though, or the steak will start to discolour.

Serve with grissini, or my Breadsticks with Leccino Black Olives (see page 180), or simply with toast.

280g lean fillet steak
extra virgin olive oil
4 egg yolks

FOR THE SAUCE
30g pitted Nocellara
  green olives, *drained
  and finely chopped*
30g capers in salt, *rinsed
  under cold water, drained
  and finely chopped*
30g gherkins,
  finely chopped
1 shallot, *peeled and
  finely chopped*
30g Dijon mustard
35g good-quality
  tomato ketchup
10ml extra virgin olive oil
1 heaped tbsp finely
  chopped flat leaf
  parsley leaves
1 heaped tbsp finely
  chopped chives
splash of Worcestershire
  sauce
splash of Tabasco sauce
salt and freshly ground
  black pepper

Using a very sharp knife, slice the fillet steak into very thin slices. Put each slice flat on a chopping board and cut into thin strips. Cut the strips into small cubes. Place in a small bowl and set aside.

Tip all the sauce ingredients into a medium-sized bowl, season well and gently stir with a metal spoon. When ready to serve, put the meat into the sauce and gently fold all the ingredients together.

Place an 8cm chef's ring in the centre of a starter plate. Spoon out one-quarter of the steak tartare mixture and place in the centre of the ring. Use the spoon to gently push the meat to the sides. Drizzle over ½ tbsp extra virgin olive oil.

Crack an egg carefully, as you will need half of its shell; refrigerate the white for another time. Place the egg yolk, keeping it in its half shell, in the centre of the steak tartare. Sprinkle over a small pinch of black pepper. Remove the ring and repeat the process for the remaining 3 plates.

Serve immediately, with a bottle of full-bodied Italian red wine.

MODERN AUBERGINE PARMIGIANA WITH BASIL + SMOKED MOZZARELLA

Melanzane alla parmigiana con basilico fresco e provola

SERVES 2

This dish is so close to my heart, as it's one that my nonna and my mamma used to make for me regularly throughout my childhood; the only difference is that they used to bake it and I like to do it in this modern, easy way, without compromising the flavours. I was very lucky to be able to cook this dish in the foothills of Mount Vesuvius, where a special, long, less bitter aubergine variety grows. I will never understand people who don't like aubergine! Please, please, give this recipe a go, I promise that you will be instantly addicted.

olive oil
2 large garlic cloves,
 peeled and very
 finely sliced
400g can of chopped
 tomatoes
24 basil leaves
100g plain flour
2 eggs, *lightly beaten*
1 large, long aubergine,
 cut into 1cm discs
150g provola cheese,
 cut into 1cm slices
about 20g Parmesan
 cheese shavings
2 tbsp extra virgin
 olive oil
salt and freshly ground
 black pepper

Pour 4 tbsp regular olive oil into a small saucepan and place over a medium heat. Add the garlic, and, as soon as it starts to sizzle, fry for 10 seconds. Pour in the chopped tomatoes and add 10 basil leaves and 1 tsp salt. Stir with a wooden spoon and allow to simmer for 15 minutes, stirring occasionally.

Meanwhile, pour enough regular olive oil into a wide frying pan, about 30cm in diameter, to reach about 1.5cm up the side. Set over a medium-high heat. Tip the flour on to a shallow dish and the eggs into another.

Take each slice of aubergine and dip it into the flour on both sides. Tap it lightly to remove any excess, then drop into the beaten egg. Gently lift the aubergine to allow some of the egg to drop off. Carefully lay the prepared aubergine into the hot oil. I do this with my hands, but use tongs if you prefer. Repeat the process with a few more slices of aubergine, being sure not to overcrowd the pan. It is quite likely you will have to cook the aubergine slices in batches.

Fry for about 2 minutes on each side, or until lightly browned and starting to crisp up on the edges, then remove to a plate covered with kitchen paper to drain any excess oil. Repeat to cook the remaining slices.

By now the tomato sauce should have thickened and have a rich tomato flavour. Switch off the heat.

Now build the Parmigiana. On each of 2 plates, lay down 3 slices of aubergine, slightly overlapped, top with 3 basil leaves, then add a slice of provola cheese and a grind of pepper. Sprinkle over large shavings of Parmesan, followed by a generous spoonful of tomato sauce. Lay 3 more discs of aubergine on top and add another slice of provola, 3 more basil leaves, more shavings of Parmesan, and finally a generous spoonful of tomato sauce. Top with a basil leaf and drizzle 1 tbsp extra virgin olive oil over each stack. Serve immediately, with warm crusty bread.

Pasta

Rice

Gnocchi

1978-81

Picnics and barbecue bliss

My favourite chapter. I could live off a plate of pasta every day and never get bored. There always seems to be a debate about where pasta originated and I'm sticking with Italy, like most food historians. Some believe that Marco Polo brought it back from his travels to China, as the earliest known pasta was made from rice flour and was more like a noodle. In Italy, pasta was made from hard wheat and shaped into long strands named *vermicelli* ('little worms'), much closer to modern-day spaghetti.

Old traditional Italian recipes are really strict about which pasta goes with which sauce and I truly believe it makes a difference. A long spaghetti suits a light vegetable-based sauce such as tomato and basil, while rigatoni (large tubes) is best with a Bolognese. In this book I have tried to give you not only varied sauces, but also to use the right pasta to go with them. The linguine with prawns in this book was one of the recipes I learned from my Aunty Clara when I was only 10, while the bucatini carbonara was among the first dishes they taught us at culinary school and was also the first time I had ever tried a creamy sauce on pasta. A must-try in this chapter, so basic but so amazing, is the spaghetti with pecorino cheese and pepper.

Rice was introduced to Sicily in the 14th century by the Arabs. Since then, its cultivation continued in Naples and eventually extended to Northern Italy, so risotto recipes stem mainly from those regions. Up until the 18th century, risotto included boiled rice; the first known version that resembles what we eat today is a recipe from 1829 that consists of rice, butter and onion, with broth added a little at a time, stirred until creamy and rich. My favourite risotto in this chapter is the seafood one, because that's what I remember my mother teaching my sister to cook while we were growing up. Maybe that was because, living in Naples, the fish was so fresh, or maybe it was just because the flavours are so amazing. A close second favourite is the baked risotto. I learned that recipe when I was 14 and our catering school took us on a food tour to Rome. The lady at the B&B cooked it for us and I made her write the recipe down. I still have the little piece of paper she gave me. I wish she had put her name on it so I could dedicate it to her.

In my opinion, gnocchi must have at least one recipe in any book I do. It goes way back to Roman times, when it was made from semolina mixed with eggs. Different variations have been created since and it became the potato dumplings familiar to us today in the 16th century, after potatoes were introduced to Europe. Nowadays you don't even have to make gnocchi, you can buy good-quality versions and boil them like pasta, or even fry them. I have a light-as-air vegetarian gnocchi recipe here, made from ricotta and a little flour, that everyone can enjoy.

SPAGHETTI WITH CREAMY PECORINO ROMANO + BLACK PEPPER SAUCE

Spaghetti cacio e pepe

I've always wanted to write this classic Roman recipe, but I was worried that it was far too simple. One evening I cooked it for myself and my son Luciano, and he made me promise that I would share it with you guys. Simplicity at its best.

Please buy bronze die-cut pasta, as it will make lots of difference to the end result; you need the roughness of the bronze die to get the sauce to stick to the pasta.

40 black peppercorns,
*plus freshly coarse-ground
black pepper, to serve*
225g dried spaghetti,
bronze die-cut
100g pecorino Romano
cheese, *finely grated*
salt

Fill a large saucepan with 3 litres water, add 1 tbsp salt and place over a high heat. Bring to the boil.

Place the peppercorns on a board and crush with a cooking hammer (or use a mortar and pestle, or the end of a rolling pin and a plastic bag).

Cook the spaghetti in the salted boiling water for 3 minutes less than instructed on the packet, stirring occasionally.

Meanwhile, place a large frying pan or a wok over a high heat and add the crushed peppercorns. Toast for 2 minutes, stirring occasionally with a wooden spoon. Pour in a full ladle of the pasta cooking water. It will immediately start to bubble; keep it bubbling for 30 seconds. Set aside.

Place the cheese in a bowl. Pour in half a ladle of the cooking water and mix/fold with a spatula for 1 minute to create a very thick creamy sauce.

Using large tongs, lift the spaghetti from its saucepan, tip into the pan with the pepper, then place over a high heat. Do not discard the pasta cooking water. Pour 2 ladles of the cooking water over the pasta and continue to mix with a wooden spoon, or toss, for 2 minutes. The more you toss/mix the pasta, the creamier the sauce will become. Switch off the heat and immediately pour the thick cheese mixture over the pasta.

Quickly start to mix all together for 30 seconds, making sure each strand of pasta is coated with the cheese. Pour half a ladle more cooking water over the pasta and stir for a further minute, creating a beautiful creamy texture. Keep tossing the pasta until you have a creamy cheese sauce. If needed, add a little more cooking water, to make it even creamier.

Serve immediately, pouring over any remaining cheese sauce from the pan, and sprinkling a little more freshly coarse-ground pepper on top.

EXTRA LARGE PASTA TUBES WITH FRESH TOMATOES, BASIL + MOZZARELLA

Paccheri Margherita

SERVES 4

Most kids love tomato and cheese pasta, but I wanted to make sure that my daughter Mia – when she was tiny – also understood that not all food is puréed... and that there is nothing quite like fresh tomatoes. From an early age, I made sure that some of her meals were cooked like this recipe, introducing her to more textures, and I really believe it's helped her to be more adventurous with food. The rest of the family like to add chilli-infused olive oil to this recipe for a little bit of kick, but the flavours are still great without it. If you can't find paccheri pasta, you can substitute rigatoni.

8 tbsp extra virgin olive oil
3 garlic cloves, *peeled and finely sliced*
30 yellow cherry tomatoes, *about 400g, halved*
30 red cherry tomatoes, *about 400g, halved*
15 basil leaves
500g dried paccheri pasta *(extra-large tubes)*
3 mozzarella balls, *about 150g each, drained and cut into 1cm cubes*
salt

Fill a large saucepan with 4 litres water, add 2 tbsp salt and place over a high heat. Bring to the boil.

Meanwhile, pour the oil into a large frying pan, add the garlic and place over a medium heat. Fry for 2 minutes, then, as soon as the garlic starts to sizzle, add all the tomatoes. Mix and cook for 3 minutes, stirring occasionally with a wooden spoon.

Tear the basil leaves over the tomatoes, sprinkle over 1 tsp salt and mix well. Continue to cook for a further 2 minutes. Take the pan off the heat and set aside while you cook the pasta.

When the water is boiling, add the pasta. Cook the pasta for 1 minute less than instructed on the packet for the perfect al dente bite, stirring occasionally. When there are only 2 minutes before your pasta is cooked, turn the heat back on under the tomatoes to warm them up again.

Drain the pasta and return it to the large saucepan. Pour over the tomatoes and mix for about 30 seconds. Sprinkle in half the mozzarella and continue to stir for another 10 seconds.

Divide between 4 warmed plates or bowls, sprinkle over the remaining mozzarella cubes and serve immediately.

MY AUNTY LINA'S PASTA GENOVESE

Pasta alla Genovese di Zia Lina

SERVES 4

The recipe for Genovese sauce is basically onions (*lots* of onions!) beef and pork cooked together for five hours to create a thick, rich 'white' sauce, by which I mean a sauce without tomatoes. The true secret of the dish is the long and very slow cooking of the onions. This is the only way to get the classic copper colour of the sauce, onions that are almost like jam, and meat that will melt in your mouth. Aunty Lina's Genovese is one of the best you will ever make and is so worth the cooking time.

Ask your butcher for cuts of beef and pork that are suitable for stews.

100ml extra virgin olive oil
750g mixture of beef and
  pork, *cut into big chunks*
200ml dry white wine
2kg onions, *peeled*
  and sliced
2 bay leaves
500g dried candele
  lunghe pasta (*long hollow*
  candles), or bucatini,
  or rigatoni
small handful of
  basil leaves
50g Parmesan cheese,
  finely grated
salt and freshly ground
  black pepper

Pour the olive oil into a large saucepan, for which you have a lid, and set it over a medium-high heat. Add all the meat and cook for 10 minutes, stirring occasionally, until it starts to brown. Pour in the wine and continue to cook for 5 minutes.

Add the onions and bay leaves. Mix well, cover the pot with the lid, reduce the heat to its lowest and cook for 5 hours. Every 20 minutes, stir the Genovese. The meat and onions should melt and amalgamate together to become a copper-coloured, creamy sauce. If the pan ever seems a little dry, splash in some water. After 4 hours, remove and discard the bay leaves. Season with salt and pepper.

Fill another large saucepan with 4 litres water, add 2 tbsp salt and place over a high heat. Bring to the boil. If using candele lunghe, break the tubes into the water. Cook the pasta in the salted boiling water for 2 minutes less than instructed on the packet, giving you that perfect al dente bite. Stir occasionally.

Drain the pasta and then pour it into the Genovese sauce. Stir well and cook over a low heat for a final 2 minutes.

Divide the pasta between 4 warmed plates. Sprinkle over the basil and Parmesan. Serve immediately with a good bottle of Italian red wine.

TROFIE PASTA WITH VITTORIA'S LEMON PESTO + CARAMELISED SPICY PRAWNS

Pasta trofie con pesto al limone e gamberoni piccanti

SERVES 2

During filming in Italy, I had the joy of meeting Vittoria. She was born and bred on the island of Procida and her family is part of the island's culinary heritage. Vittoria was the perfect guide to show me around the island's ingredients, and in particular the lemons. They have several types of lemon on Procida which carry different characteristics: some you can eat whole as you would an apple, while others verge on sweet as well as sour. Vittoria is well known for her lemon pesto, in which she uses mint and walnuts instead of the traditional basil and pine nuts. It's absolutely delicious and I couldn't resist using it for this dish.

250g dried trofie pasta
(solid twists), or fusilli
3 tbsp olive oil
16 large prawns, *heads and shells removed, tails left on, deveined (see page 18)*
1 tsp smoked paprika
2 tbsp runny honey
150g Vittoria's Lemon Pesto (see below)

FOR VITTORIA'S
LEMON PESTO
50g mint leaves
1 garlic clove, *peeled*
50g walnuts
1 small red chilli, *very finely chopped*
20g Parmesan cheese
1–1½ lemons, to taste
100ml extra virgin olive oil
salt

For the pesto, chop the mint, garlic, walnuts and chilli together, or crush in a mortar and pestle if you prefer. Grate in the Parmesan and the zest of 1 lemon, then squeeze in the juice of the lemon, drizzle in the extra virgin olive oil, add a large pinch of salt and mix together. This makes quite a chunky pesto, as mint leaves are not as soft as those of basil.

Taste and decide whether you want the pesto to have a sharper lemon flavour; if so, add the zest and juice of the remaining ½ lemon.

Now for the pasta. Fill a large saucepan with 4 litres water, add 2 tbsp salt and place over a high heat. Bring to the boil.

Cook the pasta in the salted boiling water for 1 minute less than instructed on the packet, giving you that perfect al dente bite, stirring occasionally.

Meanwhile, pour the regular olive oil into a medium frying pan and place over a medium-high heat. When hot, add the prawns and cook without moving for 1 minute.

Flip them over and sprinkle in the paprika. Drizzle over the honey and turn the heat off, letting the residual heat cook the prawns through slowly.

Pour the lemon pesto into a large clean bowl. When the pasta is cooked, use a large, slotted spoon to transfer it from the boiling water into the bowl with the pesto, carrying any of the cooking water that clings to the pasta, which will help to create a creamy sauce. Stir the trofie in the pesto until well coated.

Transfer the pasta to a large serving platter and spoon over the prawns with any of their juices from the pan. Serve immediately.

BUCATINI CARBONARA, WITH CURED PORK CHEEK/ + PECORINO ROMANO

Bucatini alla carbonara, con guanciale e pecorino Romano

SERVES 2

I must have cooked about 15 different versions of this classic Roman pasta dish, using different shapes of pasta and alternative ingredients such as pancetta, Parmesan cheese and even flat leaf parsley. Now it's time for me to show you the very classic way it's done in Rome, using cured pork cheeks, pecorino Romano and fresh eggs... yes, only three ingredients.

When you buy the pecorino Romano, ask for the original type with the black rind and make sure it is not too mature; it should be a little crumbly in texture. You can get it, as well as guanciale, from most Italian delicatessens.

100g guanciale
225g dried bucatini pasta
  (long, thick strands with a central hole)
5 very fresh egg yolks
60g pecorino Romano
  cheese, *finely grated,*
  plus more to serve
salt and freshly ground
  black pepper

Fill a large saucepan with 3 litres water, add 1½ tbsp salt and place over a high heat. Bring to the boil.

With a sharp knife, slice off and discard the tough skin around the fat side of the guanciale. Slice the remaining guanciale lengthways, about 5mm thick, then cut the slices into small strips about 3cm long. Set aside.

Cook the pasta in the salted boiling water for 1 minute less than instructed on the packet, giving you that perfect al dente bite, stirring occasionally.

Meanwhile, place a large frying pan over a high heat and add the guanciale. Fry for 6 minutes, stirring occasionally with a wooden spoon. Set aside.

Pour the yolks into a small bowl and add the pecorino Romano and ½ tsp pepper. Mix the ingredients together with a fork and keep mixing until well combined. Pour in half a ladle of the salted boiling water from the pasta saucepan and continue to mix until you create a thick creamy texture. The cheese will start melting into the egg yolks. Set aside.

Using large tongs, pick up the pasta, tip it into the pan with the guanciale and place over a high heat. Do not discard the pasta cooking water. Mix the pasta and guanciale for 10 seconds, stirring with a wooden spoon.

Switch off the heat and immediately pour the egg yolk mixture over the pasta. Quickly start to mix all together for 10 seconds, making sure each strand of pasta is coated. Pour half a ladle of the hot salted pasta cooking water over the pasta and continue to stir for a further 30 seconds, creating a beautiful creamy texture around the pasta. If needed, you can add a little more of the cooking water to make it creamier still.

Serve immediately with a little sprinkle each of black pepper and pecorino Romano on top. Fantastic served with a cold Italian beer.

OOZING BAKED RIJOTTO WITH JAUSAGE, LEEKS + GORGONZOLA

Risotto cremoso al forno con salsiccia, porri e Gorgonzola

SERVES 4

I absolutely love every kind of risotto. Coming up with new ideas is always fun and this one is fantastic. I have made it many times with different cheeses; for example, you can substitute the Gorgonzola for Taleggio or Dolcelatte, the Parmesan for pecorino. If you don't have red pesto in your cupboards (go buy some, it's a great flavour to add to things!) don't worry too much, as the baked risotto will still taste great.

1 large leek, *about 200g*
4 tbsp olive oil
6 pork sausages, *total weight about 400g, skins removed*
350g arborio rice
1.3 litres boiling water
1 chicken stock cube
1 vegetable stock cube
150g frozen peas, *defrosted*
80g Parmesan cheese, *finely grated*
5 tsp good-quality shop-bought red pesto
200g Gorgonzola cheese *(weighed after the rind has been trimmed off), chopped into small cubes*
2 mozzarella balls, *drained and chopped into small cubes*

If the leek has not been pre-trimmed, trim off 1cm from the bottom and 10cm from the top. Wash it well, as there can be dirt hidden under the top layer. Cut in half lengthways, then slice as fine as you can. Set aside.

Preheat the oven to 220°C/fan 200°C/Gas 7.

Pour the olive oil into a large saucepan and place over a high heat. Add the sausages and, with a wooden spoon, break up the meat into small pieces. Fry for 10 minutes, stirring occasionally. Remove with a slotted spoon to a bowl and set aside, leaving the flavoured oil in the saucepan.

Put the leek into the saucepan and fry for 5 minutes, stirring occasionally with a wooden spoon. Add the rice and stir well for a further 2 minutes, allowing it to become toasted and flavoured by the leek and oil. Reduce the heat to medium and pour in 900ml boiling water with both stock cubes, then stir all together. Simmer for 5 minutes, stirring occasionally.

Return the sausagemeat to the pan, add the peas, stir and continue to cook for a further 2 minutes. Pour over 400ml more boiling water, then add half the Parmesan and all the red pesto. Add half the Gorgonzola too and stir well. Continue to cook for a further 7 minutes, stirring occasionally, then switch off the heat. At this point your risotto will look quite wet and runny. This is how it should be, as it will continue to cook in the oven.

Using a ladle, place half the risotto in a large ceramic or glass ovenproof dish (mine measures 27 x 20 x 6cm). Scatter over half of the remaining Gorgonzola. Sprinkle over half of the mozzarella and half of the rest of the Parmesan. Pour the remaining risotto on top of the cheeses. Scatter over the last of the Gorgonzola and mozzarella, then finally sprinkle over the remaining Parmesan.

Place the dish in the centre of the oven and bake for 20 minutes. Remove the dish from the oven and allow to rest for 5 minutes before serving with a bottle of full-bodied Italian red wine.

PASTA SHELLS WITH POTATOES, PANCETTA + PARMESAN

Pasta e patate con pancetta e Parmigiano

SERVES 4–6

This is the ultimate hangover plate of pasta and is a must-have in the D'Acampo family if we've all been partying. The carbs and flavours make the night before disappear much more quickly... It's a one-pot wonder, full of flavours and so simple to prepare. If you want a vegetarian option, just eliminate the pancetta, use a vegetarian Parmesan and stir in some peas instead when you put in the pasta. We always have some chilli- and truffle-infused olive oil on the table, to give it an extra flavour or kick.

4 tbsp olive oil
1 large onion, *peeled and finely chopped*
100g diced pancetta
1.3kg floury potatoes, *such as Maris Piper or King Edward, peeled and cut into 3cm cubes*
2 litres boiling water
2 vegetable stock cubes
1 tbsp tomato purée
400g dried conchiglie pasta *(medium shells)*
2 tbsp roughly chopped flat leaf parsley leaves
60g Parmesan cheese, *finely grated*
salt and freshly ground white pepper

Pour the oil into a large saucepan, add the onion and pancetta and fry over a medium heat for 15 minutes, stirring occasionally with a wooden spoon.

Add the potatoes to the pan and stir all together, allowing the flavours to combine. Continue to fry for a further 8 minutes, stirring occasionally.

Pour over the measured boiling water, add the stock cubes and tomato purée and stir well. Reduce the heat, half-cover with a lid and leave to gently simmer for 35 minutes, stirring occasionally.

Remove the lid, increase the heat to medium and add the pasta, parsley, 2 tbsp salt and 1 tsp white pepper. Stir and continue to cook, without the lid, for 12 minutes, or until the pasta is al dente. (To get the perfect al dente bite, you usually need to cook the pasta for 1 minute less than instructed on the packet.)

Take the pan off the heat and stir in the Parmesan.

Serve in warmed plates or bowls and *buon appetito*.

LINGUINE WITH ЅUCCULENT PRAWNS, WHITE WINE + ЅPICY MUSHROOMS

Linguine con gamberoni, vino bianco e funghi piccanti

SERVES 4

I absolutely love earthy and fish flavours together, so, to me, mushrooms and prawns are a match made in heaven. This is a quick, easy, yet super-tasty pasta recipe. You can obviously substitute the linguine with spaghetti if you prefer, while spinach works really well instead of rocket leaves too. There is only one thing that you cannot do: sprinkle grated cheese over this dish. You will lose the freshness of the prawns and you will kill the kick from the chillies.

10 tbsp olive oil

2 large garlic cloves, *peeled and finely sliced*

2 medium-hot large red chillies, *deseeded and finely sliced*

250g mixed wild mushrooms, *roughly sliced*

250g chestnut mushrooms, *roughly sliced*

500g large jumbo prawns, *heads, tails and shells removed, deveined (see page 18)*

200ml white wine

2 tbsp roughly chopped flat leaf parsley leaves

500g dried linguine

50g rocket leaves

4 tbsp extra virgin olive oil

salt

Fill a large saucepan with 4 litres water, add 2 tbsp salt and place over a high heat. Bring to the boil.

Meanwhile, pour 6 tbsp regular olive oil into a large frying pan, add the garlic and chillies and place over a high heat. As soon as the garlic and chillies start to sizzle, fry for 1 minute. Add all the mushrooms and sprinkle over 1 tsp salt. Mix all together and fry for 13 minutes, stirring occasionally with a wooden spoon. Scoop out the mushrooms on to a plate and set aside.

Place the same frying pan back over a high heat and pour in the remaining 4 tbsp regular olive oil. Add the prawns and ½ tsp salt and fry for 2 minutes, stirring occasionally. Pour in the wine, add the parsley and continue to cook for 5 minutes, allowing the alcohol to evaporate and stirring occasionally with a wooden spoon. Return the mushrooms to the frying pan, stir and continue to cook for a further 2 minutes. Switch off the heat and set aside.

Cook the pasta in the salted boiling water for 1 minute less than instructed on the packet, giving you that perfect al dente bite, stirring occasionally. Drain and return it to the large saucepan. Tip the rocket leaves over the pasta, then pour over the prawn and mushroom sauce. Finally, pour over the extra virgin olive oil and stir well.

Use tongs to divide the linguine between 4 warmed plates. Spoon over any prawns and mushrooms left in the saucepan and serve immediately.

CREAMY PASTA BAKE WITH SUCCULENT CHICKEN + BECHAMEL SAUCE

Rigatoni cremosi al forno con pollo e besciamella

SERVES 6

Whenever one of the kids is not feeling great, this seems to be the dish that they crave. It's the ultimate comfort food. You can be as creative as you like: I often add pancetta or, for a stronger cheesy flavour, 150g Gorgonzola piccante at the same time as the Parmesan goes into the bechamel. It's the perfect dish to prepare in advance, even the day before is OK, but make sure you keep it in the fridge until needed, then bring it to room temperature before cooking.

4 tbsp olive oil

1 large onion, *peeled and finely chopped*

650g skinless, boneless chicken thighs, *cut into 4cm chunks*

200ml hot chicken stock

3 tsp English mustard

100ml single cream

200g frozen peas, *defrosted*

100g salted butter

100g plain flour

1 litre full-fat milk

130g Parmesan cheese, *finely grated*

1 tsp freshly grated nutmeg

500g dried rigatoni pasta (ridged tubes)

2 mozzarella balls, *about 150g each, drained and cut into 1cm cubes*

salt and freshly ground black pepper

Fill a large saucepan with 4 litres water, add 2 tbsp salt and place over a high heat. Bring to the boil.

Meanwhile, pour the oil into a large shallow saucepan, add the onion and fry over a medium heat for 8 minutes, stirring occasionally with a wooden spoon. Add the chicken with a pinch each of salt and pepper and fry for 10 minutes, stirring occasionally. Pour in the stock, stir well and simmer for 3 minutes. Stir in the mustard and cream and simmer for 3 minutes, again stirring occasionally. Remove from the heat and mix in the peas.

To make the bechamel, place the butter in a medium-sized saucepan set over a medium heat. Once the butter has melted, mix in the flour using a hand-held whisk and continue to cook over a medium heat for about 1 minute. Pour in half the milk and continue to mix continuously with the whisk, ensuring the paste has combined with the milk completely. Pour in the remaining milk, 100g of the Parmesan, 2 tsp salt, 1 tsp pepper and the nutmeg. Continue to stir over a medium heat until the sauce has thickened; this process should take about 10 minutes. Pour the bechamel over the chicken mixture, stir all together with a wooden spoon and set aside.

Cook the pasta in the salted boiling water for 5 minutes less than instructed on the packet, stirring occasionally. Drain and return it to the large saucepan. Pour over the chicken bechamel and mix really well, ensuring the pasta is coated perfectly with the sauce.

Spoon half of the pasta into an ovenproof dish; I use a dish that measures 30 x 20 x 6cm. Sprinkle over the mozzarella and then spoon over the remaining pasta. Sprinkle the remaining Parmesan cheese on top. Up to this point, the dish can be made in advance (see recipe introduction).

When ready to bake, preheat the oven to 220°C/fan 200°C/Gas 7. Place the pasta bake in the middle of the oven and cook for 20 minutes. Remove from the oven and let it rest for 5 minutes before serving.

PAPPARDELLE WITH NEAPOLITAN MEAT RAGÙ

Pappardelle con ragù Napoletano

SERVES 5

Growing up in Naples, this was our Sunday lunch. We only had meat once a week, due to its cost, and I can't tell you how amazing it was to wake up to these incredible aromas coming from the kitchen. Mum would start cooking really early, as this takes at least three hours to cook. It's the perfect Italian Sunday lunch: you enjoy a great-tasting plate of pasta, followed by a second course of incredible tender meats. You can cook the meat earlier in the day to serve in the evening, as the flavours just become more enhanced. This recipe means a lot to me, and I really hope you enjoy it. You can substitute the Grana Padano with Parmesan or pecorino cheese if you prefer.

5 tbsp olive oil

1 large onion, *peeled and finely chopped*

4 large pork sausages, *total weight about 300g*

8 medium-sized pork ribs, *total weight about 1kg*

500g beef topside, *fat trimmed away, cut into 3cm chunks*

200ml red wine

3 x 400g cans of chopped tomatoes

15 large basil leaves

200ml hot water

500g fresh pappardelle pasta *(thick ribbons)*

50g Grana Padano cheese, *finely grated*

salt and freshly ground black pepper

Pour the oil into a large saucepan, add the onion and place over a high heat. Fry for 7 minutes, stirring occasionally with a wooden spoon. Add the meats, then sprinkle over 3 tsp salt and ½ tsp pepper. Fry for 10 minutes, stirring often to allow all the meats to be coloured on all sides. Pour in the wine and continue to cook for a further 5 minutes, stirring occasionally.

Pour in the tomatoes and tear in the basil. Pour over the measured hot water and gently stir. As soon as it starts to bubble, reduce the heat to a minimum and simmer with the lid mostly on (leave a slight gap for steam to evaporate) for 2½ hours. Stir every 20 minutes with a wooden spoon. Remove the lid and cook for a further 30 minutes, stirring occasionally.

Switch off the heat, place the lid back on, again leaving a small gap for steam to evaporate, and allow to rest while you cook the pasta. (If you decide to serve this meal up later in the evening or the next day, reheat the sauce and meat through until warm while you cook the pasta.)

Fill a large saucepan with 4 litres water, add 2 tbsp salt and place over a high heat. Bring to the boil. Cook the pasta in the water for 1 minute less than instructed on the packet, giving you that perfect al dente bite.

Meanwhile, remove the sausages, ribs and a few pieces of beef and place on a large platter. Cover with foil and place in the centre of the table.

Drain the pasta and tip into the saucepan of ragù and remaining beef. Mix well for about 30 seconds, allowing the sauce to coat the pasta perfectly. Use tongs to divide the pappardelle, sauce and beef between 5 warmed plates. Spoon over any sauce left in the saucepan and sprinkle the Grana Padano cheese on top. Serve immediately. Enjoy the meats afterwards, with vegetables or just warm crusty bread.

CREAMY RISOTTO WITH LEEKS, ASPARAGUS + SPICY KING PRAWNS

Risotto cremoso con porri, asparagi e gamberoni piccanti

SERVES 5

When asparagus is in season, this is a recipe I love to make. It's so simple, tasty and colourful. As an alternative to prawns, I have used scallops or even crab, and you can substitute the leeks with a large onion if you prefer. As with all risotto recipes, this is quick and super-tasty and only takes 25 minutes from start to finish including the prep... but you do need to stay by the pot to stir continuously, so please make sure you have nothing else to do during that time and don't get distracted.

8 tbsp olive oil
2 medium-sized leeks, *trimmed, washed well (see page 63), halved lengthways and finely sliced*
400g arborio or carnaroli rice
200ml white wine
1.3 litres hot vegetable stock
250g fine asparagus spears, *woody ends removed, sliced diagonally into 3cm lengths*
80g mascarpone
120g salted butter, *cut into cubes*
15 raw large king prawns, *peeled and deveined (see page 18)*
2 tsp smoked paprika, or chilli powder
salt and freshly ground black pepper

Pour the oil into a large saucepan and place over a medium heat. Add the leeks and fry for 8 minutes until softened, stirring occasionally with a wooden spoon.

Tip in the rice and fry for 3 minutes, stirring continuously until all the grains are coated. Pour in the wine and let it bubble for 1 minute until the liquid has reduced by half and the alcohol has evaporated. Add 2 large ladles of hot stock, reduce the heat slightly and allow to simmer, stirring continuously until the liquid has been absorbed by the rice.

Stir in the asparagus. Continue adding the rest of the stock a couple of ladles at a time, stirring, until the rice is cooked but still has an al dente bite. This should take 16–18 minutes and you may not need all the stock.

Remove the saucepan from the heat and add the mascarpone and half the butter. Season with ½ tsp pepper and salt to taste. Stir vigorously for 30 seconds until well combined: this process in Italian is called *mantecatura* and is used to create a creamy texture. Keep warm while you fry the prawns.

Put the remaining butter into a large frying pan and place over a high heat. As soon as the butter starts to sizzle, add the prawns and sprinkle over the paprika or chilli powder. Fry for 1 minute on each side. Season with salt and switch off the heat.

To serve, equally divide the risotto between 5 warmed serving plates. Arrange 3 prawns on top of each plate and drizzle over any juices from the frying pan. Serve immediately.

LINGUINE WITH MUSSELS, WHITE WINE + CHERRY TOMATOES

Linguine con cozze, vino bianco e pomodorini

I grew up very close to the sea and was lucky to eat some of the most delicious seafood pretty much four or five times a week. My whole family is still deeply connected to the sea, not least my cousin Vincenzo who runs a stall at the Torre del Greco market. While I was there, it was only natural to buy and cook the mussels he sells, not only because he's family, but because they are truly the best. This dish is such a wonderful example of how simplicity is the best route to delicious food.

250g dried linguine,
  or spaghetti
6 tbsp olive oil
2 garlic cloves, *peeled and
  roughly chopped*
½ tsp chilli flakes
600g fresh mussels,
  *rinsed, beards and any
  barnacles removed and
  discarded*
1 glass *(about 150ml)*
  white wine
300g mixed colour
  cherry tomatoes, *halved*
large handful of flat leaf
  parsley leaves,
  roughly chopped
finely grated zest of
  1 unwaxed lemon
salt

Fill a large saucepan with 4 litres water, add 2 tbsp salt and place over a high heat. Bring to the boil. Cook the pasta in the salted boiling water for 1 minute less than instructed on the packet, giving you that perfect al dente bite, stirring occasionally.

Meanwhile, pour the oil into a large frying pan for which you have a lid, add the garlic and place over a high heat. As soon as the garlic starts to sizzle, fry for 10 seconds. Add the chilli flakes and mussels. Pour in the white wine and cover with the lid. Let the mussels steam for 4 minutes, shaking once or twice, or until cooked through (discard any that don't open).

Remove the lid and, using your hands, squeeze the tomatoes over the mussels. Stir with a wooden spoon and continue to cook for 2 more minutes. Scatter in the parsley and lemon zest and toss to combine. Switch off the heat.

Use a pair of tongs to carefully lift the cooked pasta from the boiling water straight into the frying pan with the mussels. The linguine should carry some of the starchy water with it, which will help create a sauce.

Toss all together for 30 seconds, then divide the pasta between 2 large warmed plates or bowls, pouring over any excess sauce. Serve immediately with a chilled glass of Italian white wine.

Camping
heaven

1982-84

SAFFRON RISOTTO WITH PROSECCO, PEAS + PECORINO ROMANO

Risotto allo zafferano con prosecco, piselli e pecorino Romano

SERVES 6

This is truly a traditional risotto, with the extra ingredients of prosecco and peas, just to give it a bit of a modern twist and some bright colour. Saffron risotto is one of the oldest known risotto recipes, dating back to the 15th century. There is a legend that it was created by accident from a prank, when a glass-maker in Milan added the golden spice – that he was using to stain glass for the cathedral windows – to a pan of rice being prepared for a wedding feast. What an incredibly successful prank! You can substitute the saffron threads with saffron powder and the pecorino Romano with Parmesan cheese, if you prefer.

5 tbsp olive oil
150g salted butter,
 cut into cubes
1 large onion, *peeled and*
 very finely chopped
500g arborio or carnaroli
 rice
large pinch of saffron
 threads, or ¾ tsp
 saffron powder
200ml prosecco
1.5 litres hot vegetable
 stock
250g frozen peas,
 defrosted
80g pecorino Romano
 cheese, *finely grated*
salt and freshly ground
 black pepper

Pour the oil into a large saucepan, add half the butter and place over a medium heat. Add the onion and fry for 8 minutes, stirring occasionally with a wooden spoon.

Tip in the rice and fry for 3 minutes, stirring continuously with a wooden spoon. Stir in the saffron, then pour in the prosecco. Simmer for 1 minute until the liquid has reduced by half and the alcohol from the prosecco has evaporated. Add 2 large ladles of the hot stock, reduce the heat slightly and allow to simmer, stirring continuously until the liquid has been absorbed by the rice.

Continue adding the rest of the stock a couple of ladles at a time, stirring, until the rice is cooked but still has a slight bite. This process should take 16–18 minutes and you may not need all the stock.

Remove the pan from the heat and add the remaining butter, the peas and the pecorino Romano. Season with ½ tsp pepper and salt to taste. Stir the risotto vigorously for 30 seconds until well combined, to create a creamy texture.

Serve immediately with a chilled bottle of prosecco.

ſPAGHETTI WITH CRAB, LEMON + WHITE WINE

Spaghetti con granchio, limone e vino bianco

SERVES 4

This is what a plate of pasta should be all about: simple, colourful and super-tasty. In the South of Italy, you will find this dish in many restaurants near the sea. Italians are not big on eating crab on its own, always with pasta or in a risotto. I remember, when I was a little boy, this was a real treat for us, as crab is expensive. My mother would prepare crab only and exclusively at Christmas and this is exactly the same recipe that she used to cook. Works every time!

6 tbsp extra virgin olive oil

3 garlic cloves, *peeled and finely sliced*

10 yellow cherry tomatoes, *halved*

10 red cherry tomatoes, *halved*

200ml white wine

350g fresh white crab meat

6 tbsp roughly chopped flat leaf parsley leaves

500g dried spaghetti

1 large unwaxed lemon

salt and freshly ground black pepper

Fill a large saucepan with 4 litres water, add 2 tbsp salt and place over a high heat. Bring to the boil.

Meanwhile, pour the oil into a large frying pan, add the garlic and place over a high heat. As soon as the garlic starts to sizzle, fry for 30 seconds. Add the tomatoes and sprinkle over 1 tsp salt. Mix all together and fry for 1 minute, stirring occasionally with a wooden spoon.

Pour over the wine and bring to the boil, letting it bubble for 1 minute and allowing the alcohol to evaporate. Switch off the heat and stir in the crab with the parsley and ½ tsp pepper, then set aside.

Cook the pasta in the salted boiling water for 1 minute less than instructed on the packet, giving you that perfect al dente bite, stirring occasionally. Drain and return it to the large saucepan. Pour in the crab sauce, finely grate the lemon zest over the top and stir all together.

Use tongs to divide the spaghetti between 4 warmed plates or bowls. Spoon over any sauce left in the saucepan and serve immediately.

SUPER-EASY PASTA SALAD WITH CHICKEN, HAM + RED PESTO

Insalata semplice di pasta con pollo, prosciutto e pesto rosso

SERVES 4–6

I love a pasta salad and this is a really tasty one. I must admit it came about just before we were off to Sardinia for the summer; the night before, I threw everything we had left over in the fridge or kitchen cupboards into it (which explains the apple and onions) and the outcome was delicious. That's what I love about pasta salads: anything goes and you can be as creative as you like. This is perfect for lunch on the go, it's filling and so versatile.

400g dried fusilli pasta
150g broccoli florets
100g green beans,
  trimmed and halved
5 tbsp good-quality
  mayonnaise
3 tbsp good-quality
  shop-bought red pesto
1 large red onion, *peeled*
  and finely sliced
1 large red apple, *cored,*
  cut into 1cm chunks
8 basil leaves, *torn in half*
150g cold chicken breast,
  cut into 1cm chunks
150g thick slice of ham,
  cut into 1cm chunks
5 spring onions, *trimmed*
  and finely sliced
4 tbsp extra virgin olive oil
salt and freshly ground
  black pepper

Fill a medium saucepan with water, add 1 tbsp salt and bring to the boil over a high heat. Add the pasta and cook for 2 minutes less than instructed on the packet, giving you a very al dente bite, stirring occasionally. Remove from the heat, drain in a large colander and rinse under cold water to stop it cooking. Leave to drain in the sink while you prepare the vegetables.

Fill the same saucepan with water and 1 tbsp salt and again bring to the boil over a high heat. Add the broccoli and boil for 1 minute. Add the beans and boil for a further 2 minutes. Meanwhile, pour the drained pasta into a large bowl.

Remove the broccoli and beans from the heat and drain in the same colander you used to drain the pasta. Rinse under cold water and leave to drain in the sink.

Place the mayonnaise, pesto, red onion, apple, basil, chicken, ham and ½ tsp pepper into the bowl with the pasta. Sprinkle in 1 tsp salt and mix well with a wooden spoon. Stir in the cooled broccoli and beans.

Place the pasta salad on a large serving platter. Sprinkle over the spring onions and drizzle over the extra virgin olive oil. Serve immediately, or place in the fridge until needed. Please remember always to serve this at room temperature, to appreciate the flavours of each ingredient.

RICOTTA DUMPLINGS WITH SPINACH + ROCKET IN SAGE + BUTTER SAUCE

Gnocchi di ricotta, spinaci e rucola al burro e salvia

SERVES 4

Gnocchi is so underrated and I really don't know why. If you buy the ready-made type, they are quicker to cook than pasta and can be served with lots of different sauces. This homemade special recipe has been a favourite in my family for more than three decades. Gnocchi are usually made with potatoes, but I've chosen ricotta instead to make them lighter and fluffier. You can even prepare my gnocchi the day before and leave them in the fridge until you are ready to cook them, so it's a great dish to make ahead of a dinner party, as it will take you just minutes to serve them.

200g spinach leaves
200g rocket leaves
150g ricotta, drained
100g pecorino cheese,
  finely grated, plus more
  to serve
2 egg yolks
80g '00' pasta flour
½ tsp freshly grated
  nutmeg
120g salted butter
12 large sage leaves
salt and freshly ground
  black pepper

Wash the spinach and rocket leaves and place in a large shallow saucepan with some water still clinging to the leaves. Cover with a lid, place over a medium heat and cook for 6 minutes, or until tender. Use tongs to turn the leaves and stir halfway through cooking. Drain thoroughly in a colander. Using the back of a wooden spoon, press down to extract as much water as possible. When the spinach and rocket are cool enough to handle, squeeze the leaves with your hands to extract any remaining water, then finely chop them.

Put the spinach and rocket into a large bowl and add the ricotta, pecorino, egg yolks, flour and nutmeg. Season with ½ tsp salt and ¼ tsp pepper, then mix well to combine. Line 2 large flat baking trays with baking parchment.

Scoop some of the mixture, about the size of a walnut, on to a dessertspoon. Carefully transfer the mixture to another dessertspoon, turning and smoothing each side. Repeat this turning and smoothing process several times until you have a neat, smooth egg shape with pointed ends (see photos, overleaf). Lay it on a prepared baking sheet and repeat until you have used all the mixture. You should make about 40 gnocchi. Chill for 1 hour.

Fill a large saucepan with 3 litres water, add 1 tbsp salt, place over a high heat and bring to the boil.

Meanwhile, melt the butter in a large frying pan and add the sage. Leave over the lowest heat setting on the hob to keep warm.

Drop half the gnocchi into the boiling water and simmer gently for 3 minutes. They are ready when they rise to the surface. Using a slotted spoon, lift up the gnocchi and tap the spoon on kitchen paper to get rid of any excess water. Transfer to the frying pan with the butter and sage. Repeat the process to cook and drain the remaining gnocchi.

Once all the gnocchi are in the frying pan with the butter and sage, increase the heat to high and spoon the melted butter all over the gnocchi to ensure they are well coated.

Serve on 4 warmed plates or bowls, sprinkling over more grated pecorino and a few twists of black pepper.

CHEF ROSSELLA'S RAGÙ WITH NONNA GIULIA'S FRESH EGG TAGLIATELLE

Il ragù di chef Rossella con le tagliatelle all'uovo di Nonna Giulia

SERVES 4

Making your own pasta is so satisfying, so if you have never done it before, this is definitely one for you to try! For her ragù, Rossella uses 100g each of pork and veal, which she minces herself. If you have a mincing attachment for a food processor, you can do the same, but of course your butcher will mix the meats for you if you prefer. You will need a pasta machine for this recipe. It is possible to make it with a rolling pin, but much harder as the pasta needs to be just 1mm thick.

FOR THE RAGÙ
5 tbsp olive oil
1 celery stick, *finely chopped*
1 carrot, *peeled and finely chopped*
1 onion, *peeled and finely chopped*
100g minced pork
100g minced veal
400g can of chopped tomatoes
salt and freshly ground black pepper

FOR THE PASTA
400g '00' flour, *plus more to dust*
4 tsp extra virgin olive oil
4 eggs, *lightly beaten*

Start with the ragù, as it will cook for some time. Heat the regular oil in a large, heavy saucepan, for which you have a lid, over a medium-high heat. Add the celery, carrot and onion, stir with a wooden spoon and fry for 10 minutes, or until soft. Add the minced meats and stir to combine. Cover with the lid and cook for 30 minutes, stirring occasionally. Now add the chopped tomatoes, stir, reduce the heat and allow to cook for 3 hours. Stir occasionally and top up with a little water if the sauce looks like it is sticking to the pan. When it is ready, season with salt and pepper.

Meanwhile, make the pasta. On a clean, dry work surface, create a mound with the flour and make a well in the middle. Add the extra virgin olive oil and eggs to the well and bring the flour into the wet ingredients with your hand (or use a fork, if you prefer). Mix until you create a dough. Knead vigorously by hand until smooth and elastic, around 10 minutes, wetting your hands if the dough is dry, then cover with a tea towel and rest for 1 hour.

Divide the dough in half, covering the portion you are not working with so it doesn't dry out. Take a portion of pasta dough, flatten it into a disc and dust with flour. Dust the work surface and pasta machine with flour too.

Pass the floured dough through the widest setting of the pasta machine 3 times. Now reduce the setting by 1 notch and pass the pasta through again. Continue, reducing the setting by 1 notch each time, until you reach the second thinnest setting. The pasta should be about 1mm thick. Dust both sides with flour, lay it on the floured work surface and cut into 1cm-wide strips. Repeat to roll and cut the rest of the dough.

When the ragù is nearly ready, fill a large saucepan with 4 litres water, add 2 tbsp salt and place over a high heat. Bring to the boil. Cook the pasta in the salted boiling water for 1 minute. Drain, then tip the pasta into the ragù. Mix well to combine, then equally divide the homemade pasta ragù between 4 large warmed plates. Serve immediately.

Fish

and

Seafood

1985

Catch and cook

The world's consumption of fish has doubled over the past 30 years. Fishing has become industrialised, and, as a result, 80 per cent of the world's main fish species are already at risk of disappearing. What I love about the smaller local restaurants when you travel through Italy is that they have, more often than not, sourced their fish from a local fisherman, ensuring you get the best quality seafood caught in the best possible way... normally that morning. You can really taste the difference, so please don't watch a frightening TV programme and stop eating fish or meat all together, just try to buy it from local fishmongers and butchers. That will not only keep them in business but also, I guarantee, give you a far superior quality. I know it's not always easy, and is sometimes more costly, but it's so worth it for us, and for our children in the long run.

I get really excited when I write a new book, as my wife and children become my guinea pigs and either cook the recipes I create or sample what I cook. We don't often eat fish in the UK, as my wife doesn't really like it so isn't confident in cooking it. However, every time she prepares one of my fish recipes, she not only says how easy it is but often finishes her plate. The fish pie here was her favourite and she has made it quite a few times, saying it's the only fish pie she has ever liked, so that's a huge recommendation from her.

Fish and seafood always remind me of summer, maybe because being in Italy in June filming and then in July and August on holiday, that's where I get to cook it the most; being by the sea, it would be criminal not to cook and eat fish most days. Thankfully, my children love all fish. I think a firm favourite for them are the barbecue fish skewers here. Most fish recipes are just so light and tasty – perfect for those hot days – even though, to be honest, if I had my way we would eat more fish all year round. I think my all-time favourite in this chapter, if I had to just pick one, would be the king prawns in tomato sauce. I think it's the dunking up the sauce with warm crusty bread afterwards that appeals to me the most. I am normally an advocate of allowing the main ingredient to shine without covering it in sauces, and, don't get me wrong, there is nothing more delicious than plain grilled or sautéed prawns, but I must admit, we are pretty much the dunky-dunky family. Every single one of the D'Acampos, right back to the first years I can remember, always loved a dish with a sauce that a piece of crusty bread could be dunked into and eaten. A close second favourite here is definitely the scallops, which I used to help prepare with my Nonna Assunta after school when I was a young boy. Every time I make them, it reminds me of home.

KING PRAWNS IN SPICY TOMATO SAUCE WITH OREGANO BRUSCHETTA

Gamberoni all'arrabbiata con bruschetta all'origano

SERVES 4

This recipe takes less than half an hour to cook from start to finish and looks and tastes fantastic. The bread is a must-have, to mop up the sauce after you have eaten the prawns. If you don't like the fiddly-ness of peeling prawns, you can use ready-peeled uncooked king prawns, but shorten the cooking time from six to four minutes. You can actually make two meals in one with this recipe: eat the prawns with a lovely salad or the bruschetta for lunch, then use the sauce with spaghetti or linguine for dinner.

6 tbsp olive oil

6 anchovy fillets in oil, *drained*

1 medium-sized red onion, *peeled and finely sliced*

80g pitted black Leccino olives, or other good-quality pitted black olives such as Kalamata

2 tbsp capers in salt, *rinsed under cold water and drained*

2 tsp chilli flakes

3 x 400g cans of chopped tomatoes

4 tbsp finely chopped flat leaf parsley leaves

20 large king prawns, *heads and shells on, but long antennae removed*

FOR THE BRUSCHETTA

8 slices of ciabatta, *about 1cm thick*

8 tsp extra virgin olive oil

dried oregano

salt and freshly ground black pepper

Prepare the bruschetta as on page 33, but don't grill them yet. Set aside on their baking tray.

Now for the prawns. Heat the oil in a shallow saucepan or wok over a medium heat. Add the anchovies and fry for 2 minutes, or until they break down, stirring occasionally with a wooden spoon. Add the onion and fry for 8 minutes, stirring occasionally. Stir in the olives, capers and chilli and fry for 1 minute. Pour in the chopped tomatoes and ½ tsp salt, stir and simmer for 12 minutes, stirring occasionally.

Preheat the grill to high.

Stir the parsley into the tomato sauce. Using tongs, place the king prawns into the sauce and cook for 6 minutes, turning the prawns halfway through.

Meanwhile, place the bread under the grill for 4–5 minutes until golden and toasted. Remove and set aside. You only need to toast one side of the bread.

To serve, divide the sauce between 4 warmed plates, place 5 prawns on each and 2 slices of oregano bruschetta on the side. Serve immediately.

CRAB OMELETTE WITH MASCARPONE + CHIVES

Frittatina di granchio con mascarpone e erba cipollina

<u>SERVES 2</u>

Omelettes just make eggs much more exciting, as so many different ingredients can be added to create a completely different flavour every time. I think omelettes are the perfect super-quick lunch. They aren't only the easiest recipes to make, but they can be so tasty and filling too. I had some leftover crab meat once, which is when I came up with this recipe, as I hate waste.

6 large eggs
1 tbsp mascarpone
120g fresh white crab
 meat
1 tbsp finely chopped
 chives
1 tbsp finely chopped flat
 leaf parsley leaves
15g salted butter
1 echalion shallot, *peeled*
 and finely chopped
salt and freshly ground
 black pepper

Crack the eggs into a small bowl and add the mascarpone. Lightly beat until all is combined, then stir in the crab, chives and parsley. Season with a large pinch of salt and pepper. Stir again and set aside.

Place the butter in a small frying pan and melt it over a medium heat. Add the shallot and fry for 2 minutes, stirring occasionally.

Pour in the egg and crab mixture. Using a spatula, occasionally draw in the sides of the omelette until it starts to set.

When the egg is firm and set underneath, but still slightly soft and wobbly on top, gently flip one side of the omelette over the other, to form a semicircle. Cook for a further minute.

Remove from the heat and serve with a simple crispy salad dressed with extra virgin olive oil, salt and pepper.

CREAMY FISH PIE WITH RED ONIONS + BOILED EGGS

Pasticcio di pesce con cipolle rosse e uova sode

SERVES 6-8

This is an old D'Acampo classic, a recipe that's been passed down for years. Once you are confident with the dish, you can be as inventive as you like, substituting the fish for your favourites such as hake, salmon or scallops. You can also prep the pie in the morning for later that day, which is a bonus when cooking for guests. I hope you enjoy this recipe as much as my family do and, once you have tasted the mash topping, I'm sure from now on it will be a favourite in your family.

FOR THE FILLING
1 red onion, *peeled and very finely sliced*
2 bay leaves
450ml full-fat milk
300ml double cream
500g unskinned cod fillet
250g undyed, unskinned smoked haddock fillet
150g large peeled cooked prawns, *deveined* (see page 18)
4 hard-boiled eggs, *peeled and halved lengthways*
50g salted butter
45g plain flour
5 tbsp finely chopped flat leaf parsley leaves
1 tsp freshly grated nutmeg
salt and freshly ground black pepper

FOR THE TOPPING
1.2kg floury potatoes, *such as Maris Piper, peeled and roughly cut into medium wedges*
50g salted butter, *roughly cut into 4cm cubes*
150ml full-fat milk
1 egg yolk

Put the red onion, bay leaves, milk and cream into a large shallow saucepan and place over a medium heat. Bring to the boil, then reduce the heat slightly and simmer for 10 minutes. Add the fish, skin side up, and cook for 3 minutes. Remove the fish and place on a plate.

Strain the milk through a sieve into a jug. Discard the bay leaves from the sieve and tip out the onion into a 1.75-litre capacity ovenproof dish. Flake the fish over the onion, discarding the skins. Add the prawns and gently mix all together using a wooden spoon. Place the eggs, yolks up, on top.

In the same shallow saucepan, melt the butter over a medium heat, then mix in the flour using a hand-held whisk and cook for 1 minute. Pour in the reserved milk and stir, so the flour and milk combine. Bring slowly to the boil, stirring all the time. Leave to gently simmer for 10 minutes.

Remove from the heat, stir in the parsley, nutmeg, 1 tsp salt and ½ tsp pepper and pour the sauce over the fish. Allow to cool for 15 minutes, then cover and place in the fridge to set for 45 minutes.

Preheat the oven to 200°C/fan 180°C/Gas 6.

For the topping, fill a large saucepan with 3 litres water and 1 tbsp salt. Add the potatoes and boil over a high heat for 30 minutes. Drain, and using a ricer, rice the potatoes into the pan. Add the butter, milk, egg yolk, 1 tsp salt and ½ tsp pepper and stir to a creamy mash. Spoon on top of the filling and spread using the back of a fork, creating peaks.

Place the dish on a baking tray and cook in the middle of the oven for 35 minutes.

Remove from the oven and serve immediately with any green vegetable of your choice, or a mixed salad simply dressed with extra virgin olive oil, salt and pepper.

FILLETS OF SEA BASS WITH CHIVES, LEMON + MUSTARD SAUCE

Filetti di spigola con salsa alle erbe cipollina, limone e senape

<u>SERVES 4</u>

The best thing about this recipe is that you can make the sauce in the morning, or even the day before, refrigerate it, then gently reheat it slightly when needed, allowing you to prepare an amazing dinner in literally four minutes. What a fantastic recipe after a long day. The sauce works well with any white fish such as cod, sea bream, plaice...

4 sea bass fillets, *skin on, about 150g each*
4 tbsp olive oil

FOR THE SAUCE
2 egg yolks
2 tsp plain flour
300ml double cream
2 tsp lemon juice
2 tsp Dijon mustard
1 tbsp chopped chives
salt and freshly ground black pepper

Start with the sauce. Using a hand-held whisk, mix the egg yolks and flour together in a medium-sized bowl. Whisk in the cream until smooth and combined. Transfer to a small saucepan and place over a medium-low heat. Cook gently, stirring constantly with the whisk, for 3 minutes. Add the lemon juice, mustard, chives, 1 tsp salt and ½ tsp pepper and stir with your whisk for a further 1–2 minutes until the sauce has thickened. Now either allow it to cool, cover with clingfilm and place in the fridge until needed, or simply set aside while you cook the fish.

Place the fish on a board or flat plate and pat dry with kitchen paper. Using a sharp knife, score the skin with 3 diagonal cuts enough so you can see the flesh through them. Season with a pinch of salt and pepper.

Pour the olive oil into a large frying pan and place over a high heat. When the oil is really hot, place the fillets, skin side down, in the pan and fry for 3 minutes or until the skin is golden and crisp. (The flesh should be opaque two-thirds of the way up the fillets.) Gently turn the fillets over and fry for 1 further minute.

If the sauce needs reheating, place it over a low heat and gently heat for a couple of minutes.

Equally divide the chive and lemon sauce between 4 warmed plates and gently place a sea bass fillet on top, skin side up. Serve with seasonal vegetables and some warm crusty bread to dunk up the sauce.

GRILLED CARAMELISED COD WITH HONEY, GARLIC + BALSAMIC VINEGAR

Merluzzo al forno caramellato con miele, aglio e aceto balsamico

SERVES 4

If you are new to cooking fish, this is the perfect recipe to get you started. It will take you minutes to prepare and very little can go wrong, as you simply cook it under the grill. I have used cod in this recipe for a light flavour, letting the marinade really stand out, but monkfish or salmon also work very well. Serve with new potatoes and a crispy salad, or, even better, with my Sautéed New Potatoes with Onions, Peas + Pancetta and Sicilian-Style Vegetables with Baby Plum Tomatoes, Mint + Chilli (see pages 202 and 205)... or just with some cheeky fat chips.

3 tbsp runny honey or maple syrup
5 tbsp balsamic vinegar
3 tbsp extra virgin olive oil
4 tbsp finely chopped flat leaf parsley leaves
1 garlic clove, *peeled and crushed*
1 tsp smoked paprika
4 x 200g skinless cod fillets
salt and freshly ground black pepper

Pour the honey and balsamic vinegar into a medium-sized glass bowl. Use a hand-held whisk to mix. Gradually add the extra virgin olive oil, stirring continuously with the whisk. Stir in the parsley, garlic, paprika, ¼ tsp salt and ¼ tsp pepper.

Gently place the cod fillets into the marinade. Cover with clingfilm and leave to marinate at room temperature for 30 minutes, turning the cod fillets over halfway through.

Preheat the grill to its highest setting.

Place a sheet of foil on a medium-sized baking sheet, then lay a sheet of baking parchment on top of the foil.

Gently move the fish around in the marinade, then, using tongs, carefully place the cod fillets, skinned side down, on the baking parchment. Discard the remaining marinade.

Season each fillet with a generous sprinkle of salt and pepper and grill for 10 minutes. Remove from the grill and, using a flexible spatula, gently transfer a cod fillet to each of 4 warmed plates. Serve immediately.

GRILLED SCALLOPS WITH PARSLEY + HAZELNUT BUTTER

Capesante alla griglia con burro al prezzemolo e nocciole

<u>SERVES 4</u>

This is an amazing recipe if you really want to impress your guests or your family. The butter will take you minutes to prepare in the morning or the day before, and the scallops only take four or five minutes to grill. Not only do they taste fantastic, but they look stunning. You can substitute the hazelnuts with pistachio nuts if you prefer, or if you have nut allergies and need to eliminate the nuts completely, the parsley butter will still work well.

20g unblanched (skin-on) hazelnuts
100g salted butter, *softened*
small handful of flat leaf parsley leaves, *roughly chopped*
1 tsp lemon juice
¼ echalion shallot, *peeled and roughly chopped*
12 large prepared scallops, *each sitting on a half shell*
salt and freshly ground black pepper

Preheat the grill to its highest setting.

Place the hazelnuts on a small flat baking tray and toast under the grill for 2 minutes. Shake the tray and continue to grill for a further 2 minutes. Remove the tray from the oven, place the hazelnuts on a clean tea towel and allow to cool slightly. Rub off the skins with the tea towel and roughly chop the hazelnuts.

Tip the chopped nuts into a food processor. Add the butter, parsley, lemon juice and shallot. Season with a good pinch of salt and pepper and process until well mixed. Transfer the mixture to a small bowl, cover with clingfilm and set aside, or leave in the fridge until needed. If you prepare the butter ahead of time, remember to take it out of the fridge 30 minutes before you need it, so it is not fridge-hard.

Lay out the shells with the scallops inside on a large flat baking tray and season each with a pinch of salt and pepper. Put 1 heaped tsp parsley and hazelnut butter on top of each scallop. Grill for 4–5 minutes.

Remove from the grill and either serve up 3 scallops per person, or place the shells on a large serving platter in the centre of the table. Either way, a real ooooooh moment…

MY AUNTY RITA'S BABY OCTOPUS WITH MUSSELS + CHERRY TOMATOES

Polipetti alla Luciana di Zia Rita

SERVES 4

Whenever I go home to Torre del Greco and visit my Aunty Rita, she always makes me this recipe, as I just love seafood. Even when the weather is boiling hot, this dish is always received with huge smiles and kisses. Aunty Rita uses local Vesuvian cherry tomatoes – *pomodorini del Piennolo* – as they are so very sweet, but any cherry tomatoes will work fantastically. If you struggle to find baby octopus at your local supermarket, you can buy them frozen in bags from any good fishmonger.

100ml extra virgin olive oil
3 garlic cloves, *peeled and sliced*
1 red chilli, *deseeded and finely chopped*
1kg small octopus
150ml white wine
15 cherry tomatoes
700g tomato passata
large bunch of flat leaf parsley leaves, *chopped*
1kg mussels, *rinsed, beards and any barnacles removed and discarded*
salt

FOR THE BRUSCHETTA
8 slices of ciabatta, *about 1cm thick*
8 tsp extra virgin olive oil
dried oregano
salt and freshly ground black pepper

Prepare the bruschetta (see page 33), but don't grill them yet. Set aside on their baking tray.

Pour the oil into a large shallow saucepan, set over a medium-low heat and sauté the garlic and chilli for 1 minute, until the garlic begins to give off its aroma.

Now add the octopus and let them simmer over a gentle heat, stirring with a wooden spoon, for 5 minutes, or until the tentacles withdraw a bit. Pour in the wine and simmer for about 5 minutes.

Add the whole cherry tomatoes, along with the tomato passata and half the parsley, then simmer over a low heat for 45 minutes, stirring frequently with a wooden spoon. Season with salt to taste.

After the octopus and sauce have been cooking for 40 minutes, place a large saucepan with a lid over a high heat and wait until it is hot. Tip in the mussels, cover and cook for 4 minutes, or until the shells open. (Discard any that remain closed.) Remove and discard the shells of half the mussels and add them to the pan with the octopus. Stir well with a wooden spoon. Set aside the remaining mussels in their shells.

Meanwhile, place the bread under the grill for 4–5 minutes until golden and toasted. Remove and set aside. You only need to toast one side of the bread.

To serve, place 1 bruschetta in each of 4 warmed bowls, then equally ladle the octopus and tomato between them, pouring it over the bread. Divide the mussels in their shells between the bowls, gently placing them on top. Sprinkle over the remaining parsley and serve immediately, with the remaining bruschetta for extra dunking bliss.

Holiday fun

Sunshine days

1986

SALMON FISHCAKES WITH HOMEMADE TARTARE DRESSING

Tortini di salmone con salsa tartara di senape, olive e capperi

SERVES 4

*as a main course,
or 6 as a starter*

What I love about this recipe is that you can prep the fishcakes and keep them in the fridge for a day or so until ready to fry and eat, giving you a very quick lunch or dinner after working all day. And of course, once cooked, you can also eat them cold. You can substitute the salmon with cod fillet or tuna if you prefer. The sauce is like a tartare sauce in terms of ingredients, but I have made it runnier to create more of a dressing (it also works really well as a salad dressing).

300g new potatoes,
   unpeeled but very
   well scrubbed
500g skinned salmon fillet
1 tbsp extra virgin olive oil
1 egg, *lightly beaten*
1 tbsp finely chopped
   gherkins
1 tbsp capers in salt,
   *rinsed under cold water,
   drained and chopped*
1 hard-boiled egg, *peeled
   and roughly chopped*
1 tbsp finely chopped flat
   leaf parsley leaves
¼ tsp paprika
80g fresh breadcrumbs
50ml olive oil
300ml sunflower oil
salt and freshly ground
   black pepper

Preheat the oven to 180°C/fan 160°C/Gas 4.

Pour 1.5 litres water into a medium-sized saucepan and add 1 tbsp salt and the new potatoes. Place over a medium heat and cook for 30 minutes. Drain and set aside to cool slightly.

Place a baking sheet on a small flat baking tray. Arrange the salmon fillet on the sheet and brush with the extra virgin olive oil. Sprinkle over a large pinch of pepper and a normal pinch of salt. Cook in the middle of the oven for 12 minutes. Remove from the oven and set aside to cool for 10 minutes.

Put the beaten egg, gherkins, capers, chopped egg, parsley, paprika, 1½ tsp salt and 1 tsp pepper into a large bowl. When the salmon is cool enough to be handled, flake it into the bowl. Place the boiled potatoes on a flat plate and crush them, using a fork. Tip them into the large bowl with the salmon. Gently mix the ingredients together to combine, but take care not to break up the fish flakes too much. Shape the mixture into 12 round patties, flatten them and coat them in the breadcrumbs.

Place on a flat plate or baking tray, loosely cover with clingfilm and refrigerate for at least 30 minutes, allowing the fishcakes to set.

Remove the fishcakes from the fridge 15 minutes before frying.

Pour the regular olive oil and the sunflower oil into a large frying pan and place over a medium heat until hot. Gently place 6 fishcakes into the hot oil and fry for 3 minutes on each side, until golden. Carefully lift them on to a flat plate covered with kitchen paper, allowing any excess oil to be absorbed. Repeat the process with the remaining 6 fishcakes.

FOR THE DRESSING
½ tbsp English mustard
1 tsp white wine vinegar
1 egg
150ml sunflower oil
1 tsp finely chopped
  pitted green olives
1 tsp capers in salt,
  rinsed under cold water,
  drained and finely chopped
1 tsp finely chopped
  gherkins
1 tsp finely chopped flat
  leaf parsley leaves
1 tsp finely chopped
  chives
finely grated zest of
  1 unwaxed lemon

Meanwhile, to make the dressing, put the mustard, vinegar, egg and ½ tsp salt into a small bowl and, using a hand-held whisk, whisk well for 2 minutes. Pour in the sunflower oil a little at a time, whisking constantly. Add the olives, capers, gherkins, parsley and chives and continue to mix. Fold in the lemon zest, cover with clingfilm and refrigerate until needed.

Serve the fishcakes hot or at room temperature, accompanied with the homemade tartare dressing and a crispy salad.

SWORDFISH, SALMON + PRAWN SKEWERS WITH RED ONIONS + YELLOW PEPPERS

Spiedini di pesce spada, salmone e gamberoni con cipolla rossa e peperoni gialli

SERVES 4

makes 8 skewers

This recipe makes eight skewers. I normally serve two per person with some potatoes and a mixed salad, but if there are only two of you, grill them all and allow four skewers to cool down. Remove the fish and vegetables from the skewers and place in a small bowl, cover with clingfilm and refrigerate. Add to a salad the next day and you have another great lunch. You can also try different fish such as monkfish, tuna or cod, using the same technique and cooking times.

3 tbsp olive oil

3 garlic cloves, *peeled and crushed*

handful of dill, *finely chopped*

handful of flat leaf parsley leaves, *finely chopped*

400g skinless, boneless swordfish, *cut into 3cm cubes*

400g skinless salmon fillets, *cut into 3cm cubes*

16 raw king prawns, *heads and tails removed, deveined* (see page 18)

juice of 1 lemon

1 large red onion, *peeled and cut into 16 wedges lengthways*

1 large yellow pepper, *deseeded and cut into 16 chunks*

salt and freshly ground black pepper

Mix together the olive oil, garlic, dill and parsley in a large bowl. Add the fish and prawns and, using a tablespoon, gently stir, ensuring everything is coated in the marinade. Cover and refrigerate for at least 1 hour.

Soak 8 wooden skewers in cold water for 10 minutes, so they won't burn when placed on the grill or barbecue. (Or use metal skewers.)

Remove the fish from the fridge, add the lemon juice with a big pinch of salt and pepper and stir.

Preheat a large griddle pan over a high heat for 5 minutes until very hot. Or make your barbecue ready for cooking.

Meanwhile, start threading the skewers. Thread an onion wedge, then a chunk of salmon, then a chunk of swordfish, then a chunk of pepper and then a prawn on to a skewer. Repeat the pattern so you have 2 of each ingredient on each skewer. Thread the remaining skewers. (You obviously don't have to thread the ingredients in this order, but I like the way it looks!)

Place 4 skewers on the hot griddle pan and cook for 10 minutes, turning regularly, or until the fish and prawns are cooked through. Remove from the griddle and place on a large serving platter. Keep warm. Repeat the process with the other 4 skewers. Alternatively, cook all the skewers on a barbecue for the same amount of time.

Sprinkle a generous amount of salt and pepper on the skewers and serve immediately with a mixed salad or jacket potatoes.

WRAPPED BAKED SEA BREAM WITH LEMON + CHIVES

Orata al cartoccio con limone e erba cipollina

SERVES 2

Cooking a whole fish is just so easy to do and looks so impressive. I know it can be a bit fiddly when it comes to portioning it up, but it is absolutely worth the hassle and seems to get a 'wow' response every time. Ask your fishmonger to clean the fish by descaling it and gutting it, making a slit in its belly so you can fill the cavity. If you can, I really recommend going to a fishmonger for this recipe. It truly does make a difference to the quality and size of the fish offered, and they can prep it exactly as you need it.

1 whole sea bream,
  about 650g
2 tbsp finely chopped
  chives, *plus whole chives
  to decorate*
1 garlic clove, *peeled and
  finely sliced*
¼ red chilli, *deseeded and
  finely chopped*
1 tbsp extra virgin olive
  oil, *plus more for drizzling
  over the fish*
2 unwaxed lemons
sea salt flakes

FOR THE DRESSING
5 tbsp extra virgin olive oil
juice of 1 lemon
½ garlic clove, *peeled
  and crushed*
pinch of chilli flakes
½ tsp dried oregano

Preheat the oven to 200°C/fan 180°C/Gas 6.

Place a large piece of foil – about 60 x 30cm – on a work surface and lay a same-sized sheet of baking parchment on top. Place the fish in the centre of the baking parchment.

In a small bowl, combine the chives, garlic, chilli and 1 tbsp extra virgin olive oil. Mix in the finely grated zest and juice of ½ lemon and stuff the cavity of the fish with the herby mixture. Place 2 lemon slices inside the fish, on top of the marinade. Drizzle over some extra virgin olive oil.

Arrange 5–6 chives and 2 lemon slices on top of the sea bream. Wrap tightly in the parchment and foil, ensuring the fish is completely sealed inside its package. Place on a flat baking tray and bake in the middle of the oven for 40 minutes.

Meanwhile, put all the dressing ingredients into a small saucepan. Place over a medium heat and cook for 5 minutes. Stir occasionally using a hand-held whisk, until it thickens slightly. Remove from the heat, season with salt and pour into a small bowl or jug.

Fillet the fish and divide equally between 2 warmed serving plates. Drizzle over the dressing and sprinkle sea salt flakes on top. Serve with a simple crispy salad dressed with extra virgin olive oil, lemon juice, salt and pepper, or just with your favourite green vegetables.

MEAT

AND

POULTRY

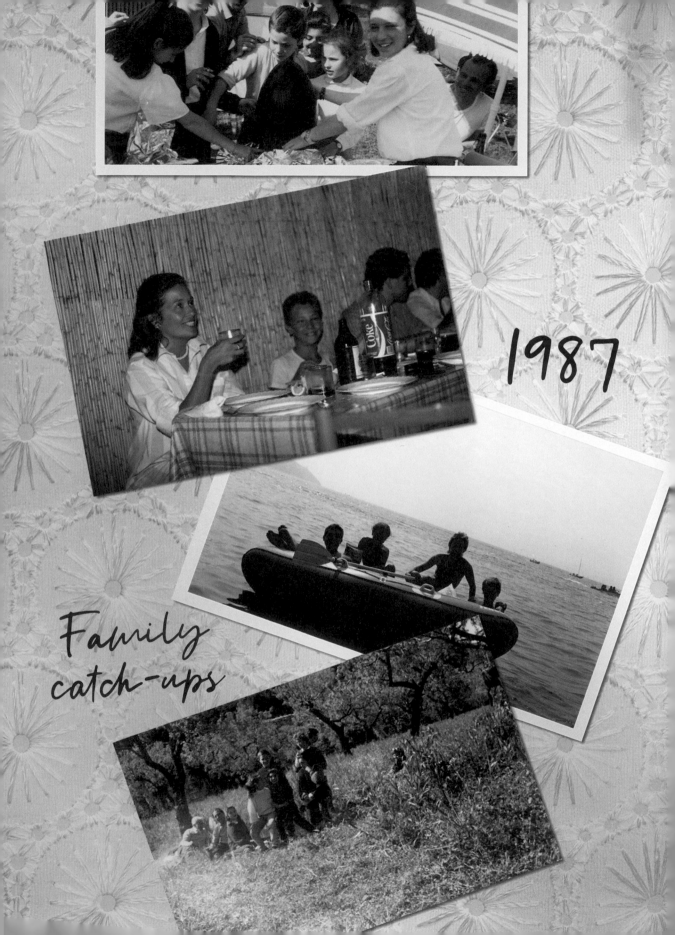

1987

Family
catch-ups

I love meat, all meat, but I have definitely eaten more of it during the last 24 years, since I left the South of Italy. There, it was fish that played the bigger part in my diet. Meat was hugely expensive for my family, so we didn't have it often, and when we did, pork or chicken was served more than the very expensive veal or steak.

Since then, travelling over the years in Italy – especially through the Central and Northern regions – I have been lucky enough to try many new meat and poultry recipes, but I still have to say that my favourites are the more traditional methods of cooking and the not-so-popular cuts on offer. I just think the meat remains the star of the show when you don't drown it in sauces or too many other flavours. My T-bone steak recipe in this chapter is proof of the ultimate flavoured steak: simple seasoning and an even simpler cooking method, but an incredible outcome.

My children are huge meat lovers and always try to get me to come up with something new. It occurred to me that, rather than the usual concoctions they are used to, they should taste some of the more traditional classic recipes that often seem to get lost along the way. Many people turn up their noses at recipes such as the Italian mixed meat stew here, but, when they actually try it, are super-satisfied, as each of the meats can truly be tasted and appreciated in their own right. I make all my recipes at home for my family before they go into a book and everyone was dreading that one... and yet they loved it. Sometimes it's best just not to tell nervous meat-eaters what you're cooking for them, instead just serve it up and let them try it! (Obviously not if they have allergies.) Take the roasted rabbit in this chapter: I had to convince my daughter Mia to try some, but, when she did, she finished her plate in minutes and even uttered that famous saying: 'Oh, it kind of tastes like chicken.' If you are a meat-eater, try everything. Sometimes you may not like it, but, in my house, it's a must to at least try things. More often than not, you will be pleasantly surprised.

My personal favourites in this section are the braised veal shin and a recipe I created in Sardinia – where pork features heavily – my amazing roast shoulder of pork. If you love pulled pork with crispy crackling, this is a must-try and it's also fantastic for dinner parties.

CHICKEN BURGERS WITH LEMON, GARLIC + PARMESAN

Hamburger di pollo con limone, aglio e Parmigiano Reggiano

SERVES 4

What an easy, tasty recipe that literally takes minutes to prepare. It is the perfect lunch, light dinner or barbecue as it's so light both in texture and flavour. You can spread mustard or mayonnaise over your bun, but, to be honest, the flavours of lemon and garlic are so good, you might not feel you need to. You can substitute the minced chicken with minced turkey if you prefer.

50ml full-fat milk
2 slices of white bread,
  total weight about 50g,
  crusts removed
450g minced chicken
4 sage leaves,
  finely chopped
leaves from 2 thyme
  sprigs, *finely chopped*
1 large garlic clove, *peeled*
  and crushed
50g Parmesan cheese,
  finely grated
1 egg, *lightly beaten*
finely grated zest
  and juice of
  1 unwaxed lemon
4 tbsp water
4 tbsp extra virgin olive oil
20g rocket leaves
  (*4 small handfuls*)
4 brioche burger buns
salt and freshly ground
  black pepper

Pour the milk into a large bowl. Break the bread up into the milk and use your fingers to mix together. Add the chicken, sage, thyme, garlic, Parmesan, egg, lemon zest, 1 tsp salt and ½ tsp pepper and mix well using your hands.

Divide the mixture into 4 and shape into burger patties. Place on a large flat plate, loosely cover with baking parchment and put into the fridge for 1 hour, to allow the burgers to 'set'.

Meanwhile, squeeze the lemon juice into a small bowl and add the measured water. Set aside.

Remove the burgers from the fridge 30 minutes before cooking them.

Pour 3 tbsp oil into a large frying pan for which you have a lid and place over a medium heat. When the oil is hot, use a slotted spatula to carefully place in the chicken patties. Fry for 3 minutes, then gently turn them over and fry for a further 3 minutes. Pour the lemon water into the frying pan, cover with a lid and cook for 3 minutes until most of the liquid has been absorbed.

Place the rocket in a small bowl and season with a pinch of salt and the remaining 1 tbsp oil. Mix well.

Place the bottom of a brioche bun in the centre of the serving plate (I like mine slightly toasted). Place a chicken burger on top. Arrange a small handful of rocket leaves on top of the burger, top with the other half of the brioche bun and serve with a nice cold Italian beer... *Salute*!

ONE-POT ROAST CHICKEN WITH PEARL BARLEY, WHITE WINE + PEAS

Pollo al forno con orzo perlato, vino bianco e piselli

SERVES 4

I always love recipes that can be made in one pot, as there is very little mess or washing up, and this one looks great. It is a good recipe to make if you are having guests over, as you can just leave it in the oven cooking for an hour while you socialise and have a few glasses of prosecco. You can use a wide-based ovenproof frying pan instead of the casserole dish, and if you prefer, substitute the white wine with a rosé.

1 tbsp sunflower oil
8 large bone-in, skin-on
   chicken thighs, *total
   weight about 1.5kg*
2 carrots, *peeled and
   finely chopped*
1 large red onion, *peeled
   and finely chopped*
225g pearl barley
200ml white wine
4 rosemary sprigs
800ml hot chicken or
   vegetable stock
juice of ½ lemon
150g frozen peas, *defrosted*
bunch of parsley leaves,
   finely chopped
salt and freshly ground
   black pepper

Preheat the oven to 150°C/fan 130°C/Gas 2.

Pour the oil into a flameproof casserole dish and place over a high heat. Add the chicken, skin side up, and fry for 4 minutes. Season the skin with a large pinch of salt and pepper and turn the thighs over. Fry for a further 4 minutes until golden. Remove the thighs and place skin side up on a plate.

Put the carrots and onion into the casserole, sprinkle over 1 tsp salt and ½ tsp pepper and fry for 7 minutes, stirring occasionally with a wooden spoon. Stir in the pearl barley for 1 minute, then pour in the wine. Stir and allow the alcohol to evaporate for about 1 minute. Add the rosemary and pour over the hot stock. Stir, cover with a lid and simmer for 10 minutes.

Remove the dish from the heat and stir the barley. Place the chicken thighs on top of the barley, skin side up, and cook in the middle of the oven, uncovered, for 55 minutes.

Take the dish out of the oven, remove the chicken thighs and place on a plate. Remove and discard the rosemary. Pour the lemon juice and peas into the barley mixture and stir well. Check for seasoning.

Place the chicken back on top of the barley and return to the oven for a final 5 minutes.

Sprinkle over the parsley and serve in the middle of the table for everyone to tuck in. A perfect one-pot dish, with vegetables, pulses and protein.

ROAST SHOULDER OF LAMB STUFFED WITH MUSHROOMS + ROSEMARY

Agnello al forno ripieno con funghi e rosmarino

SERVES 6

Who doesn't love traditional roast lamb? Adding a rosemary and mushroom stuffing gives this recipe a fabulous little extra that tastes amazing. You can substitute the rosemary with mint or thyme and the olive oil with chilli-infused olive oil. I've based the cooking time on a 2kg piece of meat, but you can work out the cooking time of a different-sized joint by allowing 20 minutes per 500g, plus 20 minutes more at a higher heat. You will also need some butcher's string to hold the shoulder of lamb together. This makes a fantastic Sunday roast.

2 large onions, *peeled,*
  1 roughly sliced,
  1 finely chopped
1 tbsp olive oil
20g salted butter
350g chestnut
  mushrooms,
  finely chopped
2 tbsp finely chopped
  rosemary leaves
100g fresh breadcrumbs
1 egg, *lightly beaten*
2kg boned shoulder
  of lamb
1 tbsp sea salt flakes
salt and freshly ground
  black pepper

FOR THE GRAVY
1 tbsp plain flour
100ml red wine
200ml vegetable stock
1 tsp Worcestershire
  sauce
1 tbsp tomato purée
1 tbsp mint sauce
1 tbsp redcurrant jelly

Preheat the oven to 180°C/fan 160°C/Gas 4. Place the sliced onion in a large baking tray and set aside.

Put the olive oil and butter into a large frying pan and place over a high heat. Once the butter has melted, add the chopped onion and fry for 6 minutes, stirring occasionally with a wooden spoon. Stir in the mushrooms and rosemary and continue to fry for a further 5 minutes. Remove from the heat and tip into a large bowl. Add the breadcrumbs, egg, 1 tsp salt and ½ tsp pepper. Mix well, then allow to cool.

Open out the shoulder of lamb and place on a work surface, skin side down. Season with a pinch of salt and pepper. Spoon the cooled stuffing into the centre of the lamb and fold the sides of the meat over it. Using butcher's string, tie a ring around one end and then another string across it like a parcel. Repeat the process at the other end of the meat so you have 4–5 strings holding the parcel together (see photos, overleaf).

Place the lamb on the sliced onion in the tray, skin side up. Sprinkle the salt flakes and a large pinch of pepper on top and roast in the middle of the oven for 1 hour 20 minutes (or see recipe introduction). Increase the oven temperature to 240°C/fan 220°C/Gas 9 and roast for a further 20 minutes. Place on a carving board, cover with foil and allow to rest.

Place the baking tray in which you cooked the lamb over a medium heat and sprinkle in the flour. Stir using a hand-held whisk for 30 seconds, then add the wine, continuing to whisk. Bring to the boil and stir in the stock, Worcestershire sauce, tomato purée, mint sauce and redcurrant jelly. Continue to boil until the gravy thickens slightly, stirring occasionally. Season with salt and pepper to taste and pour into a gravy jug.

Slice the lamb and place on a large platter for guests to help themselves. Serve with your favourite trimmings and the delicious gravy.

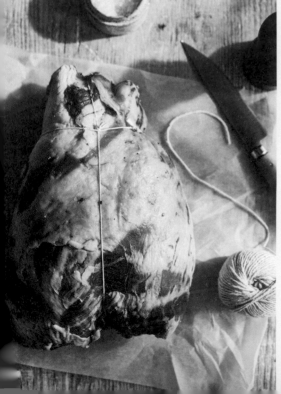

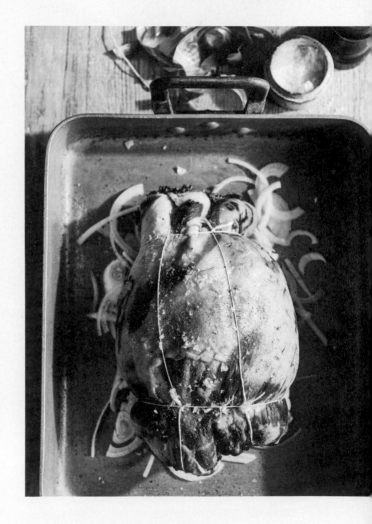

ROA$\int$T RABBIT

Coniglio al forno

SERVES 4

It's funny that many people don't seem to like the idea of rabbit and yet it is such a lovely flavour and an amazing alternative to more mainstream meats such as chicken or beef. This is the perfect recipe to try if you are a rabbit virgin, as I have created the recipe using large pieces of rabbit rather than a whole beast, making it look much more like chicken thighs or breasts, hoodwinking the children or those more squeamish people to at least try it. Most who do admit they love it. You can substitute the guanciale with pancetta, if you prefer.

1.5kg farmed rabbit, *ask your butcher to cut it into 2 hind legs, 2 shoulders and 2 saddle pieces*
2 large rosemary sprigs
10 garlic cloves
1 tbsp fennel seeds
2 large carrots, *peeled and cut into 3cm pieces*
3 large potatoes, *total weight about 700g, cut into 3cm pieces*
100g guanciale, *in a single piece, cut into lardons, or pancetta lardons*
1 celery heart, *cut into 3cm pieces*
1 fennel bulb, *cut into 8 chunks lengthways*
50ml olive oil
160ml white wine
salt and freshly ground black pepper

Wash and dry the rabbit pieces and set them in a large, deep-sided flameproof roasting tray.

Remove the leaves from 1 rosemary sprig and place on a chopping board. Peel and crush 6 garlic cloves on top. Pour on 2 tsp salt and half the fennel seeds. Using a sharp knife, finely chop to create a coarse paste, or you can use a mortar and pestle if you prefer. Rub the paste over the rabbit pieces, cover with clingfilm and allow to marinate in the fridge for at least 3 hours, or overnight.

Preheat the oven to 220°C/fan 200°C/Gas 7.

Take the rabbit out of the fridge and discard the clingfilm. Place the carrots, potatoes, guanciale, celery and fennel in the tray. Peel the remaining 4 garlic cloves, cut in half and place in the roasting tray. Scatter over the remaining fennel seeds and season with a large pinch each of salt and pepper. Pour in the oil, add the rabbit and its marinade and, using your fingers, coat all the meat and vegetables in the oil and marinade.

Place the roasting tray over a medium heat for 5 minutes, turning the rabbit over halfway so it lightly browns all over. Pour in half the wine and let it bubble for 2 minutes. Remove from the heat, turn the rabbit pieces and place the remaining rosemary sprig in the centre of the tray on top of the meat and vegetables. Loosely cover with foil and place in the middle of the oven for 30 minutes.

Remove from the oven and discard the foil. Turn the rabbit pieces over. Pour the remaining wine over the meat and roast in the middle of the oven for a further 45 minutes. After 25–30 minutes, check that there is still liquid in the tray and splash in a little water if it seems dry.

Equally divide the rabbit and vegetables between 4 warmed plates, pour over the juices and serve immediately. A perfect one-dish wonder!

CLASSIC NORTHERN ITALIAN MIXED MEAT STEW WITH CELERY + THYME

Classico bollito di carne con sedano e timo

SERVES 6–8

This is a very traditional Northern Italian style of cooking and a perfect alternative to a Sunday roast. Last summer, while filming and wandering through a market in Italy, I stopped to chat to a local butcher called Alessandro. We swapped ideas about mixing different cuts of meat in the same pot. We agreed that instead of using the more traditional cuts of meat of the region, duck, pork and chicken would complement each other perfectly, and that is how this recipe was created. If you prefer, you can substitute the pork ribs with beef ribs.

70ml olive oil

3 duck legs, *total weight about 600g, skinned, trimmed and cut into drumsticks and thighs*

800g pork ribs, *cut into 2-rib sections*

800g bone-in chicken thighs, *skinned, fat trimmed away*

1 large red onion, *peeled and roughly chopped*

2 celery sticks, *roughly chopped into 2cm pieces*

1 carrot, *peeled and roughly chopped into 2cm discs*

4 bay leaves

300ml red wine

4 thyme sprigs

1 litre hot vegetable stock

2 tbsp tomato purée

salt and freshly ground black pepper

6 spring onions, *trimmed and finely sliced, to serve*

1 red chilli, *deseeded and finely sliced, to serve*

Pour the oil into a very large saucepan for which you have a lid, or a flameproof casserole dish, and place over a high heat. Working in batches, add the duck, pork and chicken to the pan and brown on all sides. Use tongs to turn the meat. When done, transfer to a large bowl and set aside.

Reduce the heat to medium and add the onion, celery, carrot and bay leaves. Fry for 10 minutes, stirring occasionally with a wooden spoon.

Increase the heat, pour in the wine and add the thyme. Bring to the boil and let it bubble for 2 minutes, allowing the alcohol to evaporate. Add the stock, tomato purée, 2½ tsp salt and ½ tsp pepper, stir and return to the boil. Return all the meat to the saucepan with any juices that are left in the bowl.

Place the lid on the saucepan, reduce the heat and simmer for 2 hours. Stir every 30 minutes, allowing the meat to cook evenly.

Transfer the meat to a large warmed serving platter. Use a slotted spoon to spoon some of the vegetables on top of the meat and then drizzle over 3 ladles of the gravy. Sprinkle over the spring onions and chilli.

Serve with warm crusty bread and a nice glass of red wine.

Happy
place

1988

MORTADELLA BURGERS WITH CARAMELISED RED ONIONS, BALSAMIC VINEGAR + CHERRY RELISH

Hamburger di mortadella con salsina di cipolle rosse, aceto balsamico e ciliegie

SERVES 2

This burger combines some of my favourite ingredients from the Emilia Romana area of Italy. Although it may initially seem odd to combine sweet cherries with balsamic vinegar and salty mortadella, I promise you will be converted as soon as you try it. The sweet and sour relish cuts through the richness of the meat. I like to make my burgers thinner and smaller than many others. This is to increase the browned and caramelised surface area, which adds hugely to the flavour. When my sons and I have a boys' night in, we almost always cook burgers, and I promise you these will be on our menu next time.

FOR THE RELISH
1 large Tropea or red
  onion, *peeled and
  finely sliced*
3 tbsp olive oil
½ tsp chilli flakes
100g cherries, *pitted
  and halved*
2 tbsp balsamic vinegar
5 tbsp water
salt

FOR THE BURGER
250g coarse-minced beef
250g coarse-minced pork
100g mortadella, *finely
  chopped into 5mm pieces*
1 egg, *lightly beaten*
1 large garlic clove, *peeled
  and crushed to a purée*
4 tbsp finely chopped flat
  leaf parsley leaves
2 tbsp olive oil, *plus more
  for the buns*

To make the relish, tip the onion into a frying pan and set it over a medium-high heat. Sprinkle over 2 pinches of salt and dry-fry for 2 minutes until the onion begins to soften and release some of its liquid. Pour in the olive oil and sprinkle over the chilli flakes. Stir using a wooden spoon and continue to fry until the onion has softened and is lightly browned; this should take around 4 minutes.

Tip in the prepared cherries, stir and cook until they just begin to soften. Reduce the heat and pour in the balsamic vinegar. Stir and cook for another minute to reduce the balsamic a little, then pour in the measured water and stir to combine. Continue to cook for 5 minutes, or until the onions and cherries have softened and the relish has thickened. Remove from the heat and set aside to cool.

For the burgers, place all the ingredients, except the olive oil, into a large bowl and mix well with your hands. Try not to overwork the ingredients: do not pummel them, try to go with light hands. Divide the mixture into 4 and create 4 wide, flat burger patties, each about 2cm thick. Lay the burgers on a tray, cover with clingfilm and place in the fridge for a minimum of 2 hours.

When ready to cook, heat a griddle pan over a very high heat. Drizzle the 2 tbsp oil over the patties and brush it over the whole surface. When the griddle pan is hot, carefully lay the patties in. Cook for 3 minutes on one side, then flip and top each patty with a slice of cheese. Continue to cook for 4 minutes, then, using a spatula, gently remove and place on a plate to rest.

TO SERVE
4 thin slices of
  Fontina cheese,
  or burger cheese
2 burger buns, *sliced open;
  I like panino-style, but
  brioche buns work well too*
1 large ripe tomato,
  finely sliced
crisp lettuce leaves

While the burgers are resting, drizzle the burger buns with a little olive oil on their cut sides and sprinkle over a pinch of salt. Griddle the buns for about 1 minute on both sides until deeply browned. Turn off the heat and set aside.

Lay the bun bases on a board and spoon one-quarter of the relish on to each. Using a spatula, place a burger on top of the relish. Lay a slice of tomato on top and then stack on the 2 remaining burgers, creating a double cheeseburger. Top each stack with the remaining relish. Place a small handful of lettuce leaves on top and finally place the bun tops on the lettuce and gently push down. I like to skewer these burgers with large cocktail sticks before cutting straight through the middle, to help whoever is lucky enough to be eating them! These truly are the ultimate burgers and perfect with an ice-cold beer.

CHICKEN BREAST IN SWEET ITALIAN WINE WITH CAPERS + CHIVES

Scaloppine di pollo in vin santo, capperi e erba cipollina

<u>SERVES 1</u>

There is no better way to show off a quality ingredient such as vin santo than by making an incredibly simple dish that allows all the flavours to sing. After tasting the quality of the vin santo at the Terre a Mano vineyard, I knew exactly what I wanted to do with it. Vin santo is a sweet dessert wine and is easy enough to get hold of, if not from a supermarket, then in Italian delis or online. A great substitute is Marsala wine. This dish is very easy to double up to make a perfect meal for two.

1 large skinless, boneless
  chicken breast
30g plain flour
3 tbsp olive oil
30g salted butter
1 heaped tbsp capers
  in salt, *rinsed under cold
  water and drained*
3 tbsp chopped chives
6 tbsp vin santo
½ fennel bulb, *finely sliced*
½ head of chicory,
  leaves separated
2 tbsp extra virgin
  olive oil
salt and freshly ground
  black pepper

Lay the chicken breast on a work surface and place your hand flat on top of the breast. Using a sharp knife, carefully cut the breast through horizontally, creating 2 thinner pieces of chicken.

Sprinkle the flour on to a plate and season with salt and pepper. Dust the chicken in the seasoned flour, ensuring the slices are lightly coated all over.

Heat a large frying pan over a medium-high heat and add the regular olive oil and half the butter. When the butter has melted into the oil and is bubbling, pick up the breast pieces, give them a little shake to remove excess flour and gently lay them in the hot frying pan. Fry the chicken for 3 minutes. Using tongs, turn the pieces over and cook for a further 3 minutes.

Add the capers to the pan along with half the chopped chives.

Gently pour in the vin santo and carefully tip the pan towards the heat, so the wine flambés. Allow the alcohol to burn off for 30 seconds, then continue to cook the chicken for a further 2 minutes.

Meanwhile, place the fennel and chicory in a small bowl and dress with the extra virgin olive oil and season with a little salt and pepper. Toss the salad to make sure the leaves and fennel are evenly coated.

When the chicken is cooked, turn the heat off and drop in the remaining butter. Swirl the pan to emulsify the butter in the liquid.

Gently place the chicken on a serving plate, pour over the sauce and sprinkle with the remaining chives. Serve the delicious chicken with the salad.

ROAST VEAL SHIN IN
RED WINE + BAY LEAVES

Stinco di vitello al forno con vino rosso e alloro

SERVES 4

This recipe may take two and a half hours to cook, but the oven is doing all the work for you, while you get to sit on the sofa with a nice glass of wine. This is the way I like to cook: Minimum Effort... Maximum Satisfaction! Slow-cooked meats are so soft and tasty and take up very little of your time. Ossobuco is an all-time favourite of mine and cooking the whole veal shin in one piece is just another (and easier) way to make a similar tasting dish. The gravy that accompanies it is extremely versatile and can be used with any roast meats.

3 tbsp olive oil
1 whole veal shin, *about
 1.4kg, ask your butcher to
 saw off the knuckle at one
 end and the end of the bone
 at the other, to expose the
 bone marrow*
200g salted butter,
 *chopped, plus more for the
 baking sheet*
400ml red wine
6 bay leaves
salt and freshly ground
 black pepper

FOR THE GRAVY
3 tbsp olive oil
1 large red onion, *peeled
 and finely chopped*
4 thyme sprigs
1 tbsp runny honey
300ml red wine
250ml hot beef stock
2 tbsp balsamic vinegar
2 tsp cornflour, *mixed with
 3 tbsp water*
2 tbsp cherry jam, or
 strawberry jam

Preheat the oven to 200°C/fan 180°C/Gas 6.

Pour the olive oil for the veal into a flameproof roasting tray and place it over a high heat for 20 seconds. Place the veal shin in the tray and brown it on all sides, using tongs to turn it. This process should take around 5 minutes. Remove the veal from the tray and put it into a medium bowl.

Place the butter in the tray and allow it to melt over a medium heat. Add 1 tsp salt and ½ tsp pepper and return the veal to the tray with any juices collected in the bowl. Turn the meat in the salted butter. Pour in 300ml red wine and add the bay leaves. Cook for 2 minutes, allowing the alcohol from the wine to evaporate.

Remove from the heat, cover loosely with a buttered baking sheet and place in the middle of the oven for 1 hour.

Remove from the oven, turn the meat over and place back in the middle of the oven, again with the baking sheet on top, and continue to cook for 1 hour. Meanwhile, make the gravy.

Pour the oil for the gravy into a medium-sized saucepan. Place over a medium heat and add the onion and 1 tsp salt. Fry for 8 minutes, stirring occasionally with a wooden spoon. Add the thyme and honey, stir and fry for 1 minute. Pour in the wine and bring to the boil. Reduce the heat to low and simmer gently for 15 minutes, stirring occasionally. Pour in the hot stock and the balsamic and simmer for 20 minutes, stirring occasionally.

Place a sieve over a medium-sized bowl or jug and pour the gravy through, using the back of the wooden spoon to press it all through. Return the gravy to the saucepan and place over a low heat.

Pour in the cornflour mixture and stir continuously for 1 minute until the gravy has thickened slightly. Now add the jam and stir for a further 2 minutes. Turn off the heat.

Remove the veal from the oven, turn the meat over one last time, pour over the remaining 100ml red wine, cover with the baking sheet again and place back in the centre of the oven for a final 30 minutes.

Remove from the oven and slice the meat. Reheat the gravy if needed and drizzle it over the veal slices. Serve with creamy mash and your favourite green vegetables, or my amazing Stuffed Peppers with Sautéed Mixed Vegetables + Parmesan (see page 208).

CALF'S LIVER IN SALTED BUTTER SAUCE + CRISPY SAGE

Fegato burro e salvia croccante

SERVES 2

Many people, including my wife, will go to restaurants and order pan-fried calf's liver as a special treat, which is really strange because it actually only takes minutes to cook for yourself at home. You can serve it with my amazing boiled potatoes here, or with my Creamy Mashed Potatoes with Spicy 'Nduja Paste (see page 193). This meat is so tender and tasty, full of iron and goodness, and it's a must-try for your family. I hope you love it as much as we do.

6 slices of calf's liver, *1cm thick, total weight about 500g*

3 large waxy or red potatoes, *total weight about 700g*

2 tbsp extra virgin olive oil

4 tbsp plain flour

4 tbsp olive oil

8 large sage leaves

50g salted butter, *cut into cubes*

salt and freshly ground black pepper

Take the liver out of the fridge 15 minutes before you want to cook it.

Peel the potatoes, cut in half, rinse in cold water, then place in a small saucepan. Fill the saucepan with water so it comes to 1cm above the potatoes, add ½ tbsp salt and place over a medium heat. Half-cover with a lid and bring to the boil, then reduce the heat, gently simmering the potatoes for about 35 minutes until cooked al dente. Drain and carefully place the potatoes on a plate. Generously season with salt and pepper, drizzle over the extra virgin olive oil and cover with clingfilm. Set aside.

Place the flour on a plate and season with ½ tsp pepper and 1 tsp salt. Mix well.

Put a large frying pan over a high heat and pour in the regular olive oil. As soon as the oil is hot, add the sage leaves and gently fry for 1 minute, pressing the leaves down flat with a fork. Turn them over and continue to fry for a further minute. Gently remove the crispy sage leaves and set aside on a small plate.

Coat the slices of liver in the seasoned flour on both sides. Shake off any excess flour and place in the hot oil. Fry for 2 minutes. Turn the slices over, add the butter, generously season with salt and pepper and continue to fry for a further 2 minutes, giving you the perfect medium liver.

Place 3 slices of calf's liver on each serving plate, pour over the flavoured buttery oil and decorate with the crispy sage. Serve immediately with the boiled potatoes.

SLOW-COOKED PORK SHOULDER WITH SUPER-CRISPY CRACKLING

Spalla di maiale cotta lentamente al forno, con cotenna super-croccante

SERVES 6-8

I am very lucky that I get to spend at least four months of the year in Sardinia. The people there are huge pork lovers and it will feature on nearly every menu. Rather than spit-roasting the pork, which is their speciality, I wanted to create a slow-cooked pork that still had the amazing crunchy crackling that we all love. This is the perfect recipe for that. You can marinate the meat the night before and literally all you then have to do is put it into the oven. Minutes to prepare and four and a half hours to cook, but no actual time taken away from your day. Perfect for lazy Sundays.

In the D'Acampo household we serve this with brioche buns and coleslaw, but anything goes, from crispy salad to roast potatoes to just simple boiled rice. I promise this will be the best pork you have ever made, however you decide to serve it!

2.2kg pork shoulder, *with skin on; ask your butcher to score the skin*
2 large onions, *halved horizontally*
3 large carrots
5 rosemary sprigs
200ml red wine
200ml water
1 tsp cornflour
sea salt flakes

FOR THE DRY RUB
1 tbsp garlic powder
1 tbsp smoked paprika
2 tsp English mustard powder
1 tsp ground turmeric
2 tsp vegetable stock powder
salt and freshly ground black pepper

FOR THE GLAZE
3 tbsp barbecue sauce
3 tbsp honey
1 tbsp dark soy sauce
1 tsp chilli powder

Place a sheet of baking parchment on a baking tray. With a sharp knife, separate the skin from the pork and set aside. Trim off and discard any excess fat around the meat.

Place all the dry rub ingredients in a large baking tray with ½ tbsp each salt and pepper and use your fingertips to mix well. Take the pork skin and put it into the mixture, making sure it is completely covered on both sides. Place it on the baking parchment, skin side up, cover and put into the fridge for at least 2 hours. Now put the pork shoulder in the mixture and cover it completely with the dry spices, ensuring the meat is coated on all sides, including in all the little crevices. You should have used up all the dry rub, leaving a clean baking tray. Set the pork aside on a plate.

Arrange the onions, carrots and rosemary in the baking tray where the spices were, creating a natural rack for the meat to sit on. Place the pork shoulder on top. Pour in the wine and measured water at the sides of the tray to make sure the meat stays dry. Cover with foil, making sure the tray is completely sealed, and rest it in the fridge for at least 2 hours.

Preheat the oven to 170°C/fan 150°C/Gas 3½. Place the pork in the bottom of the oven and cook for 2½ hours. Take the skin out of the fridge. Generously sprinkle over 2-3 pinches of sea salt flakes and place at the top of the oven. Cook the pork and skin for another 1½ hours.

Meanwhile for the glaze, pour the ingredients into a small bowl. Mix well.

Remove the crackling from the oven and drain any excess fat. Remove the pork shoulder from the oven. Remove and discard the foil and, using a pastry brush, coat the pork shoulder with the glaze.

Increase the oven temperature to 220°C/fan 200°C/Gas 7 and place the crackling back on the top shelf and the shoulder on the bottom. Cook for a final 30 minutes.

Remove the crackling from the oven and place 2 forks or spoons under it, allowing air to circulate around. Set aside. Remove the shoulder of pork from the oven and carefully lift the meat on to a large serving platter. Cover with foil and let it rest.

Drain the juices from the pork shoulder baking tray through a sieve into a small saucepan. Place over a medium heat and bring to the boil. Put the cornflour into an espresso cup and fill up halfway with water. Mix well and pour into the gravy. Using a hand-held whisk, stir until the gravy has thickened, about 3 minutes. Turn off the heat.

Remove the foil from the pork and, with the help of 2 forks, shred the meat into pieces. Drizzle the gravy all over the meat.

Finally chop the crackling into small pieces and sprinkle over the meat. Serve immediately.

VEAL ESCALOPES WITH LEMON + PARSLEY SAUCE

Piccatina con salsa al limone e prezzemolo

SERVES 4

If you are looking for a super-fast and super-tasty dinner, this is the one. From start to finish, it will take you less than 10 minutes to cook this wonderful classic Italian dish. The sweetness of the veal and sharpness of the lemon is a combination made in heaven. You can substitute the parsley with dill, but please make sure you use freshly squeezed lemon juice and not lemon juice from a plastic bottle; the two are incomparable.

50g plain flour
8 small, thinly sliced veal escalopes, *total weight about 600g*
5 tbsp olive oil
100g salted butter
juice of 2 lemons
60ml warm vegetable stock
5 tbsp finely chopped flat leaf parsley leaves
salt and freshly ground black pepper

Put the flour on a large plate, season with ½ tsp each salt and pepper and mix. Coat each side of the veal escalopes with the seasoned flour. Gently tap the veal to discard any excess flour.

Place a large frying pan over a medium heat, pour in the olive oil and add half the butter. Once the butter has melted, place the veal in the pan and fry for 2 minutes on each side.

Remove the veal and keep warm while you make the sauce. (The best way to keep the meat warm is to place the cooked veal slices on a large serving plate and cover with foil or clingfilm.)

Pour the lemon juice and the stock into the same frying pan and, with the help of a wooden spoon, scrape all the browned bits from the edges and bottom into the sauce. Bring to the boil and stir for 1 minute.

Add the chopped parsley and remaining butter and continue to stir for a further minute until you create a creamy texture. Taste to check if it needs a little more seasoning.

To serve, place 2 slices of veal on each of 4 warmed serving plates and drizzle over the lemon and parsley sauce. Serve immediately with a crispy salad of your choice and my Baked Sliced Potatoes with Butter + Fresh Rosemary (see page 186).

T-BONE STEAK WITH GARLIC, CHILLI + ROSEMARY GLAZE

Bistecca alla Fiorentina con glassa di aglio, olio al peperoncino e rosmarino

SERVES 4-6

To be called *bistecca alla Fiorentina*, a T-bone cut must be dry-aged for 25–30 days. It must be 5–8cm thick, so you can stand the steak up on the flat side of its 'T': this is very important, because you will need to cook the steak on its end for five minutes.

The Fiorentina should be always cooked *al sangue*: rare. If you prefer medium-rare, cook it for one minute longer on each step. After medium-rare you are practically ruining the Fiorentina, so I will not tell you how to do it.

When you cook meat on the barbecue or griddle pan, you must follow five very important rules: 1. Make sure your meat is at room temperature, take it out of the fridge five hours before cooking. 2. Do not season the meat with salt before cooking, it will draw out the moisture and make the steak tough. 3. Do not move the meat around too often during cooking, every time you move it you will lose moisture and natural juices. 4. You must allow the meat to rest after cooking to ensure it is tender and juicy, so wrap the steaks with foil and rest for at least five minutes. 5. Do not poke or make holes in the meat, or it will lose its natural juices and flavours.

2 T-bone steaks,
  about 1.4kg each
sea salt flakes

FOR THE GLAZE
2 large garlic cloves,
  peeled and crushed
1 tbsp finely chopped
  rosemary leaves
3 tbsp extra virgin
  olive oil
3 tbsp chilli-infused
  olive oil

Preheat the barbecue until very hot, at least 30 minutes before cooking. Alternatively, preheat a large griddle pan over a high heat.

For the glaze, place the garlic and rosemary in a small bowl and pour over the oils. Mix and set aside.

Place the meat on the barbecue or griddle for 2 minutes. Do not move the meat, as you want to create grill marks on the steaks.

Turn the meat 90°, keeping it on the same side, and continue to grill for a further 5 minutes.

Turn the steaks over and repeat, following the same technique and cooking times. Preheat the grill to high.

Now stand the T-bone steaks on the flat side of the 'T' and continue to cook for 5 minutes. This is a very important process as the central bone of the steak will conduct heat through the meat. Your Fiorentina should now be cooked to perfection, the meat should have a crispy dark brown colour all over and the fat should be oozing down the sides.

Place the Fiorentina steaks on a medium-sized tray and brush the glaze all over the meat. (Always glaze the meat when resting, never when cooking or you will lose the freshness of the glaze.) Wrap the steaks with foil and rest for 5 minutes at room temperature.

Meanwhile, place a baking tray in the oven under the hot grill and keep it hot.

Carve the T-bone steaks in thick slices and place on the hot tray, drizzling over any juices left from the resting tray and sprinkling over a couple of pinches of salt flakes. Serve immediately with sautéed potatoes, or my Baked Sliced Potatoes with Butter + Fresh Rosemary and Sicilian-Style Vegetables with Baby Plum Tomatoes, Mint + Chilli (see pages 186 and 205).

PIZZA AND BREAD

Perfect memories

1989

Yeah, pizza: everyone's favourite quick meal and, really, once you have the dough mastered, anything goes except pineapple... WHY?! I know you can buy some fantastic pizzas nowadays, I even have my own range so I know they can be truly great, but making pizza from scratch gives you so much satisfaction, especially if you have friends or children to make them with. It actually becomes an entertaining part of the day or evening in itself, as everyone gets stuck in with the toppings.

Pizza was invented in my home region, Naples, as a fast, tasty, affordable meal for the working class on the go. While topped flatbreads were consumed in ancient Egypt and Rome, it was in Naples during the 17th and 18th century when what we recognise as pizza was born. Naples was a bustling waterfront city, where overcrowding forced local people to find quick, cheap ways to feed their families; pizza was considered a street food for the poor and not suitable for the upper class. I bet they wish they had invested in it now, as such a simple creation has turned into a global phenomenon and I've never met anyone who doesn't love a proper Italian pizza. I wonder if the rich and famous back then used to sneak out to get a slice and pretend it was for their staff...?

I have chosen six quite traditional pizzas for this book, but to this day my all-time favourite, and the one you must please try, is the traditional Neapolitan pizza. If you have never been to Italy or tasted a 'proper' homemade Italian pizza, it is as close as you will get. It was the first recipe I was taught, the first I ever tried (at about 18 months or two years old) and the ultimate pizza for me. Give it a try: it's fun, I promise, and everyone will love you forever if you make my naughty sweet Nutella calzone afterwards!

I'm not going to write about the history of bread here, as it is such a vast and varied subject, but I do think it is interesting to know that ancient Romans took the art of breadmaking to a much higher level. Rome even opened a baking school in the 1st century AD. I have written a book solely on baking, so to pick just a few recipes to feature here was quite challenging. I had to put in my Nonna Flora's amazing focaccia or I'm sure she would have come and visited me in my dreams to tell me off, and, to be honest, it's one of the best focaccias I've ever tasted. My other favourite is the olive breadsticks, which go fantastically with antipasti dishes. Making bread is not as hard as you might think and I can't urge you enough to give it a go. As with pizza, once you have mastered your preferred flavoured dough, you can be as creative as you like... and it is so much fun.

THE REAL NEAPOLITAN PIZZA MADE AT HOME

La vera pizza Napoletana fatta in casa

MAKES 5

Over the past 25 years I have tried so many different recipes for traditional Neapolitan pizza using a domestic oven, and I can now confidently say that... this is the one!

As you can see, I am including two ingredients not commonly used to make a traditional Neapolitan pizza base: oil and sugar. Both give the base a beautiful golden colour, considering we cook it in a domestic oven and not a proper wooden pizza oven. You will, though, need a pizza stone to bake this. If you're going to make a lot of pizza, it will be worth it, and they often come with a pizza shovel, too.

If you can't find fresh yeast in a deli or supermarket, ask at your local bakery.

FOR THE NEAPOLITAN PIZZA DOUGH
3g fresh yeast
550ml water
800g '00' flour, *plus more to dust*
10g caster sugar
25ml extra virgin olive oil
salt

FOR THE TOPPING
2 x 400g cans of chopped tomatoes
15 basil leaves, *plus 10 leaves to scatter on top*
5 tbsp extra virgin olive oil, *plus 10 tbsp more to drizzle on top*
3 mozzarella balls, *drained and cut into 5mm strips*

Dissolve the yeast in the measured water in a large jug.

Tip the flour into a large bowl and sprinkle over the sugar and 25g salt. Pour over the yeasty water and start mixing all together for about 1 minute. Drizzle over the oil and continue to mix for 2 minutes. Once all the ingredients are combined, transfer the dough to a well-floured work surface. If the dough is too sticky, sprinkle over a little more flour.

Gently knead with your hands for 10 minutes until you create an elastic and smooth dough, which should still be slightly sticky. Gently roll it into a big ball on the work surface and cover it by placing the mixing bowl upside down on top. Leave for 1 hour.

Remove the bowl and divide the dough equally into 5 pieces. Each piece should weigh about 290g. Roll each piece into a tight ball, making sure there are no air bubbles in the middle.

Lightly dust a large, deep tray (it should be at least 10cm deep) with flour and place the balls inside, about 10cm apart from each other. Cover with clingfilm, making sure the clingfilm does not touch the dough balls. Place a large tea towel over the tray and let rest at room temperature for 5 hours.

Meanwhile, place all the ingredients for the topping, except the mozzarella, into a medium-sized bowl, with 1 tsp salt. Using your fingertips, crush the tomatoes into a fine pulp, mix and set aside.

Preheat the oven grill to maximum, as hot as it will go. Place a pizza stone on the top shelf of the oven, about 10cm away from the grill element.

Make sure you preheat the grill and the pizza stone for 30 minutes before you are ready to cook the pizza.

Gently pick up a dough ball and place it on a lightly floured surface. Use your fingertips to gently push the dough ball out from the centre, creating a 'crown' or border around the rim. The pizza should be about 30cm in diameter.

Lightly dust a pizza shovel, or flat baking sheet with no lip, with flour and gently slide the pizza base on to the shovel or baking sheet. Use your fingers to neaten up the shape of the base.

Use a large kitchen spoon to spread 1½ tbsp tomato mixture on top of the pizza base. The best way to do this is to pour the tomato mixture into the middle of the pizza and spread it from the centre outwards, using the back of the large kitchen spoon. Leave the crown clean.

Equally scatter one-fifth of the mozzarella over the tomato mixture and evenly drizzle over 2 tbsp extra virgin olive oil. Finally place 2 basil leaves on top.

Slide the pizza on to the very hot pizza stone and cook for 5–6 minutes.

Congratulations: you have just made a traditional Neapolitan pizza.

WHITE PIZZA WITH TALEGGIO, WILD MUSHROOMS + TRUFFLE OIL

Pizza bianca con Taleggio, funghi di bosco e olio al tartufo

MAKES 5

I love a white pizza without any tomatoes and I can't understand why people are sometimes so against it and won't give it a try. The flavour of the Taleggio cheese with wild mushrooms and truffle is a match made in heaven, and lately in all my restaurants this is becoming a very popular choice with the younger generation. My boys Luciano and Rocco can't get enough of this pizza and they literally forced me to write this recipe for you guys... I really hope you will give it a go. As before, you will need a pizza stone for this. I have a tip for you: to properly slice the Taleggio – or any soft cheese such as Brie – make sure it's really cold and not at room temperature.

FOR THE BASE
1 quantity Neapolitan
  Pizza Dough (*see
  page 156*)
'00' flour, *to dust*

FOR THE TOPPING
5 tbsp olive oil
1 tsp thyme leaves
500g mixed wild
  mushrooms, *sliced*
400g Taleggio or Brie
  cheese, *weighed
  after the rind has been
  trimmed off, thinly sliced*
5 tbsp truffle-infused
  olive oil
salt and freshly ground
  black pepper

Make the dough and leave it to prove in a deep tray, as on page 156.

Meanwhile, pour the olive oil and thyme leaves into a large frying pan and place over a high heat. Add the mushrooms and sprinkle over 1 tsp salt and ½ tsp pepper. Fry for 8 minutes, stirring occasionally with a wooden spoon. Set aside to cool.

Preheat the oven grill to maximum, as hot as it will go. Place a pizza stone on the top shelf of the oven, about 10cm away from the grill element. Make sure you preheat the grill and the pizza stone for 30 minutes before you are ready to cook the pizza.

Gently pick up a dough ball and place it on a lightly floured surface. Use your fingertips to gently push the dough ball out from the centre, creating a 'crown' or border around the rim. The pizza should be about 30cm in diameter.

Lightly dust a pizza shovel, or flat baking sheet with no lip, with flour and gently slide the pizza base on to the shovel or baking sheet. Use your fingers to neaten up the shape of the pizza base.

Equally and quickly scatter one-fifth each of the Taleggio and the mushroom mixture over the pizza base and slide on to the very hot pizza stone. Cook for 5–6 minutes.

Drizzle 1 tbsp truffle oil over each pizza and serve immediately with a glass of full-bodied Italian red wine, while you cook the rest.

QUICK SPICY PIZZA WITH TOMATOES, CHILLI, GARLIC + EXTRA VIRGIN OLIVE OIL

Pizza veloce con pomodori, peperoncino, aglio e olio extra vergine

MAKES 2

An easy pizza with a fantastic kick – what a fab recipe to cook at the weekend with your kids – which will take less than an hour from start to finish. Much better than waiting for the delivery man. This pizza has no cheese, so is slightly lighter than a regular pizza. You can also add your favourite extra toppings such as anchovies, pepperoni, mozzarella, olives or salami, but please do try this simple version first, as sometimes less is more and you won't be disappointed.

FOR THE BASE
2 tbsp extra virgin olive oil, *plus more for the baking sheets and dough*
200g strong white bread flour, *plus more to dust*
7g sachet of fast-action dried yeast
140ml warm water
salt

FOR THE TOPPING
200g canned chopped tomatoes
4 tbsp extra virgin olive oil
3 garlic cloves, *peeled and finely chopped*
2 tsp chilli flakes
1 tsp dried oregano

Brush 2 large baking sheets with a little oil and set aside.

To make the dough, place the flour into a large bowl with the yeast and ½ tsp salt. Make a well in the centre and add the 2 tbsp oil. Slowly pour in the measured warm water, mixing with the handle of a wooden spoon until you have a wet dough. Flour a work surface well and turn the dough out on top. Knead for about 10 minutes, or until smooth and elastic.

Halve the dough and shape each piece into a ball. Place each ball in the centre of an oiled baking sheet. Brush the tops with a little oil and cover with clingfilm. Leave to rest at room temperature for 30 minutes.

Preheat the oven to 240°C/fan 220°C/Gas 9.

Meanwhile, for the topping, pour the chopped tomatoes into a medium bowl. Add 2 tbsp extra virgin olive oil and all the garlic, chilli flakes and oregano. Season with ½ tsp salt and stir. Using your fingertips, squeeze the tomatoes to create a fine pulp. Set aside.

Use your hands to push each dough ball out from the centre, stretching the dough to create 2 round pizza bases about 25cm in diameter and 1cm thick. Make a small rim by pulling up the edges slightly.

Equally divide the tomato mixture between the pizza bases. Using the back of a tablespoon, spread the tomato mixture over the pizza bases, from the centre outwards, leaving about 1cm clear for the rim.

Place the pizzas in the centre of the preheated oven and bake for 13–15 minutes or until golden brown.

Remove from the oven, drizzle 1 tbsp extra virgin olive oil over each pizza and return to the oven for a further minute. Enjoy!

GLUTEN-FREE PIZZA WITH AVOCADO, SEMI-DRIED TOMATOE/, ROCKET LEAVES + BAL/AMIC GLAZE

Pizza senza glutine con avocado, pomodori semi secchi, rucola e glassa di aceto balsamico

<u>MAKES 2</u>

So many people nowadays seem to have intolerances to gluten, including my niece Ella, while many others choose to eat gluten-free products, so it's only fair that a gluten-free pizza should feature in this book. I have chosen to top it with cold ingredients, which gives the pizza a different dimension to what we are used to or expecting, and I just love the combinations. We often have an avocado, mozzarella, tomato and balsamic glaze salad as an antipasti with crusty bread, so this recipe was just an extension of our usual flavours and we all love it.

FOR THE BASE
2 tbsp extra virgin olive
  oil, *plus more for the*
  baking sheets and dough
200g gluten-free bread
  flour, *plus more to dust*
7g sachet of fast-action
  dried yeast
140ml warm water
salt

FOR THE TOPPING
200g tomato passata
6 tbsp extra virgin
  olive oil
2 x 125g mozzarella
  balls, *drained and cut
  into small strips*
1 avocado, *halved, pitted,
  peeled and sliced*
10 wedges of semi-
  dried tomatoes in oil
40g rocket
shop-bought balsamic
  glaze
freshly ground black
  pepper

Brush 2 large flat baking sheets with a little oil and set aside.

To make the dough, place the gluten-free flour into a large bowl with the yeast and ½ tsp salt. Make a well in the centre and add the 2 tbsp oil. Slowly pour in the measured warm water, mixing with the handle of a wooden spoon until you create a sticky dough. Turn out the dough on to a well-floured work surface and knead for 10 minutes, until smooth.

Halve the dough and shape into 2 equal balls. Place each ball in the centre of an oiled baking sheet. Brush the top of each ball with a little oil and cover with clingfilm. Leave to rest at room temperature for 45 minutes.

Preheat the oven to 240°C/fan 220°C/Gas 9.

Use your hands to push each dough ball out from the centre, stretching the dough to create 2 round pizza bases about 25cm in diameter and 1cm thick. Make a small rim by pulling up the edges slightly.

Equally divide the passata on top of the pizza bases. Using the back of a tablespoon, spread the passata over the pizza bases, from the centre outwards, leaving about 1cm clear for the rim. Drizzle 1 tbsp extra virgin olive oil over each pizza.

Scatter over the mozzarella and bake in the middle of the oven for 13 minutes. Remove from the oven and place on a large serving plate or chopping board. Top each evenly with avocado, semi-dried tomatoes and rocket and sprinkle over ½ tsp salt and some pepper. Drizzle 2 tbsp extra virgin olive oil over the pizzas and some (or a lot of, if you are my son Rocco) balsamic glaze. Serve immediately.

PIZZA TRAY TOPPED WITH CHARGRILLED PEPPERS, OLIVE∫ + MOZZARELLA

Pizza in teglia con peperoni grigliati, olive e mozzarella

MAKES 8–12 SLICES

This is the perfect pizza to share with friends and family. You can even slice it into small finger-food bites and serve as an antipasti, which works fantastically. If you like a bit of a kick, drizzle over some chilli-infused olive oil, or scatter over a few slices of spicy salami. You can top this with any leftover vegetables, or any jarred vegetables in oil, get as creative as you like!

FOR THE BASE
6 tbsp extra virgin olive oil, *plus more for the bowl, the dough and the tray*
450g strong white bread flour, *plus more to dust*
7g sachet of fast-action dried yeast
300ml warm water
salt

FOR THE TOPPING
200g tomato passata
1 tsp dried oregano
3 tbsp extra virgin olive oil
200g mozzarella block, *cut into strips*
150g mixed chargrilled peppers in a jar, *(drained weight), cut into slices*
20 pitted Leccino or good-quality black olives, or other good-quality pitted black olives such as Kalamata

Brush a large bowl with oil and set aside.

To make the dough, place the flour, yeast and 2 tsp salt into a separate large bowl. Pour in 3 tbsp extra virgin olive oil and then gradually add the measured warm water, mixing with the handle of a wooden spoon until you create a sticky dough. Flour a work surface well and turn the dough out on top. Knead for 10 minutes, or until smooth and elastic. (You can add a touch more flour if the dough is really sticky.)

Shape the dough into a ball and place into the oiled bowl. Brush the top with a little olive oil, cover with clingfilm and leave to rise in a warm, draught-free place for 1 hour. Brush a large baking tray, 40 x 25cm, with oil and set aside.

With the dough still in the bowl, knead 3–4 times to knock out the air. Transfer to the oiled tray and, using your fingertips, gently flatten the dough until it extends to the sides of the tray. Press your fingers into the dough to make indentations, as you would when making a focaccia bread. Brush over the remaining 3 tbsp extra virgin olive oil, cover with a tea towel and leave to rise again for a further 1 hour.

Preheat the oven to 240°C/fan 220°C/Gas 9.

For the topping, pour the passata into small bowl and add the oregano, extra virgin olive oil and ½ tsp salt. Mix well.

Remove the tea towel from the pizza and make more indentations in the dough with your fingertips. Use a tablespoon to spread over the passata, leaving a 1cm border all round. Scatter over the mozzarella, peppers and olives. Bake in the middle of the oven for 20 minutes, or until golden. Transfer to a wire rack to cool slightly. Cut into 8 or 12 slices, as you prefer, and serve hot or at room temperature.

FOLDED PIZZA WITH NUTELLA, BANANA + MASCARPONE

Calzone con Nutella, banana e mascarpone

MAKES 2

to share between 4

I have to dedicate this recipe to my son Rocco. He absolutely loves chocolate-hazelnut spread, and the combination of chocolate and banana has always been his favourite, whether simply spread on toast or put on top of pancakes. If you are having a pizza party and trying out my other pizza recipes, this is the perfect way to serve dessert. Your dough is already made and you just create a lovely surprise for your guests. I promise they will love you forever!

If you prefer, you can substitute the banana for mango.

FOR THE DOUGH
2 tbsp extra virgin olive
   oil, *plus more for the*
   sheets and the dough
200g strong white
   bread flour, *plus more*
   to dust
7g sachet of fast-action
   dried yeast
140ml warm water
salt

FOR THE FILLING
4 heaped tbsp (about
   150g) chocolate-
   hazelnut spread, such
   as Nutella
4 tbsp full-fat milk
2 bananas, *peeled and*
   sliced into 5mm discs
   on the diagonal
100g mascarpone
40g hazelnuts, *crushed*
icing sugar, *to dust*
vanilla ice cream,
   to serve

Brush 2 large baking sheets with 1 tbsp oil and set aside.

To make the dough, place the flour, yeast and ½ tsp salt into a large bowl. Make a well in the centre and add the 2 tbsp oil. Slowly pour in the measured warm water, mixing with the handle of a wooden spoon until you create a sticky dough. Turn out the dough on to a well-floured surface and knead for about 10 minutes, until smooth and elastic.

Halve the dough and shape into 2 equal-sized balls. Place each ball in the centre of an oiled baking sheet. Brush the top of the dough with a little oil and cover with clingfilm. Leave to rest at room temperature for 30 minutes.

Meanwhile, for the filling, spoon the chocolate-hazelnut spread and milk into a small saucepan and place over a low heat. Using a wooden spoon, stir continuously for 5 minutes until the chocolate-hazelnut spread has melted into the milk, creating a thick chocolate sauce: you are looking for it to be the same consistency as double cream. Remove from the heat and set aside at room temperature.

Preheat the oven to 240°C/fan 220°C/Gas 9.

Use your hands to push each dough ball out from the centre, stretching the dough to create 2 round pizza bases, each about 25cm in diameter.

Spread 2 tbsp of the chocolate sauce over half the surface of a pizza base, leaving a border of 1cm all round. Scatter half the banana slices over the chocolate. Place 5 tsp mascarpone, dolloped separately, randomly over the banana and finally sprinkle over one-quarter of the crushed hazelnuts (see photos, overleaf). Repeat the process for the other pizza base, reserving some sauce and nuts for decoration.

Fold over the empty sides to enclose the filling. Pinch the edges to seal, creating a rope-like effect if possible. Bake in the middle of the oven for 16 minutes, or until golden brown.

Remove from the oven and place each sweet calzone on a large plate. Drizzle over the remaining chocolate sauce in a zigzag. Sprinkle over the remaining chopped hazelnuts and dust with icing sugar. Serve immediately, with scoops of vanilla ice cream.

FRIED SANDWICH WITH OOZING FONTINA CHEESE + SPECK HAM

Tramezzino fritto con fontina e speck

MAKES 6

This recipe reminds me of summers with my family and friends on the island of Sardinia. I am so lucky to be able to spend every summer in Sardinia and even luckier to be able to visit the beach and take my boat out for a spin on the incredible Mediterranean Sea. This classic fried sandwich is served at Baia Caddinas Hotel, where I often visit, and there is nothing better than grabbing a couple of fried triangles with a cold beer and sitting on the beach or boat, just enjoying the moment. I can literally have these sandwiches for breakfast, lunch or dinner. If you prefer, you can substitute the speck with Parma ham, or with any cooked ham.

200g fontina cheese *(weighed after the rind has been trimmed off)*
3 tbsp double cream
2 tbsp Worcestershire sauce
1 tbsp Dijon mustard
1 egg yolk
¼ tsp cayenne pepper, or chilli powder
12 slices of sourdough bread
12 slices of speck ham *(or see recipe introduction)*
200ml olive oil
salt

Cut the cheese into small cubes and place in a small bowl. Leave it in a warm place for 30 minutes.

Put the cheese and cream into a food processor and pulse-blend for about 30 seconds, then stir. Pour in the Worcestershire sauce, Dijon mustard, egg yolk, cayenne pepper or chilli powder and a pinch of salt. Pulse-blend for a further 30 seconds until you create a spreadable thick sauce. Set aside.

Trim off and discard the crusts from the bread. Spread the cheese mixture equally over all the 12 slices. Lay 2 speck slices on top of each of 6 of the bread slices, making sure the speck covers the cheese completely. Cover with the remaining bread slices, cheese side down on top of the speck. Press down firmly, creating 6 sandwiches. Cut each sandwich into 2 triangles.

Pour the oil into a large frying pan and place over a medium heat until hot. Add as many triangles as will fit and fry for 2 minutes. With the help of 2 forks, turn the triangles over and fry for a further 2 minutes until light brown and crisp on both sides. Remove and place on a plate lined with kitchen paper. Repeat the process with the remaining triangles.

Serve on a large platter with crisps of your choice and cold beers... unless you decide to eat these for breakfast.

1990-92

The simple things

ƒOFT BREAD ROLLS WITH EXTRA VIRGIN OLIVE OIL

Panini soffici con olio extra vergine di olive

MAKES 8

These little panini rolls are amazing and, because I am using extra virgin olive oil, it makes the flavour just incredible and also gives them a super-soft texture. You can eat these rolls to accompany any soups, fill them with any cheeses or hams or, even better, chocolate-hazelnut spread... anything goes. If you are new to making bread, this is definitely the recipe to start with. The biggest tip I can give you is to make sure you use a good-quality extra virgin olive oil; believe you me, it will make a lot of difference. Happy baking!

500g strong white
  bread flour, *plus
  more to dust*
7g sachet of fast-action
  dried yeast
170ml full-fat milk
80ml good-quality extra
  virgin olive oil, *plus
  more for the bowl*
100ml tepid water
salt

Line a large baking sheet with baking parchment and set aside.

Place the flour in a large bowl. Add 1 tsp salt to one side of the bowl and the yeast to the other side. Make a well in the centre and pour in the milk and extra virgin olive oil. Use a metal tablespoon to stir, drawing the flour in. As the dough starts to come together, pour in the measured tepid water.

Continue to use the spoon and fold all the ingredients together for a couple of minutes, until you have a sticky wet dough, then use your hand to fold the dough, bringing in the sides to the centre for a few minutes, turning the bowl as you go so all the sides are equally treated. Dust a work surface with a little flour and tip the dough out on to that. Knead for about 10 minutes, or until it becomes smooth and silky.

Brush the inside of a large bowl with 1 tbsp extra virgin olive oil and place the dough back into the bowl. Cover with clingfilm and leave to rise in a warm dry place for 1½ hours, or until it has at least doubled in size.

If needed, dust your work surface with flour again. Tip out the dough on to the floured surface. Divide it into 8 equal pieces and work each into a ball. Place the balls on the prepared baking sheet, making sure they are spaced well apart. Cover with a tea towel and leave to prove for 1 hour.

Preheat the oven to 200°C/fan 180°C/Gas 6.

Remove the tea towel from the baking sheet and place the bread rolls in the middle of the hot oven. Bake for 16–18 minutes, then remove to a wire rack. Serve warm or at room temperature.

FOCACCIA WITH ROSEMARY + SEA SALT FLAKES

Focaccia al rosmarino fresco e fiocchi di sale

MAKES 1 LARGE FOCACCIA

There is nothing quite like the smell of baking bread, and the sheer satisfaction of making it yourself is amazing. I love focaccia and it is a must-have when I serve antipasti such as hams, pickled vegetables and cheeses. This is the ultimate recipe that never goes wrong. You can top it with oregano, cooked onions or even little cherry tomatoes; once you have mastered the dough, most things can be added on top. If you have any leftover roasted vegetables, they will also make a fantastic topping.

extra virgin olive oil
500g strong white
 bread flour
7g sachet of fast-action
 dried yeast
360ml tepid water
4 rosemary sprigs
sea salt flakes
salt

Drizzle 2 tbsp extra virgin olive oil into a medium baking tray (mine was 25 x 20 x 3cm). Use your fingers to coat the base and sides of the tray. Pour 1 tbsp extra virgin olive oil into a 3-litre capacity square plastic container. Again use your fingers to coat the base and sides.

Place the flour in a large bowl. Add 1 tsp salt to one side of the bowl and the yeast to the other side. Make a well in the centre and pour in 40ml extra virgin olive oil and three-quarters of the measured water. Use a metal spoon to draw the flour in. As the dough starts to come together, pour in the remaining water. With the spoon, fold all the ingredients together for a couple of minutes, until you have a sticky wet dough, then use your hand to fold the dough, bringing in the sides to the centre for a few minutes, turning the bowl as you go so all sides are equally treated.

Pour 4 tbsp extra virgin olive oil on a work surface and tip the dough out on top. Knead for about 10 minutes, or until it becomes smooth and soft. Place into the oiled plastic container, cover with a tea towel and leave to rise in a warm dry place for 2 hours until it has at least doubled in size.

Tip the dough out into the oiled tray and, with your fingers, gently push it out to fill the tray. Cover with a tea towel and leave to prove for 1 hour.

Preheat the oven to 240°C/fan 220°C/Gas 9.

Remove the tea towel and make deep dimples in the focaccia with your fingertips, pushing them all the way through to the bottom. Leave about 1cm without dimples around the border. Pour over 5 tbsp extra virgin olive oil and use a pastry brush to ensure you coat all the top of the dough. Place a few rosemary needles in each dimple. Sprinkle over a generous pinch of sea salt flakes and place in the middle of the hot oven.

Bake for 10–12 minutes. Cool slightly on a wire rack. Drizzle over some more extra virgin olive oil and serve warm or at room temperature.

BREADSTICKS WITH LECCINO BLACK OLIVES

Grissini soffici con olive Leccino

MAKES 14

These are very different from regular breadsticks; my grissini are soft on the inside and crunchy on the outside. They look great, are really easy to make and you can be as creative as you like. I have used pitted black olives in this recipe, but you can use sundried tomatoes, green olives, fennel seeds or a mixture of herbs such as oregano and rosemary. They keep for a few days and are fantastic to serve with soups, salads or any dips.

4 tbsp extra virgin
   olive oil
500g strong white
   bread flour, *plus*
   more to dust
10g fast-action
   dried yeast
400ml tepid water
250g Leccino pitted
   black olives, or other
   good-quality pitted
   black olives such as
   Kalamata, *drained*
salt

Line 2 baking sheets with baking parchment and set aside. Pour 1 tbsp oil into a 3-litre capacity square or rectangular plastic container, rub it all around the edges and set aside.

Place the flour in a large bowl. Add 12g salt to one side of the bowl and the yeast to the other side. Make a well in the centre and gradually pour in 300ml of the measured tepid water, using a metal spoon to stir, drawing the flour in. As the dough starts to come together, pour in the final 100ml water.

Continue to use the spoon to fold the ingredients together for a couple of minutes, until you have a stretchy wet dough, then use your hand to fold the dough, bringing in the sides to the centre for a few minutes, turning the bowl as you go so all the sides are equally treated. Pour in the remaining 3 tbsp oil with the olives and use your hand to combine all the ingredients. It will be quite wet and sticky and stretch easily when pulled. Pour out the dough into the oiled container, loosely cover with a tea towel and allow to triple in size for at least 1 hour at room temperature.

Dust a work surface heavily with flour. Tip out the dough on to the floured surface. It will still be wet and loose. Dust the top of the dough with a little flour and, using your fingertips, stretch it out gently to a rough rectangle 28–42cm long and 20–25cm wide. Cut the dough into 14 strips each 20–25cm long and 2–3cm wide. The dough will still be wet and sticky to handle, so use a large knife or palette knife to help you lift the breadsticks and place them on to the prepared baking sheets, leaving about 3cm between each breadstick.

Place each baking sheet inside a large clean plastic bag, tucking the open ends under the sheets, and leave to prove for 30 minutes.

Meanwhile, preheat the oven to 240°C/fan 220°C/Gas 9. Place the breadsticks in the middle of the hot oven and bake for 16–18 minutes. Cool on a wire rack, then serve.

Salads

SIDES

Small

PLATES

1992-94

UK here I come

Our ancestral Romans loved feasting. Banquets were a huge social event, from small family gatherings to grand spectacles, and the more food there was on the table, the better. Feasts were occasions when new dishes were served and tasted. The Empire embraced flavours and ingredients from other cultures, such as spices from the Middle East, so imperial Rome was a hot spot for the ultimate fusion cuisine. The Romans often liked complex, intricate flavours and used sophisticated techniques to prepare food. Ostrich meat, roasted game and wild rabbit were just a few of the favourites. These dishes would be placed at the centre of the table... but what would always catch your eye were the huge abundance of side dishes that would accompany them. Each told its own story and was a meal in itself. Just as much care and attention to detail was given to these dishes as to the main courses. Only fresh seasonal ingredients were ever used, freshly baked breads were served and each dish was just as important as the next. I would love to travel back in time and sit at the table during those times for just one feast; I would relish every moment. Food for Italians has always been a symbol of two things: wealth and love. Everyone who eats a meal prepared by someone who loves them, and that is shared with someone they love, is the wealthiest man alive. This tradition still remains with Italians today.

One thing you will never see Italians do is to pile all the dishes on to one plate. Side dishes and salads normally have their own separate plates, where they shine in their own right. Side dishes are really important to Italians and, more often than not, are a separate section on restaurant menus. You choose your main meal, then you decide what you want to accompany it. Each side will be priced separately, as each choice has been carefully cooked and is just as important to the chef as a main dish.

Some of the recipes in this chapter can be eaten on their own for lunch, such as the cod salad, while others are great for starters, for example the green bean and goat's cheese salad. Others are perfect side dishes with fish or meat recipes, such as my 'nduja mash. I think, for me, the most important recipe in this chapter, which has been made by all the women in my family dating back for years, has to be caponata. My grandmother Flora remembered her grandmother teaching her how to cook it, and was told that her grandmother was taught by her great-grandmother, so this recipe literally goes back years. A definite favourite of my kids is the sautéed new potatoes with onions, peas and pancetta: it really is a lovely alternative way of doing potatoes and tastes amazing. There are hundreds of Italian side dishes and salads, but here I've tried to pick the more traditional recipes, those that are truly 'like mamma used to make'.

BAKED SLICED POTATOES WITH BUTTER + FRESH ROSEMARY

Patate al forno con burro e rosmarino fresco

SERVES 4–6

This potato recipe is so tasty, looks really impressive and can be made in the morning for later that night, leaving you with more time with your guests. It is a lovely substitute for traditional roast potatoes. It is also great as an alternative topping to a fish pie, or even a chilli con carne. You can substitute rosemary for thyme, or even add a couple of teaspoons of English mustard to the butter mixture if you like a bit of a kick.

2kg medium-sized waxy
  potatoes, *peeled but
  left whole*
70ml olive oil
200g salted butter,
  melted
2 tbsp finely chopped
  rosemary leaves
salt and freshly ground
  black pepper

Preheat the oven to 220°C/fan 200°C/Gas 7.

Fill a large saucepan with 3 litres water, add 1 tbsp salt and bring to the boil. Make sure your potatoes are roughly the same size; if you have one much bigger than the others, cut it in half. Reduce the heat to medium, add the potatoes and boil for 25 minutes. Drain and allow to cool slightly, so you can handle them.

Meanwhile, pour the oil and melted butter into a medium-sized bowl, add the rosemary and ½ tsp pepper, mix well and set aside.

Cut each potato into 1cm-thick slices and dip each slice into the rosemary butter. Place the potato slices upright in lines that run the length of a roasting tin, packing them so they can support each other.

Pour over any remaining rosemary butter and season with 1 tsp salt and 3 more twists of black pepper. If cooking them later that day, loosely cover with clingfilm and set aside until needed, but remember to preheat the oven for at least 10 minutes before baking. Bake in the middle of the oven for 25 minutes.

Remove from the oven and serve in the centre of the table for your family and friends to help themselves.

CHARGRILLED PEPPERS WITH GARLIC, OLIVES, CAPERS + PARSLEY

Peperoni grigliati con aglio, olive, capperi e prezzemolo

SERVES 4–6

The most amazing side dish you will ever taste: colourful, delicious sweetness from the peppers, very easy to prepare, works perfectly with fish or meat and – in my house – we also use it to top bruschetta. My son Luciano goes crazy when I prepare these and always tells me off that we don't do it often enough. You can cook this recipe with only one colour of pepper, but if you do, please use yellow, orange, or red, as green peppers can be a little bitter on their own. You can definitely prepare this dish the day before you want it; the longer it marinates the better it is.

2 medium-sized
  yellow peppers
2 medium-sized
  red peppers
2 medium-sized
  green peppers
2 medium-sized
  orange peppers
8 tbsp extra virgin
  olive oil
3 tbsp pitted Leccino
  olives in brine or oil,
  or other good-quality
  pitted black olives
  such as Kalamata,
  drained and halved
large handful of flat
  leaf parsley leaves,
  roughly chopped
1 tbsp capers in salt,
  rinsed under cold water,
  drained and chopped
3 large garlic cloves,
  peeled and very
  finely sliced
salt and freshly ground
  black pepper

Grill the peppers on a high open flame, barbecue, or griddle pan. With the help of cooking tongs, turn them occasionally and cook until they are completely chargrilled, literally black all over.

Immediately place the peppers in a large bowl, cover tightly with clingfilm and set aside for 30 minutes. (The steam created inside the bowl from the hot grilled peppers will later help you to separate the burned skin from the flesh.)

Pick up each pepper and gently rub off and discard the burned skins. Open the peppers and discard the stalks and seeds. (Be careful, as there will be hot liquid inside.)

Place the cleaned peppers on a chopping board and slice into 5mm strips. Transfer the strips to a medium-sized ceramic dish.

Sprinkle 1½ tsp salt and ½ tsp pepper over, pour in the oil and scatter over the olives, parsley, capers and garlic. Mix it all together and cover with clingfilm.

Refrigerate for 3 hours, every hour mixing it all together, allowing the flavours to combine properly.

Serve at room temperature to accompany any main course, or simply enjoy on its own with warm crusty bread.

COD SALAD WITH ORANGE DRESSING + NOCELLARA OLIVES

Insalata di merluzzo con arance e olive Nocellara

SERVES 4

Cod is such a lovely textured fish but can be quite simple in flavour, which allows you to be really creative with its sauces and dressings. I wanted to create a cod salad that can be eaten warm or at room temperature; using orange instead of the traditional lemon or lime really does give it a fabulous taste. You can eliminate the chilli if you're serving this to younger children, or adding capers will also work very well.

700g cod fillet
5 tbsp extra virgin
   olive oil
1 garlic clove, *peeled and*
   very finely sliced
handful of flat leaf
   parsley leaves,
   finely chopped
finely grated zest
   and juice of 1 large
   unwaxed orange
12 pitted Nocellara
   green olives in brine,
   drained and halved
1 small chilli, *deseeded*
   and finely chopped
15 red baby plum
   tomatoes, *quartered*
salt

Pour 2 litres water and 1 tbsp salt into a medium-sized saucepan and bring to the boil over a medium heat. Reduce the heat to a gentle simmer and add the cod. Poach for 6 minutes. Use a large, slotted spoon to gently pick up the fish, tap against the saucepan a couple of times in order to drain any excess water and place on a plate. Make sure there are no loose bits of fish still in the saucepan that you can spoon out. Reserve the cooking water. Use a fork to separate the cod flakes and set aside. (Discard the skin, if there was any.)

Pour the extra virgin olive oil into a small bowl with the sliced garlic, 1 tsp salt, the parsley, 3 tbsp orange juice and 3 tbsp cod-poaching liquid. Whisk to combine together and set aside.

Arrange the cod flakes on a serving dish (I like an oval one for this) with the olives, chilli and tomatoes. Pour over the dressing and sprinkle the zest of the orange on top. Serve at room temperature with some warm crusty bread.

If serving later that day, cover with clingfilm and place in the fridge, but remember to take it out at least 20 minutes before serving, to allow it to return to room temperature.

CREAMY MASHED POTATOES WITH SPICY 'NDUJA

Purè di patate cremoso con 'nduja piccante

SERVES 6–8

We love mashed potatoes in our house, and I came up with this recipe to go with a very simple chicken dish. I wanted a side dish with lots of flavours, so added 'nduja for an extra kick, and we all loved the results. It also turns the mash a beautiful red colour, so looks fantastic, and is great to accompany any kind of meals.

2kg floury potatoes, *peeled and roughly cut into 5cm chunks*
50ml full-fat milk
100g salted butter
40g (about 2 tbsp) 'nduja
salt

Fill a large saucepan with 2.5 litres water and add 1 tbsp salt. Add the potatoes and place over a high heat. Boil for 35 minutes, stirring occasionally. Drain and set aside.

Put the milk and butter into the hot empty saucepan. Use a potato ricer to mash the potatoes on top of the milk and butter. Add 1 tsp salt and the 'nduja. With the help of a wooden spoon, mix really well to combine all the ingredients, until you have a smooth creamy mash.

Serve hot.

GREEN BEAN + GOAT'S CHEESE SALAD WITH MINT

Insalata di fagiolini e formaggio di capra con menta fresca

SERVES 2

*as a light lunch, or
4 as a side dish*

I created this warm salad one lunchtime when I wanted something quick, tasty and easy to make. I often cook beans this way as a side dish, but adding cold goat's cheese turns it into a completely new prospect. If you prefer, you can substitute the goat's cheese with feta cheese, or use a drizzle of balsamic glaze instead of the lemon and mint, which also works fantastically.

300g fine green beans,
  trimmed each end
25g fresh white bread,
  weighed without crusts
3 tbsp olive oil
2 shallots, *peeled,
  quartered lengthways
  and finely sliced*
8 mint leaves,
  finely sliced
juice of ½ lemon
100g hard goat's cheese
salt and freshly ground
  black pepper

Pour 1 litre water into a medium-sized saucepan, add ½ tbsp salt and bring to the boil over a medium heat. Tip in the beans and boil for 5 minutes. Drain and plunge into cold water to ensure they stop cooking and keep their bright green colour.

Place the bread in a food processor and blitz to create breadcrumbs.

Meanwhile, pour the oil into a medium-sized frying pan, place over a high heat and when the oil is hot (about 30 seconds), add the shallots. Fry for 3 minutes, stirring occasionally with a wooden spoon.

Drain the beans and add to the frying pan. Season with ½ tsp salt and 5 twists of black pepper, mix well and stir-fry for 2 minutes.

Reduce the heat to medium and stir in the breadcrumbs, mint and lemon juice. Fry for a further minute.

Spoon the beans on to a large serving platter or 4 individual small plates.

Crumble over the goat's cheese and serve immediately with some warm crusty bread.

GRILLED VEGETABLE SALAD WITH LEMON + MUSTARD DRESSING

Insalata di verdure grigliate con condimento al limone e senape

SERVES 2

*as a light lunch, or
4 as a side dish*

This has to be one of my favourite salads of all time. For me it's a real combination of Italy and the UK. The grilled vegetables and artichokes, which we eat almost daily in the South of Italy, mixed with the very popular avocado, honey and mustard are truly a perfect match. This really is a meal in itself, but of course you can add tuna, or a cheese such as feta or goat's cheese, or even pieces of cooked chicken if you prefer. If you're preparing this in advance, don't add the avocado, dressing or lemon until ready to serve, or it will discolour the salad.

1 Little Gem lettuce

2 courgettes, *1cm
trimmed off each end,
halved horizontally, then
finely sliced lengthways*

1 red pepper, *deseeded
and cut into 3*

2 tbsp olive oil

280g chargrilled
artichokes in oil,
sliced, oil reserved

10 mint leaves,
finely sliced

1 tsp grainy mustard

2 tbsp white wine
vinegar

1½ tsp runny honey

1 large avocado

juice of ½ lemon

salt and freshly ground
black pepper

Preheat the oven grill.

Separate the leaves from the lettuce, roughly tear them in half and place on a serving platter, creating a bed. Set aside.

Cover a large baking sheet with foil. Place the courgette slices on the sheet. Put the pepper pieces, skin side up, on the same sheet if you have room (if not, grill the vegetables in 2 batches). Brush the pepper and courgettes with olive oil and season with a pinch of salt and pepper. Turn the courgettes over and brush with the remaining olive oil and sprinkle over a small pinch of salt and pepper. Place under the grill for 7 minutes.

Remove from the grill, turn the courgettes over and grill for a further 5 minutes, or until the courgettes are golden and the peppers are black. Remove the baking sheet from the oven and place the peppers in a small bowl. Cover with clingfilm and set aside, allowing to cool. Place the courgettes on top of the prepared lettuce leaves.

Pour the artichokes and their oil into a bowl. Remove the artichokes and scatter them over the courgettes and lettuce. Once the pepper has cooled, peel off and discard the skin, finely slice and add to the salad.

Sprinkle half the mint leaves into the bowl of artichoke oil. Add the mustard, vinegar and honey and mix well. Peel and pit the avocado and finely slice. Place in the bowl and gently toss together.

When ready to serve, place the avocado slices on top of the salad, drizzle over the dressing and the lemon juice and sprinkle over the remaining mint.

Season with 4–5 twists of pepper and serve with some simple toasted ciabatta bread, rubbed with a garlic clove. I could literally eat this every day. Enjoy!

RAINBOW CARROTS WITH SPICY RED PESTO + HONEY GLAZE

Arcobaleno di carote con glassa piccante di pesto rosso e miele

SERVES 4

I have taken a simple concept of roasted carrots and completely given them a makeover. I think this side is so good looking. Using rainbow carrots really does jazz up the dish and adding a touch of chilli and red pesto means it has such a fantastic flavour. You can give your carrots a bit more of a kick if you prefer, by using 2 tbsp chilli-infused olive oil and 3 tbsp olive oil. A perfect side dish to go with any meal.

900g rainbow carrots,
  unpeeled but very
  well scrubbed
1 tbsp chilli-infused
  olive oil
4 tbsp olive oil
1 tbsp good-quality
  shop-bought
  red pesto
2 tbsp runny honey
sea salt flakes

Preheat the oven to 220°C/fan 200°C/Gas 7.

Cut off and discard 1cm from each end of the rainbow carrots. Place in a medium baking tray. I like to arrange them so the colours are all mixed up.

Pour over the chilli oil, olive oil and 1 tbsp sea salt flakes. Use your fingertips to make sure the carrots are equally coated. Place in the middle of the oven and roast for 30 minutes.

Meanwhile, spoon the red pesto and honey into a small bowl and mix well.

Remove the carrots from the oven and, using a pastry brush, equally baste the red pesto and honey glaze all over them. Return to the oven and roast for a further 15 minutes. Serve immediately with any meat, fish or vegetable dish.

RICE /ALAD WITH TUNA CHUNKS, QUAIL'S EGG/ + PECORINO

Insalata di riso con pezzettoni di tonno, uova di quaglia e pecorino

SERVES 6–8

This recipe is very versatile, it can be used as a starter, main course, picnic lunch, office lunch, school lunch… and if you remove the tuna, it makes a great accompaniment to any meat or fish dish. It's also very easy to prepare and can be kept in the fridge for a couple of days. I recommend eating this salad always at room temperature, so make sure you take it out of the fridge 30 minutes before serving it.

300g long grain rice
100g frozen peas,
  defrosted
100g green beans,
  *trimmed and cut into
  2cm lengths*
3 x 150g cans of tuna
  chunks in olive oil,
  drained
100g pitted Leccino
  olives, or other
  good-quality pitted
  black olives such as
  Kalamata, *drained
  and halved*
100g gherkins,
  finely chopped
1 red pepper, *deseeded
  and finely chopped*
1 yellow pepper, *deseeded
  and finely chopped*
15 red cherry tomatoes,
  quartered
5 tbsp good-quality
  mayonnaise
5 tbsp extra virgin
  olive oil
60g pecorino cheese
  shavings
24 quail's eggs, *hard–
  boiled for 3–4 minutes,
  then peeled*
salt and freshly ground
  black pepper

Fill a medium-sized saucepan with 2.5 litres water, add 1 tbsp salt and bring to the boil. Pour in the rice and cook for 12 minutes, stirring occasionally with a wooden spoon. Add the peas and beans and continue to gently boil for a further 2 minutes. Remove from the heat and drain through a sieve. Rinse the rice and vegetables under cold running water to cool, then leave to drain thoroughly.

Meanwhile, put all the remaining ingredients, except the pecorino and quail's eggs, into a large mixing bowl. Add the drained rice and vegetables. Sprinkle in half the cheese shavings (try and reserve good-looking larger shavings for the decoration), ½ tsp pepper and 1 tsp salt. Stir gently with a wooden spoon until it is all mixed together.

Transfer the rice salad to a large serving platter. Arrange the quail's eggs on top of the rice and scatter over the remaining pecorino shavings. Sprinkle over 10 twists of pepper and serve. If needed later, or the next day, loosely cover with clingfilm and refrigerate.

SAUTÉED NEW POTATOES WITH ONION, PEAS + PANCETTA

Patate novelle saltate con cipolla, piselli e pancetta

SERVES 4

My wife Jessica absolutely loves potatoes in any way they come, from jacket, to mash, to roast, but the first time I made this recipe for her... well, let me just say that I had a fantastic night. If you fancy a vegetarian option, you can substitute the pancetta for a large courgette, chopped into 1cm cubes.

1kg new potatoes of a
  similar size, *halve any*
  that are a little large
60g salted butter, *melted*
3 tbsp olive oil
1 large onion, *peeled and*
  finely sliced
200g diced pancetta
150g frozen peas,
  defrosted
salt and freshly ground
  black pepper

Fill a medium saucepan with 1.5 litres water, add ½ tbsp salt and bring to the boil over a high heat. Add the potatoes and gently boil for 17 minutes. Drain and carefully tip them into a large bowl with the melted butter. Grind in 10 twists of pepper and mix well using a wooden spoon.

Meanwhile, pour the oil into a large shallow saucepan and place over a medium heat. Add the onion and fry for 8 minutes, stirring occasionally with a wooden spoon. Add the pancetta and fry for a further 6 minutes, stirring occasionally.

Add the buttered potatoes to the pan and mix well. Fry for 2 minutes. Pour in the peas, stir and fry for 2 minutes, combining all the flavours.

Equally divide the potatoes between 4 plates to accompany any meat or fish recipe, or place on a large serving platter and let your family and friends help themselves.

ſICILIAN-STYLE VEGETABLES WITH BABY PLUM TOMATOES, MINT + CHILLI

Caponata

SERVES 4–6

There are many ways to make a traditional caponata, some people add pine kernels, others like raisins or parsley, but aubergines, celery and onion always feature in any recipe. You can serve this dish warm as an accompaniment, or at room temperature, and it is particularly fantastic with fish. I also like to serve it warm with toasted ciabatta slices: a perfect bruschetta.

2 aubergines, *total weight about 500g*
300g celery
2 tbsp capers in salt, *rinsed under cold water and drained*
2 tbsp white wine vinegar
10 tbsp extra virgin olive oil
1 large red onion, *peeled and finely sliced*
1 large garlic clove, *peeled and very finely sliced*
15 baby plum tomatoes, *halved*
1 tsp chilli flakes
2 tbsp pitted Leccino olives in brine or oil, or other good-quality pitted black olives such as Kalamata, *drained*
20 mint leaves, *finely sliced*
sea salt flakes
salt and freshly ground black pepper

Cut off and discard both ends of the aubergines, then cut them into 1.5cm cubes. Place in a colander, sprinkle over 1 tbsp sea salt flakes and drain over a bowl or in the sink for 30 minutes.

Meanwhile, cut off and discard both ends of the celery sticks. Cut them into 2cm pieces, place in a small saucepan and cover with water. Add 1 tsp salt, bring to the boil, then cook for 3 minutes. Drain and set aside.

Place the capers in a small bowl and add the white wine vinegar. Set aside.

Pour 3 tbsp oil into a large shallow saucepan and place over a medium heat. When the oil is hot, add half the aubergines and fry for 8 minutes, turning occasionally with a wooden spoon, ensuring all pieces are brown on all sides. Remove and drain on some kitchen paper to absorb any excess oil. Repeat the process with the remaining aubergines and another 3 tbsp oil.

Pour 2 tbsp more oil into the same shallow saucepan and add the onion. Fry for 6 minutes, stirring occasionally with a wooden spoon. Add the celery and garlic and cook for a further 5 minutes. Add the tomatoes, chilli flakes, ½ tsp salt and ½ tsp pepper and stir all together. Add the fried aubergines and mix well with a wooden spoon. Cook for 5 minutes.

Remove from the heat, add the olives, capers – including their vinegar – and the mint. Stir well with a wooden spoon.

Tip the vegetables into a small serving dish, drizzle over the remaining 2 tbsp oil and either serve immediately or cover, allow to rest and eat at room temperature.

/PICY MUSHROOM BRU/CHETTA
WITH CHEE/Y FRIED EGGS

Bruschetta con funghi piccanti e uova fritte al formaggio

SERVES 2

This is the D'Acampo version of breakfast bruschetta. My boys Rocco and Luciano absolutely love eggs and would eat them every day if they could, so I try to come up with different ideas to make them a little bit more exciting. This is definitely one of their firm favourites, so quick to do and with amazing flavours to kick-start your day. You can substitute the Parmesan cheese with pecorino if you prefer and, if you can only get small slices of bread, make two toasts for each person, topping each slice with an egg.

8 tbsp extra virgin
  olive oil
¾ tsp chilli flakes
1 large garlic clove,
  peeled and finely sliced
250g chestnut
  mushrooms,
  finely sliced
leaves from 4 thyme
  sprigs
2 extra-large slices of
  country style bread,
  *22cm x 10cm, sliced
  1cm thick (or see recipe
  introduction)*
4 large fresh eggs
20g Parmesan cheese,
  finely grated
salt

Pour 5 tbsp oil into a large frying pan. Add the chilli flakes with the garlic and place over a high heat. As soon as the garlic starts to sizzle, fry for 1 minute, then add the mushrooms and thyme. Sprinkle over ½ tsp salt and mix well. Fry for 10 minutes, stirring occasionally with a wooden spoon. Tip the mushrooms on to a plate and set aside.

Toast the slices of bread on both sides.

Meanwhile, using the same frying pan as for the mushrooms, pour in the remaining 3 tbsp oil and place over a medium heat. As soon as the oil is hot, crack in the eggs and fry for 1 minute. Sprinkle the Parmesan cheese over the eggs and continue to fry for a further minute.

Place 1 slice of toasted bread on each serving plate.

Equally divide the mushrooms on top of the bread and then gently place 2 cheesy fried eggs on top of each slice. Serve immediately.

STUFFED PEPPERS WITH SAUTÉED MIXED VEGETABLES + PARMESAN

Peperoni ripieni di verdure e Parmigiano Reggiano

SERVES 4

*as a main course, or
8 as a side dish*

4 yellow peppers
2 tbsp olive oil

FOR THE STUFFING
4 tbsp olive oil
1 large onion, *peeled and
    finely chopped*
1 small aubergine,
    *ends trimmed off, cut
    into 1cm cubes*
1 large red pepper,
    *deseeded and cut into
    1cm cubes*
2 large courgettes, *total
    weight about 600g,
    ends trimmed off, cut
    into 1cm cubes*
10 red cherry tomatoes,
    quartered
100g Parmesan cheese,
    finely grated
salt and freshly ground
    black pepper

Whenever I cook this dish it reminds me of my father Ciro, he loved peppers with any kind of stuffing. This recipe is delicious and super-easy and can be eaten as a main course or is a fantastic side dish to accompany any meat or fish recipe. It is also perfect the day after cooking, for a packed lunch to go to the office: just warm it up slightly in a microwave and you are ready to go. You can substitute the Parmesan cheese with goat's cheese, or even strips of mozzarella.

Preheat the oven to 200°C/fan 180°C/Gas 6.

To make the stuffing, pour the 4 tbsp oil into a large frying pan and place over a medium heat. Add the onion and fry for 3 minutes until softened. Add the aubergine and continue to fry for 8 minutes, stirring occasionally with a wooden spoon. Add the pepper and continue to fry for 6 minutes, again stirring occasionally. Add the courgettes, tomatoes, 1½ tsp salt and ½ tsp pepper, mix well and fry for a further 8 minutes. Keep stirring occasionally, then remove from the heat and set aside.

Cut the yellow peppers in half lengthways, then remove and discard the seeds and membrane. Try to leave the stalks intact if you can, as it looks great when serving. Place the peppers on a medium baking sheet, skin side down. Drizzle over the 2 tbsp olive oil and sprinkle with salt and pepper. Loosely cover with foil and roast in the middle of the oven for 20 minutes.

Remove from the oven and discard the foil. Equally divide the vegetable mixture between the half peppers and return to the centre of the oven for 20 minutes.

Remove the tray from the oven and equally sprinkle the Parmesan on top of each stuffed pepper. Place back in the centre of the oven for 5 minutes. Remove and serve immediately.

DESSERTS

Promises made,
traditions continued

2000

Italian desserts range in flavours and textures from sweet to slightly bitter, but somehow they never seem to be too sickly. Most of them have an amazing balance, so you can eat lots of them. That's what I tell myself anyway... Many experts believe that the first Roman desserts were basically bread sweetened with honey and fruits, as sugar was too costly. The famous panforte was born using these ingredients. I think the most famous Italian dessert today has to be tiramisu. Over the years, writing books, I have created so many different versions of tiramisu that I actually haven't featured one in this book. I decided to pick lesser known but still very traditional Italian desserts instead, hoping that you may not have tried some of them before. I promise you won't be disappointed.

This chapter in the book is definitely Rocco's and Mia's favourite. It was one of the easiest chapters to write because there are so many amazing Italian desserts; sometimes I even get inspired by English puddings, using Italian ingredients to create something new. Everyone who has tried these recipes has a different favourite, so I know I have something here for everyone.

I think the recipe closest to my heart is the lemon cream cake. It's an old traditional recipe that my mother used to love. When she was ill, my sister Marcella and I went down to Sorrento to get the best lemons we could find, we reminisced about our trips there growing up, came home and made this cake together for my mum. I remember sitting in the garden and enjoying a huge slab of this amazing light cake and we laughed about silly memories we all had. It was a really lovely day. It always makes my day, when I come home from a really busy week to find that cake is sitting there, waiting for me to tuck in.

Another old traditional favourite of our family is the pistachio and rum ice cream, while my dad's personal favourite was his mum's amazing recipe for a plum pie. I have served it here with homemade custard (basically because I love it), but traditionally we would eat it with a huge dollop of mascarpone cream, which is also delicious. I couldn't write this book without my Nonna's classic Florentine biscuits too. This chapter means a lot to me. I hope you try every recipe and that you come to love them all as much as we do.

BANOFFEE PIE WITH AMARETTI BISCUITS

Torta di banana e caramello con amaretti

SERVES 6–8

My son Rocco has always loved this dessert and often asked me why it has never featured in one of my cookery books. I explained that it isn't an Italian recipe, but he was so adamant that people should be able to make this that he convinced me to make a slight amendment by adding amaretti biscuits to the base. Rocco asked me to send you this message from him: *You're welcome everyone x*

200g digestive biscuits
50g hard amaretti
   biscuits
100g salted butter,
   melted
400ml double cream
400g canned caramel
3 large ripe bananas
100g dark chocolate,
   coarsely grated

Crush both types of biscuits into crumbs by either using a food processor or putting them into a sealed food bag and, using a cooking hammer or rolling pin, smashing them until you get a crumb texture.

Place the melted butter in a medium-sized bowl. Tip in the crushed biscuits and use a flexible spatula to mix well, ensuring the butter has coated all the crumbs. Pour into a rectangular glass or ceramic dish (mine measured 24 x 20cm) and press down firmly. Place in the freezer for 10 minutes.

Meanwhile, whip the cream in a medium-sized bowl until soft peaks form. Set aside.

Remove the biscuit base from the freezer and gently pour over the caramel. Use a spatula to distribute the caramel evenly, covering the biscuit base entirely.

Slice the bananas into 1cm-thick discs and place on top of the caramel.

Spoon over the whipped cream and use a spatula to evenly distribute it to cover the bananas completely. Try and create a smooth flat top. Sprinkle the chocolate over the cream to cover completely.

Cover with clingfilm and refrigerate for at least 1 hour before you serve it to your family or guests.

STRAWBERRY + PANETTONE CHEESECAKE WITH AMARETTO LIQUEUR

Torretta di panettone e fragole con mascarpone e Amaretto

MAKES 2

to share between 4

After I tasted Stefania's panettone while filming the show in Italy that accompanies this book, I knew I had to do something with it. Normally, panettone is prepared and eaten at Christmas time, but this recipe gives it a summer twist. You can substitute the strawberries with raspberries, if you prefer. I believe that desserts are best shared, so this makes two large puddings that can be shared between four.

2cm-thick slice of
  panettone
5 tbsp Amaretto liqueur
250g mascarpone
2 tsp runny honey
seeds from 1 vanilla pod
3 tbsp finely chopped
  pistachio nuts
14 small strawberries,
  *trimmed, hulled
  and halved*
icing sugar, *to dust*

Use two 8 x 5cm chef's rings to cut out 2 circles of the panettone. Place the rings on a tray lined with baking parchment and push a circle of panettone into the base of each. Drizzle ½ tbsp Amaretto over each and leave it to soak in.

Meanwhile, work the mascarpone in a large bowl with a fork until it loosens. Add the honey, vanilla seeds and 2 tbsp chopped pistachios and mix together.

Using 6–7 halved strawberries, line the sides of both the chef's rings, placing the cut sides of the strawberries against the rings. Be careful, as these will create the final look of your dish. Equally divide the mascarpone mixture over the top of the strawberries by gently pouring it into the moulds. Give the tray a little tap to remove air bubbles, then finally use the back of a knife to evenly flatten the surface.

Cover, put into the fridge and leave to set for 2–3 hours.

Place the remaining halved strawberries into a bowl and pour over the remaining Amaretto. Give the ingredients a mix, cover the bowl and leave to macerate for 1 hour.

When ready to serve, place the cheesecakes on 2 individual plates. Use warm hands, or a kitchen blowtorch, to loosen the moulds, then gently slide them off.

Top each pudding with the macerated strawberries, sprinkle with the remaining pistachios and dust with icing sugar. Get close to the person you're sharing with and dive in.

BISCOFF + ESPRESSO CHEESECAKE

Torta al formaggio con biscotti e caffè

<u>**SERVES 10–12**</u>

This has to be one of my wife's favourite desserts of all time. She is a huge cheesecake lover and I often catch her dunking one of these biscuits in her coffee, so I decided to come up with something that would combine them both and it was a great success. I have used a strong coffee liqueur in this recipe, but it also works very well with Irish cream liqueur. Anything goes really. You can make a chocolate cheesecake by using chocolate-hazelnut spread instead of Biscoff spread, or substitute the Biscoff biscuits for digestives. This is an amazing cheesecake recipe that you can really get creative with.

250g Lotus Biscoff biscuits, *plus 3 biscuits to decorate*
100g salted butter, *melted*
300ml double cream
80g icing sugar
500g full-fat cream cheese
2 tsp vanilla extract
20ml strong espresso coffee
10ml coffee liqueur, *such as Kahlua*
150g Biscoff spread

FOR THE COFFEE SYRUP
50ml strong espresso coffee
50ml coffee liqueur, *such as Kahlua*
50ml caster sugar

Crush the biscuits into crumbs by either using a food processor or putting them into a sealed food bag and, using a cooking hammer or rolling pin, smashing them until you get crumbs. Tip them into a medium-sized bowl with the melted butter and, using a flexible spatula, mix well, ensuring the butter has coated all the crumbs. Pour into a loose-based cake tin – I used a deep tin with a diameter of 24cm and a depth of 6cm – and press down firmly over the base and sides, ensuring the sides are even, as that is the part you will see when the cheesecake is finished. Place in the freezer while you prepare the filling.

Pour the cream and icing sugar into a large bowl and whip until soft peaks form.

In a separate large bowl, whisk the cream cheese and vanilla extract until smooth. Pour the whipped cream into the cream cheese mixture and use a spatula to mix.

Pour half the cream cheese filling into another large bowl. Add the coffee and liqueur to one bowl and use a spatula to mix gently until smooth in colour. Take out the biscuit base from the freezer and pour over the coffee cream mixture. Spread evenly using a spatula and return to the freezer for 10 minutes.

Place the Biscoff spread into the remaining cream cheese mixture and use a spatula to mix well, again until smooth in colour. Remove the biscuit base from the freezer and gently spread on top of the coffee cream mixture, creating a 2-layer cheesecake. The layers are very similar in colour, but the balance of flavours is perfect. Smooth the top and place in the fridge for at least 5 hours, allowing the cheesecake to set.

To make the syrup, pour all the syrup ingredients into a small saucepan and place over a medium heat. When bubbling, reduce the heat and simmer for about 6 minutes, creating a thick runny syrup, stirring occasionally with a wooden spoon. You can test it is ready by making sure it coats the back of a metal spoon. Pour into a small jug and allow to cool completely.

When ready to serve the cheesecake, drizzle over the coffee syrup and arrange 3 biscuits standing up in the centre.

This will be OK to eat for 3 days if kept, covered, in the fridge... if it lasts that long.

CLASSIC CREAMY TART WITH RICOTTA + VANILLA

Torta della Nonna

SERVES 12

Every Italian grandma somehow knows how to make this perfectly. I'm not sure if it's taught or if they are born with it and it automatically becomes a technique they find they know by heart as soon as their first grandchild is born. I am yet to meet a nonna that doesn't make this a few times a year for her family. I still remember today my Nonna Flora in the kitchen covered with flour and the smell of vanilla throughout the whole house, a great memory I will never forget.

FOR THE PASTRY
500g caster sugar,
  plus 1 tbsp
7 large eggs
500g salted butter,
  softened, plus more
  for the tin
1kg plain flour, *plus*
  more to dust
1 tbsp icing sugar
1 tbsp baking powder
finely grated zest of
  2 unwaxed lemons
20g pine kernels, *soaked*
  in water for 5 minutes

FOR THE FILLING
200g caster sugar
70g plain flour
3 large eggs
200ml full-fat milk
1 unwaxed lemon,
  zest removed with a
  vegetable peeler, plus
  the lemon juice
1 vanilla pod, *split*
  lengthways
350g ricotta, *lightly*
  beaten with a fork

Start with the pastry. In a large bowl, beat the 500g sugar and 6 of the eggs together with an electric whisk. Gradually add the softened butter, 3 spoons at a time, and keep whisking. Add the flour, icing sugar, baking powder and lemon zest. Mix together as quickly as you can using your hands: it will be very wet and sticky to begin with, but persevere and start to bring the mixture together to form a dough. Lightly flour a work surface and knead the dough to form a smooth ball. Wrap in clingfilm, place back in the bowl and put into the fridge for 1 hour.

Meanwhile, to make the creamy filling, put the sugar and flour into a medium-sized bowl and mix to combine. Whisk in the eggs one at a time.

Pour the milk into a medium-sized saucepan. Add the lemon zest and the vanilla pod. Place over a low heat until almost at boiling point. Remove the lemon zest and vanilla pod, scrape the vanilla seeds into the pan and discard the pod. Pour the egg, flour and sugar mixture into the saucepan and simmer for 5–6 minutes, stirring continuously with a hand-held whisk, until you have a thick, smooth custard. Do not cook it too fast, or it will split. Pour into a bowl or jug and allow to cool completely. Once completely cooled, stir in the beaten ricotta and the lemon juice.

Preheat the oven to 200°C/fan 180°C/Gas 6.

Butter a 30cm loose-based tart tin, then dust it with 1 tsp flour.

Remove the dough from the fridge and place just over half of it on a well-floured surface. Roll it into a circle about 1cm thick. The circle should be slightly bigger than the tin, allowing the dough to come up the sides.

The trick to lift the pastry away from the work surface is to gently roll it around the rolling pin. Lift the pastry up and carefully place over the tart tin. Gently press down with your fingertips to make sure it completely covers the base and sides. Trim the edges with a knife.

Spoon the custard into the tart tin over the dough. Roll out the remaining dough into another rough circle, but thinner this time, about 5mm thick. Carefully place on top of the cream and pinch the pastry seams between the top and bottom pastry circles to ensure the filling is encompassed completely in the dough.

Beat the remaining egg in a small bowl and use a pastry brush to lightly brush it over the top of the tart. Sprinkle over the 1 tbsp caster sugar and scatter with the drained pine kernels.

Bake in the middle of the oven for 40 minutes.

Remove from the oven and allow the tart to rest on a wire rack for 2 hours. Remove the tart from the tin and serve at room temperature. This will keep, covered and refrigerated, for up to 4 days.

EΣPRESSO + AMARETTO PANNA COTTA

Panna cotta con Amaretto e caffè espresso

SERVES 4

I can't write an Italian cookbook without at least one of the classic desserts in it, but of course, I always make them different; I need to create new concoctions to give you a vast choice throughout all my books. Sometimes new recipes don't work, but this one was a huge success in my opinion, as I love coffee! You can substitute the Amaretto with an Irish cream liqueur if you prefer. These little desserts are perfect for a dinner party, as you can prepare them the day before.

2 gelatine leaves
300ml double cream
100ml full-fat milk
30ml Amaretto liqueur
70ml strong espresso
  coffee
80g caster sugar
2 tbsp flaked almonds

In a small bowl, soak the gelatine leaves in cold water for 5 minutes.

Meanwhile, pour the cream, milk, liqueur, espresso and sugar into a small saucepan and warm gently over a low heat, stirring continuously with a hand-held whisk until the sugar dissolves and the cream starts to bubble lightly at the sides of the saucepan, about 5 minutes. Do not boil the milk mixture. Remove from the heat.

Take the gelatine leaves from the bowl of water and squeeze out any excess water. Place in the warm cream mixture and stir gently with the whisk until dissolved.

Divide the cream between 4 small ramekins or moulds and set aside to cool. Once cooled, gently cover with clingfilm and place in the fridge for at least 5 hours or, even better, overnight.

When ready to serve, place the flaked almonds in a small dry frying pan and toast for 2 minutes over a medium heat. Remove from the heat and set aside.

Take the panna cottas out of the fridge and discard the clingfilm. Dip the bases of the moulds in warm water for 20 seconds, being careful not to get any water in the panna cottas themselves, then carefully turn out on to dessert plates. Sprinkle over the toasted almonds equally and serve.

FLORENTINE BISCUITS

Biscotti alla Fiorentina

MAKES 16

These remind me of Christmas. We have them in Italy all year round, but my Nonna Flora always had them on a little plate covered with a net, in the centre of her coffee table, for everyone and anyone to come in and help themselves during the festive season. I remember as a kid licking off the chocolate but not being too bothered about the dried fruit biscuit, which is funny, as nowadays I think the best bit is actually the biscuit with or without the chocolate. I really love these and not only because they remind me of good times... they are truly delicious.

100g demerara sugar
100g golden syrup
100g salted butter
100g plain flour
100g flaked almonds
75g pistachio nuts,
 roughly chopped
finely grated zest of
 3 unwaxed oranges
120g glacé cherries,
 chopped
200g dark chocolate,
 70% cocoa solids

Preheat the oven to 200°C/fan 180°C/Gas 6. Line 2 large baking sheets with baking parchment.

Put the sugar, golden syrup and butter into a small saucepan. Place over a medium heat until the butter has melted, stirring frequently with a hand-held whisk; it should take about 2 minutes. Remove from the heat, then whisk in the flour. Add the flaked almonds, pistachios, orange zest and cherries. Use a wooden spoon to mix well.

Place 8 heaped tbsp of the Florentine mixture on to each baking sheet. Leave plenty of room in between each, allowing them to spread during cooking time. Bake for 10 minutes, or until golden brown. Remove from the oven and leave to cool for 5 minutes. With the help of a rigid spatula, gently transfer them to a wire rack to cool completely.

Meanwhile, break the chocolate into small pieces and place in a medium-sized heatproof bowl. Heat a small saucepan of simmering water over a medium heat and place the bowl on top, making sure the bowl does not touch the water. Melt the chocolate, stirring occasionally with either a flexible spatula or wooden spoon. Allow to cool for a few minutes.

Turn the Florentine biscuits over and use a tablespoon to help you spread a little melted chocolate over the flat bottom side of each, ensuring you cover it right to the edges. Place in the fridge to set for 1 hour. Serve on a plate, some chocolate side up and some chocolate side down. Perfect with a lovely cup of coffee. If there are any left over, store in an airtight container in a cool dry place; they should last up to 4 weeks.

DELICIOUS LEMON CREAM CAKE

Delizia al limone

Close your eyes and this cake will transport you to Sorrento, where the famous lemons feature in anything and everything. I first tried this as a young boy with my mother; we had visited Pompeii (definitely a must-see if you can), then travelled on to Sorrento for some lunch. We passed an amazing bakery and she bought this cake to bring home for my dad, sister, nonna and nonno. It's the best memory I have with them all, so I love making this cake and telling my family and friends all about that amazing day. If you don't like pistachios or cannot have nuts, decorate this with lemon zest instead.

FOR THE CAKE
butter, *for the baking tray*
5 large eggs
2 tsp lemon extract
finely grated zest of
  1 unwaxed lemon
70g caster sugar
35ml olive oil
35ml vegetable oil
50g plain flour

FOR THE CREAM
500ml double cream
finely grated zest of
  2 unwaxed lemons
4 tsp lemon extract
250ml natural yogurt
80g icing sugar

FOR THE SYRUP AND DECORATION
3 tsp limoncello
1 tsp water
1 tsp caster sugar
40g pistachio nuts,
  crushed
3 mint leaves

Preheat the oven to 180°C/fan 160°C/Gas 4. Lightly butter a large (40 x 30cm) baking tray and line it with baking parchment.

Separate the eggs, placing the egg whites in a large bowl and the yolks in a small bowl. Whisk the egg whites until stiff. Lightly beat the yolks. Using a flexible spatula, fold the lemon extract, lemon zest and caster sugar into the egg whites. Now fold in the egg yolks, half at a time. Pour in the oils and, again, gently fold. Finally, sift in the flour and fold to combine all the ingredients. Pour into the prepared baking tray and bake in the middle of the oven for 12 minutes until golden. Remove from the oven and turn out on to a wire rack. Allow to cool.

Meanwhile, pour the cream into a large bowl and whip to form soft peaks. Add the lemon zest, lemon extract and yogurt and sift in the icing sugar. Using a flexible spatula, fold to combine, then set aside.

When the cake is cold, to make the syrup, pour the limoncello, measured water and caster sugar into a small saucepan. Place over a medium heat and stir until the sugar has dissolved, 1–2 minutes. Remove from the heat.

Remove the baking parchment from the cake and place it on a work surface. Use a pastry brush to brush the hot syrup all over the sponge, then cut it lengthways into 4cm-wide strips. Spread some cream on the first strip, carefully roll it up and place upright in the middle of a flat serving plate. Spread some cream on a second strip and roll it around the first rolled strip on the plate (see photos, overleaf). Continue until all the strips are used. Don't be tempted to put cream on all the strips at once, as the sponge can get too soggy to handle, just do one at time.

Using a palette knife, gently spread the remaining cream all over the cake, covering it completely. Flatten the top as much as possible. Sprinkle the crushed pistachios on top and place 3 mint leaves in the centre. Place in the fridge for 2 hours, then serve. From me to you, via the Amalfi coast.

FLOURLESS CHOCOLATE FONDANTS

Tortino con cuore di cioccolato senza farina

SERVES 4

Fondants have to be a firm favourite with most kids and, of course, adults. They look really impressive and are a fantastic choice if you can't eat wheat flour. Many people think they are really difficult to make, but actually this is one of the easiest dessert recipes in this book. It is also a good choice for a dinner party, as you can prepare the fondants in the morning until the chilling stage and just put them into the oven when needed. I love serving them with my Pistachio + Rum Ice Cream (see page 240).

115g salted butter
15g cocoa powder,
 plus more to dust
100g dark chocolate,
 70% cocoa solids
2 eggs, *plus 2 egg yolks*
50g caster sugar

Place 15g of the butter in a small microwaveable bowl and melt it in the microwave. With a pastry brush, use it to butter 4 individual pudding basins. Dust with cocoa powder and set aside.

Roughly cut the remaining 100g butter into 3cm cubes and place in a heatproof bowl. Break in the chocolate and set over a small saucepan of simmering water, making sure the bowl doesn't touch the water. Using a flexible spatula, stir until the chocolate and butter have melted and combined. Remove from the heat, sift in the 15g cocoa powder, mix well and set aside to cool slightly.

Meanwhile, put the eggs and egg yolks into a medium bowl. Pour in the caster sugar and, with an electric whisk, mix until thick and pale, about 3 minutes. Fold the melted chocolate mixture into the egg mixture. Equally divide the mixture between the 4 prepared moulds, cover with clingfilm and place in the fridge to chill for 1 hour, or until required.

When ready to serve, preheat the oven to 200°C/fan 180°C/Gas 6.

Take the fondants straight out of the fridge, remove and discard the clingfilm and bake in the middle of the oven for 13 minutes. Remove from the oven and set aside to rest for 2 minutes.

Gently run a knife around the sides of each basin to release the fondants. Turn them out on to individual dessert plates and serve immediately with my amazing Pistachio + Rum Ice Cream.

MARBLE CAKE WITH AMARETTO LIQUEUR

Ciambella con liquore Amaretto

SERVES 12

I know that, traditionally, cakes like this are for an afternoon tea or a mid-morning snack but, for me, they have to be a breakfast option as well. I am also aware that you should allow a cake to rest for at least half an hour before serving, but again, I like to break the rules and have a cheeky warm slice of this five minutes after removing it from the oven, with a cup of coffee or even a glass of cold milk. You can eliminate the Amaretto liqueur if you prefer. In the past, I have also added 50g chocolate chips to the chocolate mixture, which is fantastic.

40ml olive oil, *plus 1 tbsp*
100g plain flour, *plus 1 tsp*
5 large eggs
200g caster sugar
1 tbsp baking powder
200g ground almonds
seeds from ½ vanilla
  pod
3 tbsp Amaretto liqueur
3 tbsp cocoa powder
2 tbsp full-fat milk
salt

Preheat the oven to 200°C/fan 180°C/Gas 6.

Pour the 1 tbsp oil and 1 tsp flour into a small bowl and mix well. Use a pastry brush to spread the mixture around the sides and base of a medium-sized (24cm diameter) bundt tin. Set aside.

Separate 4 of the eggs. Put the whites into a large bowl and the yolks into a small bowl. Whisk the egg whites until stiff. Add the egg yolks and sugar and whisk until pale and thick. Sift in the 100g flour and the baking powder and use a flexible spatula to stir until combined. Add the ground almonds, vanilla seeds, 40ml olive oil and the Amaretto liquor and stir to combine. Pour half the mixture into a medium bowl.

Crack the egg white of the remaining egg into a small bowl with a pinch of salt. Whisk until stiff. Add this to one of the bowls of mixture. Add the cocoa powder and milk to the same bowl and use a spatula to combine all the ingredients.

Pour half the pale batter into the prepared tin and make sure to cover the bottom of the tin. Gently blob the chocolate batter on top. Pour the remaining pale batter on top of the chocolate and use a palette knife to create a marbled effect. (Do not overdo it as you want the flavours to remain separate.) Bake in the middle of the oven for 40 minutes.

Remove from the oven and allow to rest for as long as you can wait for, normally at least half an hour. Carefully run a knife around the edges of the cake and tip it upside down on to a serving plate.

MY MOTHER'S VANILLA BREAKFAST CAKE

La torta alla vaniglia di mia madre

SERVES 8–10

I have called this a breakfast cake because my mother, Alba, always used to make it on a weekend and serve it for breakfast with a pot of chocolate-hazelnut spread and a glass of cold milk. I have kept the tradition going with my children: Rocco is especially happy when this cake is at the breakfast table. When I was a little boy, it used to last a whole week, but in my house we are lucky if it lasts a couple of days. It is so easy to do and takes minutes to prepare. You can substitute the vanilla with the finely grated zest of an unwaxed orange or lemon, if you prefer.

175g salted butter, *softened, plus more for the tin*
175g caster sugar
175g self-raising flour
2 tsp vanilla extract
4 large eggs
50g ground almonds

Preheat the oven to 160°C/fan 140°C/Gas 3. Butter an 18cm, deep, round loose-based cake tin. Line the bottom of the tin with baking parchment, butter the parchment, then set aside.

Place all the ingredients in a large bowl and use an electric whisk to mix until smooth. Pour the mixture into the prepared tin and gently tap on a flat surface a couple of times, allowing any air bubbles to disappear. Level the top using a flexible spatula and place in the centre of the oven for 1½ hours, as this cake is cooked very slowly at a fairly gentle temperature.

Remove from the oven and allow to cool in the tin for 10 minutes.

Turn out on to a wire rack and cool completely for about 1 hour.

Serve with a glass of cold milk and do not forget the chocolate spread!

PISTACHIO BISCUITS

Pistacchiotti

MAKES 15

Yes, this recipe only requires four ingredients, and you will make the most delicious biscuits ever. I came across spreadable pistachio cream as I was travelling around Sicily, and it was love at first sight. It is like chocolate-hazelnut spread, but made with pistachio nuts: incredible. I often spread it on toasted bread and also make a delicious ice cream from it (see overleaf). Not an easy ingredient to buy in shops or supermarkets, but get online and you will find it immediately. My *pistacchiotti* can be stored in an airtight container for four or five days.

180g pistachio cream,
  plus more for the filling
1 large egg, plus
  1 egg yolk
150g '00' flour, *plus more
  if needed*
30g unsalted pistachio
  nuts, *chopped*

Line a large baking sheet with baking parchment.

Spoon the pistachio cream into a bowl and add the egg and egg yolk. With the help of a fork, mix all together until well combined.

Tip in the flour and continue to mix until you have created a dough that does not stick to your hands. If needed, add a little more flour.

Divide the dough into 15 balls and place on the prepared baking sheet. Leave space between the balls, as they will slightly expand during cooking.

With the handle of a wooden spoon, create a hole in the middle of each ball by pressing three-quarters of the way down, smoothing out any cracks that start to appear with your fingers. Chill for 1 hour.

Preheat the oven to 190°C/fan 170°C/Gas 5. Bake in the middle of the oven for 11 minutes exactly. Do not cook for longer, otherwise you will start to see cracks around the biscuits. Leave to cool completely.

Fill each hole with 1 tsp pistachio cream and sprinkle over the chopped pistachio nuts.

Serve with your favourite cup of coffee or tea.

PISTACHIO + RUM ICE CREAM

Gelato al pistacchio e rum

SERVES 8

... or 6 greedy people

10 egg yolks
100g caster sugar
300g pistachio cream
500ml double cream
100g chopped pistachio
  nuts, *plus more*
  to decorate
6 tbsp good-quality
  rum

I love discovering new ingredients and was so excited to find this pistachio cream. It is absolutely delicious and can be used in so many different ways. You can even just spread it on toast. I have made amazing Pistachio Biscuits with the same cream (see the previous page) which you also must try. I cannot sell this recipe enough. It looks great, is easy to prepare and tastes amazing! Fantastic served with cantuccini biscuits.

Put the egg yolks and sugar into a large heatproof bowl and set the bowl over a saucepan of simmering water. Ensure the base of the bowl does not touch the water. Using an electric whisk, whisk for 3–5 minutes, or until the sugar has dissolved and the mixture is pale and thick.

Remove the bowl from the heat and whisk in the pistachio cream. Leave to cool completely.

Meanwhile, pour the cream into a separate large bowl and lightly whip for about 5 minutes, until thick enough to just hold its shape and form soft peaks. Using a flexible spatula, fold the whipped cream into the pistachio mixture in 3 stages. Finally, fold in the chopped pistachios and rum.

Pour the mixture into a 1-litre freezerproof plastic container that has a lid, cover with the lid and place in the freezer for 6 hours, or until set, preferably overnight.

About 10 minutes before you are ready to serve, remove the ice cream from the freezer. Serve in dessert bowls and top each serving with some chopped pistachios... or, if you're in my house, grab some spoons and let everyone just dig in.

PLUM PIE + VANILLA CUSTARD

Torta di susine con crema alla vaniglia

SERVES 6–8

Who doesn't love a pie? I am a huge fan of this recipe because it is a fantastic alternative to the more popular apple, rhubarb or berry choices. Plums are slightly sour, so work perfectly with my vanilla custard. You can bake the pie and reheat it later if you wish, and if you are making the custard in advance – or want to serve the custard cold – take the saucepan off the heat and place a sheet of clingfilm on top, touching the custard, to ensure a skin does not form. If you don't have a vanilla pod, 2 tsp vanilla extract will definitely do the job.

FOR THE PASTRY
225g plain flour
75g icing sugar,
 plus more to dust
100g salted butter,
 chopped
1 egg, lightly beaten,
 plus 1 more to glaze

FOR THE FILLING
25g cornflour
100g caster sugar
11 ripe plums, *total
 weight about 780g,
 halved and pitted*

FOR THE CUSTARD
4 large egg yolks
60g caster sugar
2 tbsp cornflour
700ml full-fat milk
200ml double cream
1 vanilla pod

To make the pastry, put the flour, icing sugar and butter in a large bowl. Using your fingertips, rub together to form a crumb texture. This can also be done in a food processor. Add the beaten egg and, with the handle of a wooden spoon, stir until the pastry combines and forms a soft dough. Use your hands to shape it into a ball, wrap in clingfilm and refrigerate for 30 minutes.

Preheat the oven to 200°C/fan 180°C/Gas 6.

To make the filling, place the cornflour and sugar into a small bowl and mix well. Dip each plum half, flesh down, into the sugar mixture and arrange in a shallow 25cm diameter round ovenproof dish, skin sides up. Sprinkle the remaining sugar mixture all over the top of the plums.

Remove the pastry from the fridge and discard the clingfilm. Roll out the chilled pastry to create a circle 2cm bigger than the ovenproof dish. Gently place on top of the plums, loosely tucking in the edges. Brush the top with the beaten egg to glaze and place on a flat medium-sized baking tray, to catch any juices that might spill over instead of dirtying your oven.

Bake in the middle of the oven for 40 minutes, or until golden.

Meanwhile, to make the custard, place the egg yolks, sugar and cornflour into a medium-sized bowl and, using an electric whisk, whisk until pale.

Pour the milk and cream into a medium-sized saucepan, add the vanilla pod and place over a medium heat. Very carefully bring to just below boiling point. Basically, when you see a couple of bubbles forming, take off the heat.

Remove the pod and slice in half lengthways. Using a sharp knife, scrape the seeds into the creamed milk mixture and either discard the pod or dry it out and place it in a sugar jar. You have just made vanilla-flavoured sugar.

Add the warm creamed milk slowly to the beaten egg mixture, constantly stirring using a hand-held whisk. Once combined, pour back into the saucepan and place back over a low heat.

Gently simmer, still constantly stirring with the hand-held whisk, until the custard thickens. This is up to individual preference, but I find about 8 minutes is perfect. If you cook it for too long, you run the risk of curdling the custard.

Remove the pie from the oven and allow it to cool for 5 minutes.

Sprinkle with icing sugar and serve with a generous helping of your homemade vanilla custard. Enjoy!

RASPBERRY + LIMONCELLO SORBET

Sorbetto di lamponi e limoncello

SERVES 6

Whenever I make a sorbet, I like to use as few ingredients as possible, allowing the fruit to be the star of the show and also leaving the recipe as natural as possible, so it contains fewer calories than an ice cream. Sorbets are perfect after a heavy meal or even in between courses. You can substitute the limoncello with Pimm's, or even eliminate it completely, while blackberries instead of raspberries work fantastically well too.

800g fresh raspberries
5 tbsp limoncello
3 tbsp runny honey
1 tbsp caster sugar

Place all the ingredients in a food processor and blitz until you create a smooth purée.

Pour half the mixture through a sieve into a freezerproof plastic container that has a lid, using a tablespoon to press the juices through. Discard the seeds and repeat the process with the remaining mixture.

Stir and cover with the lid. Freeze for 4 hours.

Take the sorbet out of the freezer 15 minutes before serving.

Scoop into glass bowls and enjoy.

INDEX

ACNOWLEDGEMENTS

ACNOWLEDGEMENTS

Thank you

ACNOWLEDGEMENTS

I would like to start by thanking my agent and son Luciano D'Acampo at MEMS Agency. You have taken on the new role of looking after me incredibly well and I'm so grateful and proud of you. Thank you also to all the women in my life that have inspired some recipes and kept traditions alive, from my grandmothers Nonna Assunta and Nonna Flora, my mother Alba, my mother-in-law Elizabeth, my sister Marcella and my wife and daughter Jessica and Mia. I love you all so much, and, for those of you who are no longer with us, you are never forgotten. I promise you that Mia and my boys, Luciano and Rocco, will learn every one of your signature dishes!

Thank you to ITV for continuing to believe in me and let me still bring, after all these years, traditional Italian cuisine, culture and history to the screens of the UK, I never take for granted how lucky I am. A huge thank you to all at Betty for their amazing vision, creativity and hard work on the TV production that goes with this book. *Grazie* always to my beautiful country Italy and especially the nonnas and mammas there for always receiving me with love, warmth and great food.

Much love, always, to Abbi Rose for being my right-hand girl on every shoot and for continuing to make me look less shiny and half decent. You really do make my days that little bit more stress-free.

Thank you to all at Bloomsbury Publishing. It's been an absolute privilege to work with you all again. A special mention to Lena Hall, Rowan Yapp, Rose Brown, Laura Brodie in Production, Di Riley in Marketing and Sarah Bennie in PR. A massive shout-out to Lucy Bannell, my Editor, who is absolutely fantastic. Special thanks to Emma Wells and Nikki Dupin at Studio Nic & Lou for interpreting the brief so beautifully; you've created a book that is also a work of art. Thanks to Liz and Max for the amazing photography, Claire, Rob and Ellie for interpreting the dishes with such flair, and Jen Kay for your flawless taste! Loved working with you all again this year, let's keep doing it!

Finally, as I do for every book, I have to show huge gratitude to all of you. I am always humbled at how much you support me, laugh with me and cook with me. You make those hard shoot days worthwhile and I hope that you feel a little closer to Italy when travelling with me through my shows and my cookery books. Thank you all!

BLOOMSBURY PUBLISHING
Bloomsbury Publishing Plc
50 Bedford Square, London, WC1B 3DP, UK
29 Earlsfort Terrace, Dublin 2, Ireland

BLOOMSBURY, BLOOMSBURY PUBLISHING
and the Diana logo are trademarks of Bloomsbury Publishing Plc

First published in Great Britain in 2022
Text © Gino D'Acampo, 2022

Photographs © Haarala Hamilton, 2022

A catalogue record for this book is available from the British Library.
Library of Congress Cataloguing-in-Publication data has been applied for.

ISBN: HB: 978-1-5266-3263-O; eBook: 978-1-5266-3264-7;
2 4 6 8 10 9 7 5 3 1

Project Editor: Lucy Bannell
Designer: Emma Wells, Studio Nic & Lou
Photographer: Haarala Hamilton
Food Stylists: Rob Allison, Claire Bassano and Eleanor Mulligan
Prop Stylist: Jennifer Kay
Indexer: Vanessa Bird

Printed and bound in Germany by Mohn Media

MIX
Paper from
responsible sources
FSC® C011124

To find out more about our authors and books,
visit www.bloomsbury.com and sign up for our newsletters.

all american

all american

a style book by

TOMMY HILFIGER
with DAVID A. KEEPS

A MADHOUSE PRODUCTION

UNIVERSE

A MADHOUSE PRODUCTION
PRODUCED BY B. JEFFREY MADOFF
CREATIVE DIRECTOR: DEREK UNGLESS
EDITORIAL DIRECTOR: GILLIAN YOUNG
PRODUCER OF PHOTOGRAPHY: PATRICK DEEDES-VINCKE

EDITOR: JAMES STAVE
PRODUCTION DIRECTOR: ELIZABETH WHITE

ART DIRECTOR: ALEX MIN
BOOK DESIGNER: MICHAEL ENGLISH AT ME DESIGN
COVER DESIGNER: TRACEY TANGO AT TOMMY HILFIGER

STILL-LIFE PHOTOGRAPHERS: BILL STEELE AND DAVID BASHAW
CLOTHING STYLISTS: DEBBI MASON AND ARABELLA GUNDRY-MILLS
PHOTOGRAPHIC RESEARCHERS: SHARI CHERTOK AND IAN SOUTHWOOD AT RE:SEARCH

First published in the United States of America in 1997
by UNIVERSE PUBLISHING
A Division of Rizzoli International Publications, Inc.
300 Park Avenue South
New York, NY 10010

97 98 99 00 01 / 10 9 8 7 6 5 4 3 2 1

Library of Congress Catalog Card Number: 97-61339

Printed in Japan

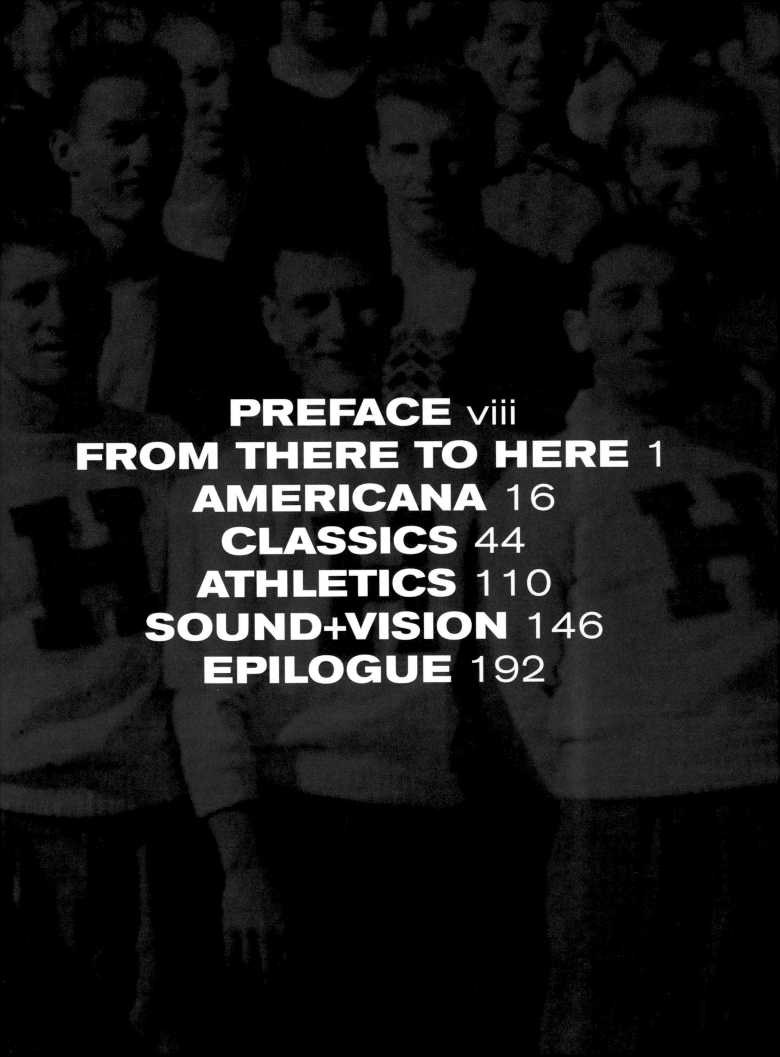

*Elmira heroes, left to right: Mark Twain;
Ernie Davis, All-American halfback from
Syracuse University and native of Elmira,
New York, won the Heisman Trophy in 1961,
but tragically, his promising future was cut
short by leukemia 18 months later; my
father, Richard Hilfiger*

WHEN IT CAME TIME TO PUT MY NAME ON A LINE OF CLOTHING, I LOOKED BACK TO THE BASICS I WAS BROUGHT UP WITH, THE CLEAN-CUT IVY LEAGUE LOOK OF THE EARLY SIXTIES. IN SOME VERY SIMPLE YET ELEGANT CLOTHING—BLAZERS AND SWEATERS FROM THE COLLEGE PLAYING FIELDS, CHINOS AND DENIMS FROM THE BLUE-COLLAR WORKFORCE—I FOUND A VOCABULARY OF COMFORTABLE, CASUAL DRESSING, THE ESSENCE OF AMERICAN SPORTSWEAR AND THE FOUNDATION OF POPULAR STYLE.

WE HAVE ARRIVED AT A UNIQUE MOMENT IN THE HISTORY OF MENSWEAR. WITH THE ADVENT OF CASUAL FRIDAYS, THE WORKPLACE HAS BECOME LESS FORMAL. OUR PREOCCUPATION WITH FITNESS AND SPORTS HAS MADE ATHLETIC CLOTHES ESSENTIAL WEEKEND WEAR. AND WE FREELY DRAW FROM THE FLASH AND GLAMOUR OF DECADES PAST TO BRIGHTEN UP OUR NIGHTS OUT ON THE TOWN. IN SOME WAYS, WE ARE MOVING BEYOND FASHION TO A CELEBRATION OF PERSONAL STYLE. FASHION IS FOR THE MOMENT, BUT STYLE IS INNATE AND ENDURING. PEOPLE WITH STYLE AND GOOD TASTE NEVER HAVE TO TRY TOO HARD. YOU CAN WEAR A T-SHIRT WITH A PAIR OF JEANS, A PAIR OF SOCKS, AND TENNIS SNEAKERS AND LOOK ABSOLUTELY PERFECT.

THIS BOOK IS A VOYAGE THROUGH THE CULTURAL CHANGES THAT HAVE SHAPED FASHION, AND THE FASHIONS THAT HAVE SHAPED OUR CULTURE FROM THE 1950S TO TODAY. IT IS A PERSONAL JOURNEY THROUGH THE ELEMENTS OF STYLE THAT HAVE INFLUENCED MY WARDROBE AND FORMED MY DESIGN SENSIBILITY. THINK OF THIS BOOK AS A REFERENCE GUIDE, A WAY TO UNDERSTAND WHERE FASHION COMES FROM AND WHERE IT'S GOING. SEE HOW THE IMAGES OF THE PAST RESONATE IN THE PRESENT, HOW YOU CAN PUT TOGETHER A MODERN WARDROBE THAT SUITS YOUR LIFESTYLE BY USING TAILORED CLOTHES AND SPORTY GEAR. LET THIS BOOK BE AN INSPIRATION EVERY TIME YOU OPEN YOUR CLOSET.

IN PREPARING THIS BOOK I WOULD LIKE TO EXPRESS THANKS TO SUSIE, MY WIFE AND BEST FRIEND OF 18 YEARS, WHO TAUGHT ME NEVER TO SETTLE AND ALWAYS TO SEEK PERFECTION, WHICH IS WHY WE MAKE SUCH A GREAT TEAM. SHE IS MY INSPIRATION. AND TO MY FAVORITE ASSETS IN THE WORLD, MY CHILDREN: ABBY, WHO TELLS ME WHAT TO WEAR SO I DON'T LOOK LIKE A NERD; RICHARD JAMES, WHO LIKES TO BE CALLED KING RICHARD JAMES—HE DOES NOT UNDERSTAND WHY HE SHOULD HAVE TO WEAR FANCY CLOTHES AT TIMES AND WISHES I MADE TOYS; ELIZABETH (FOO FOO), WHO IS MY 5:30 A.M. WAKEUP CALL AND WOULD RATHER BE A BOY; AND KATHLEEN, MY MASCOT AT HOME, WHO MOST RESEMBLES HER DAD. I WOULD ALSO LIKE TO THANK MY FATHER, RICHARD, AND MY MOTHER, VIRGINIA, FOR BRINGING ME INTO THIS LIFE AND SUPPORTING ALL MY WILD DREAMS, AND MY EIGHT BROTHERS AND SISTERS: KATHLEEN (KATHY), DOROTHY (SUSIE), ELIZABETH (BETSY), WILLIAM (BILLY), ROBERT (BOBBY), MARIE (DEE DEE), ANDREW (ANDY), VIRGINIA (GINNY). SPECIAL THANKS TO GINNY FOR BEING SUCH AN IMPORTANT PART OF MY DESIGN TEAM AND ANDY FOR CONNECTING ME TO THE MUSIC WORLD. THANKS TO AUNT ANNIE FOR TEACHING ME TO DO MY BEST IN EVERYTHING I DO. TO MY PARTNER SILAS CHOU, WHO FOUND ME IN BEVERLY HILLS AND BELIEVED IN ME; LAWRENCE STROLL, WHO TAUGHT ME HOW TO THINK BIG; AND JOEL HOROWITZ, MY ROCK OF GIBRALTAR. AND THANKS TO MIKE AND JOE, MICHAEL H. AND BUBBLES. THANKS TO MY ELMIRA CONTINGENCY, MY FRIENDS FOR 40-PLUS YEARS: FRENCHY, SPANGS, BLOOMER, RATSY, K.D., THE COLGIES, AND PAPPY. SPECIAL THANKS TO MY FORMER PARTNER LARRY STEMERMAN FROM PEOPLE'S PLACE AND HIS ENTIRE FAMILY FOR THEIR TREMENDOUS SUPPORT IN THE EARLY DAYS. I WOULD ALSO LIKE TO THANK MY LAWYER AND CONFIDANT TOM CURTIN AND HIS ASSOCIATE JOE LAMASTRA FOR THEIR ADVICE AND CONSULTATION. AND I CANNOT FORGET MOHAN MURJANI, WHO BELIEVED IN ME; STU KOMER, WHO FINALLY PERSUADED ME TO LEAVE ELMIRA; ANGELO, EMIL, AND ALEX FOR MAKING NEW YORK FUN. IT IS ALSO IMPORTANT TO THANK MY WONDERFUL AND DEDICATED STAFF AT TOMMY HILFIGER WHO HAVE HELPED ME REALIZE MY DREAMS AND HAVE BECOME PART OF MY FAMILY. UNFORTUNATELY, THERE ARE TOO MANY NAMES TO NAME, BUT I KNOW YOU KNOW WHO YOU ARE. SPECIAL THANKS TO QUINCY JONES, RUSSELL SIMMONS, MICK JAGGER, PETE TOWNSHEND, AND DAVID BOWIE. AND TO THE TEAM WHO PUT THIS BOOK TOGETHER WITH ME: CHARLES MIERS OF UNIVERSE PUBLISHING, JEFF MADOFF, DEREK UNGLESS, GILLIAN YOUNG, PATRICK DEEDES-VINCKE, JIM STAVE AND DAVID A. KEEPS.

FROM THERE TO HERE

I was born in Elmira, a small town in upstate New York. I'm a third-generation American.

My father's ancestors are from Bavaria—part Dutch and part German. My mother is English, Irish, and Scottish. Growing up in Elmira was sort of like living in "Leave It to Beaver–land." Everyone knew each other, and all the neighbors were very close. Our doors were always open, never locked. People would just come and go as they pleased; you trusted everybody. My mom still lives in the same house I grew up in. The house has five bedrooms, and our family had nine children. So figure out the math! We teamed up together, learned how to share, and how to respect one another—and we are all still very close. My mother taught us the golden rule: Do unto others as you would have them do unto you.

Just imagine five girls and four boys under one roof. Our house really rattled. All the boys loved music; the girls loved clothes. My parents were very open and liberal. We had sleepovers and slumber parties. In the basement we'd have band practice. In the backyard we'd have baseball practice. The driveway would be full of kids on bicycles, and my sisters would be in one of the bedrooms playing with Barbie. We had a cat named Barney and a dog named Garnet.

I played Little League baseball, small-fry football, went ice skating and skiing with the family. I loved collecting sports equipment—baseball gloves, bats, football helmets, shoulder pads. And, of course, I needed my six-shooters—every boy has his guns—and chaps and cowboy hats. And I had to have a Davy Crockett coonskin cap. Every little boy wanted to look like this

ELMIRA
NEW YORK
THE GLIDER CAPITAL OF AMERICA

hero. As I can attest, the concept of people dressing to look like their heroes is not new at all: I used to wear Billy the Kid–brand jeans.

I loved Roy Rogers and Sky King, all the American favorites. I read mysteries, the Hardy Boys and Nancy Drew, and I read about Tom Sawyer and Huck Finn because Mark Twain had kept a summer house in Elmira and was a local hero. I was in Cub Scouts and Boy Scouts, but not seriously—I didn't like it: I liked the scout uniforms and pocketknives, but not the discipline of scouting. I'm dyslexic, so I couldn't tie those damn knots. I would look at the diagrams and stare at the rope and I just didn't get it. When somebody tried to show me how to do it, I just got frustrated.

Christmas was very "storybook." On Christmas morning we would wake up and run downstairs, thinking Santa Claus had really been there. Over the years, I got a red bicycle, a red truck, airplanes, cowboy hats, a football—all the traditional Christmas presents. And I got marionettes, which I loved. I played with them until I was 11 or 12. Of course, I liked the Howdy Doody Show because Howdy was a marionette. Then someone told me I looked like Howdy Doody—after that I never watched the show again.

When I was very young, my favorite program was the Mickey Mouse Club. I was in love with Annette Funicello. I always wanted a Mickey Mouse hat with real Mickey Mouse ears, and finally I got one for my birthday. I wore it everywhere, but one day I dropped it in the toilet. I was so upset, I didn't stop crying until my mother took it out, rinsed it off, and ironed it so the ears would stay up.

We were a totally American family. We drove around in a Ford Country Squire station wagon and my dad would drive fast. This was before cars came with seat belts, so I'd be sliding all over the front seat. He'd go slamming the gas pedal into the floor, come right up to a stop light, and then hit the brakes. We ate all the American grocery-store brands: Campbell's soup, Jiffy peanut butter and Welch's grape jelly on Sunbeam bread, Ritz crackers, Ring Dings, Hostess Twinkies, and Snickers, Milky Way, and Hershey bars. In the summer we'd have barbecues: hot dogs, potato chips, Coca-Cola, potato salad with Hellmann's mayonnaise.

Watching Ozzie and Harriet was a family ritual. On Sunday night we'd gather in front of the TV set and watch the Wonderful World of Disney, with movies like OLD YELLER, and of course we'd watch the Ed Sullivan Show. I remember when the Beatles came on. My sisters and brothers and I thought they were the coolest; my parents thought they were obnoxious, with that moppy, floppy hair. TV played a big role in my life then. I loved The Twilight Zone. Rod Serling was Ivy League all the way, but with a slicker look. I loved The Fugitive, Bonanza, and western movies. The show I have the worst memories of was Lawrence Welk, which I will always associate with my parents getting ready to go out on Saturday nights and my having to stay behind.

My dad worked in a jewelry store, fixing watches and jewelry, and my mother was a nurse. They were very cautious about spending money and very proud. They didn't spoil our fun, but they had their rules. They didn't want us ever to use bad manners, get in trouble, do poorly in school, have long hair, or leave our bicycles on the front lawn. They tried to be very buttoned up about the whole thing. Even though they both worked a lot, it seemed like we were always broke, down to our last dime. It was stressful, and therefore I cherished having a job, not having to ask my father for money, being able to buy my own clothes.

Having a job also meant I could pay for my own haircuts. Going to the barber cost $1.25 back then, so my father used to sit my brothers and me down on a high chair in the kitchen on a Sunday night, put the sheet around our necks, turn on clippers, and say, "Hold still." While a lot of other kids had

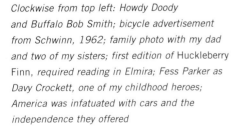

Clockwise from top left: Howdy Doody
and Buffalo Bob Smith; bicycle advertisement
from Schwinn, 1962; family photo with my dad
and two of my sisters; first edition of Huckleberry
Finn, *required reading in Elmira; Fess Parker as
Davy Crockett, one of my childhood heroes;
America was infatuated with cars and the
independence they offered*

It was sort of like living in

Tony Dow and Jerry Mathers as Wally and Theodore "Beaver" Cleaver

"Leave It to Beaver–land."

One of my favorite TV programs was the Mickey
Mouse Club, with Jimmie Dowd and the Mousketeers

haircuts where the sides were cut but there was still something on top, I was buzzed all over. During the early Beatles period, I started to grow it out in front a little bit, and a bit more, and then a bit more. Finally, when I could pay for my own haircut, I didn't let my father do it anymore.

My first job, at age nine, was mowing lawns. It was buggy and hot and terrible. At ten, I had a newspaper route. When I was 14, I got a job at Pal's Sporting Goods, at $1.25 an hour as a stock boy. Mr. Paltrowitz, the owner, taught me everything there was to know about sporting goods and how to operate a retail business. That's where I fell in love with sports equipment. When I was 16, I got a job at a Hess service station. When a customer pulled in, we'd run up to the car and ask them if they wanted us to fill it up. We had to wash the windows and check the oil whether they wanted us to or not. I made $2.50 an hour, which was a lot in those days, and I got to work with older kids. I remember feeling very proud wearing my uniform with the big Hess logo on the back. Ever since, the graphics of the automobile world has been an influence on my designs.

In those days I was very interested in clothing, particularly the Ivy League look: chinos, madras, oxford cloth shirts. I had all the grooming stuff too: Old Spice, Canoë, English Leather, Jade East, Wildroot, Brylcreem, Vitalis. I wanted to look rich, and I wanted to look cool because I was always very small for my age. People used to say, "Oh, isn't he cute?" I didn't want people to refer to me as a little boy. I wanted to be a teenager, but I wasn't quite there. Until I was 18, people didn't think I was even 15. I didn't shave; I didn't even have whiskers until I was 17. I wanted to grow sideburns so badly. After all, this was the sixties.

I mostly wanted to look my age because I was interested in girls. Courtship was pretty uncomplicated back then. There was a local radio station, WENY, 1200 AM, that played a lot of Motown and used to have record hops. In those days the boys really didn't like to dance. It was boys on one side, girls on the other. There were a few people who danced, but it wasn't the cool thing to do. Later on, when we got driver's licenses, we used to go to drive-in movies. I vaguely remember some of the films we saw, but we were really there to drink, make out with girls, and smoke cigarettes.

I think my high school friends thought I would never make it. I was always in trouble with teachers, parents, and friends, always into mischief—my friends used to call me Eddie Haskell when they introduced me to their parents—not severely illegal mischief, but I skipped school a lot and caused trouble with my friends' parents. The minute I got my driver's license, I bought my own car—a 1960 Olds '98. After driving it for a while, I decided I really wanted a Volkswagen Beetle, so I traded my Olds for an old beat-up Beetle. Since it was completely rusted, I painted it olive drab.

When I was 17 years old, I went to Cape Cod with my friends to hang out. I got a job at a boutique in Hyannis. It was a sort of poster, incense, candles, and flower shop called the Sunflower, with Hendrix, Jefferson Airplane, Blind Faith playing in the background, the smell of incense, the glare of psychedelic colors everywhere, and strobe lights. The dress was sandals, bell bottoms, long hair. I was into it all. One of my icons at the time was the poster for the surfing film THE ENDLESS SUMMER. That was the first time I had ever been away from home alone, and it was really the summer of the beginning of my new life.

When I came back from Cape Cod I had much longer hair than when I left, and my father was just shaking his head, no way. My parents did not want to hear about it. They were a combination of June and Ward Cleaver and the image you see in the Norman Rockwell painting of the guy in the station wagon with the kids and dogs. When I came back that summer, my father did not want even to look at me. My friends all had long hair, too, and we were all into dressing really mod. After school we'd go to my basement, or to one of my friends' houses, to listen to the Who and the Stones and the Beatles.

We were in our senior year in high school. Every morning one of my friends, Larry Stemerman, would come to my house to pick me up for school, and we would look at each other and say, "Do you really feel like going today?" "No." So we'd go to Ithaca, a college town with cool people, boutiques, record shops, and a lot of activity. We found a head shop selling bell bottoms, and we started talking to the people who ran the store, and I said, "Wow, can we buy these from you and sell them to our friends?"—which is exactly what we ended up doing. Then Larry and I and our friend Jon Allen came up with the idea of opening our own business. I had saved $150, Larry had $150, and Jon had $150. We opened a shop in Elmira called People's Place, painted the walls black, burned incense, played music, and sold candles and bell bottoms. It was a fun place where all the cool people came in and hung out. The music was loud, the incense was burning, it was a great place to be for young people at that time.

Business got very good. I thought, "This is unbelievable." And then business started getting even better. We opened another store, and then another after another, all throughout upstate New York college towns. Larry's father, who owned a shoe store, was very helpful in guiding us into becoming official retailers. And my father was a bit more tolerant after he saw that I could make something of myself. In the beginning, I did just about everything creative myself. I redecorated the store and the windows on a regular basis, I romanced and displayed the merchandise, sold it, rang it up on the register, wrapped it, and walked the customers to the door. But I wasn't really happy with what we were selling. And I thought maybe I should be designing the merchandise too. I wanted the clothes to be cooler, so I began sketching my own ideas

Above: I still treasure my varsity jacket from my high school days at
Elmira Free Academy; facing page: freshman-class yearbook photo,
1967; advertisements for grooming essentials (R. Kravette, Jericho,
NY/used with permission of the Procter & Gamble Company; © 1963
Bristol-Myers, reproduced with permission of the Bristol-Myers
Squibb Company)

"CHILLS AND SPILLS CROWD THE SCREEN.
LEAVES A VIEWER BREATHLESS."
Time Magazine

"A PERFECT MOVIE."
The New Yorker

"BREATHTAKING! SWEEPING AND EXCITING."
Newsweek

The Endless Summer

A true motion picture about surfing.
Filmed in Africa, Australia, New Zealand, Tahiti, Hawaii and California.
A BRUCE BROWN FILM IN COLOR
Distributed by Cinema V

WOODSTOCK
MUSIC & ART FAIR
presents
AN
AQUARIAN
EXPOSITION
in
WHITE LAKE, N.Y.

3 DAYS of PEACE & MUSIC

AUGUST
15, 16, 17.

Larry Stemerman (from left), Tom Hilfiger and John Allen, owners of The People's P

Bell Bottom Business Booming

'Mod, Mod World' for 3 Youths

By DICK MITCHELL

"To the old, anything new is bad news."

This is the philosophy of three "mod" youths—Larry Stemerman of 86 Greenridge Drive, Thomas Hilfiger of 606 W. Clinton St. and John Allen of 600 Cornell Road, all seniors at Elmira Free Academy.

They parlayed a $400 investment into a thriving downtown business known as the People's Place.

Despite their profit making venture the long-haired, mod dressed youth say they have not joined "the establishment"—nor are they fighting it.

Stemerman said that as proof, the three youths aren't conforming to the established procedures of business.

"What business would hire youths with long hair?" he asked. "We're not white collar conservatives."

Other youths describe the People's Place as more of an experience than a chore—what with the odor of incense, leather and suede and sounds of the latest records. Discussing this environment

Hilfiger commented, "The members of the establishment are committed to their generation and we're servants to ours."

"I'm my own boss," added Allen. "I don't have the hassles older, established store workers and bosses have, because of my age.

Long-haired mods sometimes are harassed by the older generation, the three agree, "because they think this makes us degenerates."

Stemerman recalled that he and Hilfiger recently sat at a coffee shop next to two women.

"Do you have jobs?" one of the women asked the two boys.

The other woman laughed and commented: "Who would hire them with hair like that?"

Hilfiger recalls that at this point they told the two women they owned their own business. "It really blew their minds," he said with a chuckle.

He said it will be necessary for his generation to suffer disrespect and humiliation

from older persons until discover that "some y really have something for them."

The three plan co educations but will wait they consider thems mature enough for the perience.

"Kids are rushed into lege when they are mature enough to unders the responsibility of a co education," Stemerman tends.

Who would buy a pa striped bell bottoms, Fonda glasses, white body shirts, flutes or s candles?

Quite a few people wou For example, since opened Dec. 1, they have more than 300 pairs of bottoms and more tha body shirts.

They say that the e stock has been sold times and their invest has grown 10 times.

During the Christ season they averaged $5 day in sales.

They are doing so they have enlarged the to twice its original size.

The Endless Summer poster, 1968; Woodstock poster, 1969;
the press takes notice of our budding enterprise;
facing page, clockwise from top: with my business partner Larry
Stemerman; conducting business at People's Place; print advertisement for
People's Place

and found a manufacturer that could make apparel to my specifications.

The best moment was in 1972, when we were informed that there was a risk of heavy flooding. Our store was on a lower level, so Larry and I moved all the merchandise from the basement to the top floor of the building. Elmira was soon flooded under 30 feet of water. There wasn't a stitch of merchandise left in the entire city. People were out of their homes with no food, no clothes, no furniture. We were the only people with merchandise left. So we sold all this funky clothing to little old ladies and all different types of people. The Red Cross gave them money to get back on their feet, so they came to the store and bought our bell bottoms, beaded blouses, crochet vests, and patchwork leather jackets. All of Elmira was dressed in super-cool clothes. If you were passing through, you'd have thought you were on Carnaby Street. Everyone was dressed to the nines.

Eventually I started losing interest in the store. When I was 25, it went bankrupt. It was very sobering. I paid off my debt and went back into business, but it was never the same. I ended up selling my shares in the stores a few years later. I think you have to learn from your mistakes. You also have to just dive into something you believe in.

People's Place also brought me the love of my life, Susan Cirona, whom I met when she got an after-school job at the boutique in Ithaca. I'd just come back from a trip to London. I had very long hair, platforms, all the cool, mod gear and jewelry from the Kensington Market. To Susie, I looked like some overblown spectacle, a creature on a total rock-star trip. Eventually, she became less afraid of me when she figured I wasn't from Mars, and we became very close. She was remarkably creative, and I thought we could make a great team. We decided to move to New York City and to look for design work. Susie and I had a working honeymoon in Bombay, where we designed clothes for our new company, Tommy Hill.

When we returned, we joined Jordache Jeans, but they didn't understand what we were trying to do, and we were basically out on the streets. I was knocking on doors every day looking for design work. As I had only two months of official experience, at Jordache, I decided the only way to overcome this would be to create my own company. Eventually, I met a clothing-factory owner who was making fuddy-duddy women's clothes and whom I persuaded to start a more contemporary line. We began 20th Century Survival, which was all military gear with swashbuckler shirts, very new wave. Then at the height of the Japanese fashion craze in 1982, Susie started O'Tokyo and I started Click Point, both of us doing very architectural women's clothing, mine inspired by David Bowie's "China Girl" period.

We had our first child in 1985, so I was considering taking a steady design job with either Calvin Klein or Perry Ellis. I had offers from both, and I was completely confused about which to go with. In desperation I called a psychic named Zvia, whom we had met in Los Angeles, from a pay phone on Seventh Avenue and 40th Street. Zvia dismissed my concerns. "But you don't understand," I insisted. "This is CALVIN and PERRY. These are fashion ICONS." "Hold on, something better will be coming," Zvia intoned. And the next day I was called to a meeting with Murjani, who offered me my own company. That was the same week I got a summons for jumping the turnstiles in the subway. We were three months behind in the rent, and I had no money. By then I knew what I really wanted to do. My vision turned full circle from the trendy clothes of the eighties back to my preppy roots. Picturing a more New England, outdoorsy, and classic campus look that I knew would last, I launched Tommy Hilfiger.

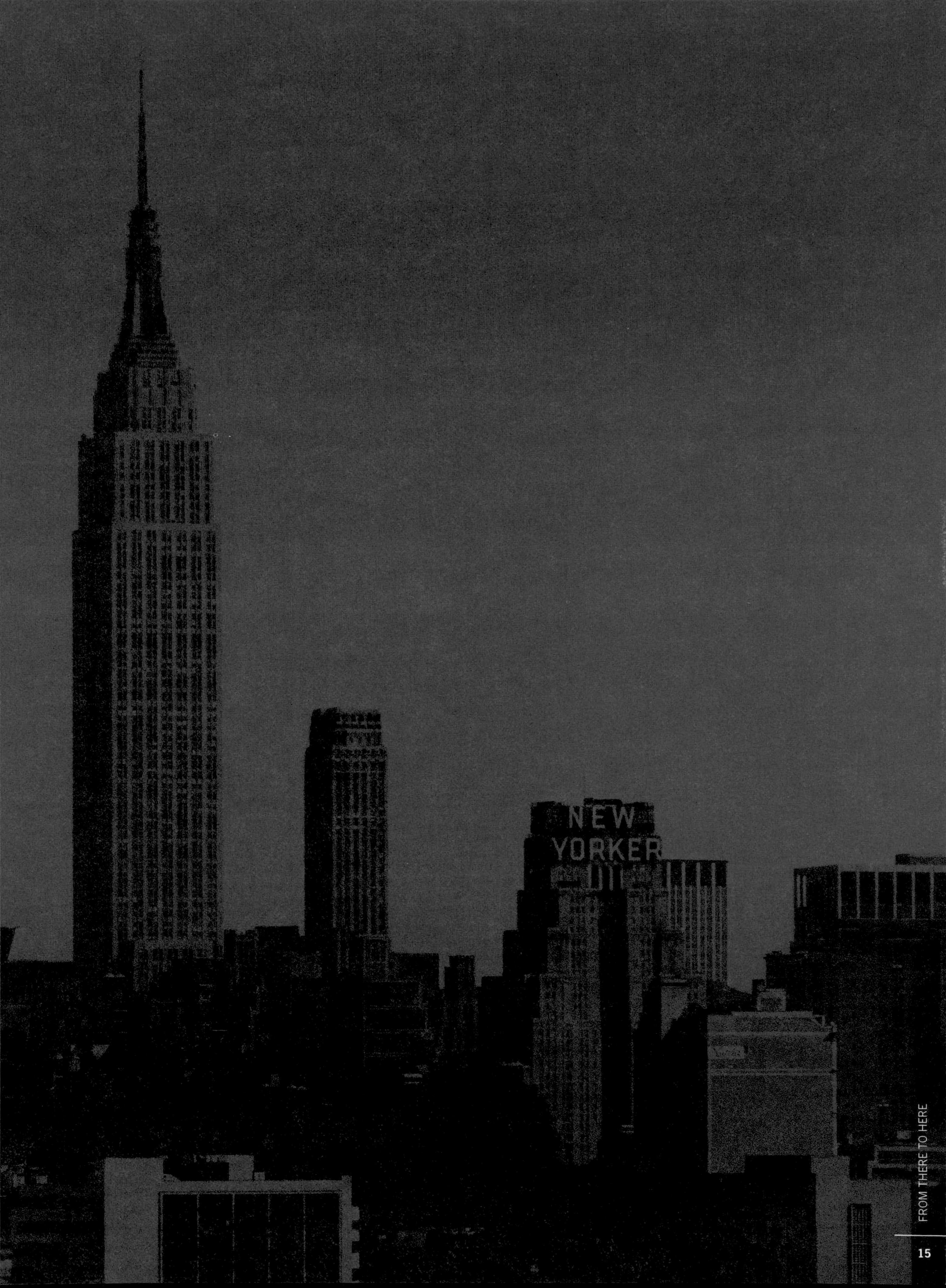
NEW
YORKER

AMERICANA

Whenever I look at the Statue of Liberty, the Empire State Building, Mt. Rushmore, whenever I see a pair of blue jeans or a '65 Mustang, I realize that these are all icons that make me proud to be American.

The history of our country has always been about vast, progressive changes in society and in the way people live. I think we all recognize that there are short-comings to the system, but as a nation we hold ourselves up to an ideal. I think Americans are proud of their country and their lives and honest about their desires: a lot of people take it for granted that we live in this bliss, to which many others look yearningly as a dreamland. We have generous living standards, a treasury of music and art, a bounty of style and fashion, and a lot of freedom and enthusiasm within our lives. We have spontaneity, but we also have rules to protect us.

America's finest metaphor always has been, and always will be, that it is one great big melting pot. I love that idea. I like things to be mixed-up—not confused, but diverse. There are all different types of people in this American melting pot: gay, straight, black, white, Hispanic, Asian—all making up a whole that gives American life its incredible vibrancy. Maybe my love for the mix comes from having so many brothers and sisters, all with different personalities. And even though Elmira, the town where I was raised, only had some 40,000 people, there were all types.

Growing up in a middle-class, white-bread neighbor-hood of numerous Irish Catholic families with a lot of kids, I knew there were traditional values to absorb as well as a world full of modern products to fall in love with. There were hot dogs, baseball, and apple pie. TV and rock and roll. The game I didn't really understand was that of the rich. Mysterious to me were certain well-to-do, old-world families that I delivered newspapers to: I would see more than one car in the driveway or a swimming pool in the backyard; a maid would answer the door; the family would take vacations in Florida or the Bahamas or go away for the whole summer. Sometimes when I'd go to the door to collect for the paper, the mother would be all dressed up in the middle of the day.

That was just one part of the America I grew up with—the American Dream. At school there were rich kids, but there were also hoods and jocks and preppies. The preppy group was much more cool to be in; you could still get up to all kinds of mischief, but because you looked Ivy League you weren't suspected of being a troublemak-er. Then there was the black crowd. They were into really cool stuff, music and sports, and they had a way about them that interested me. It was almost mysterious, a culture that I had never been exposed to in a respectful way.

Today, of course, we all know each other better. America has seemingly gone from a simple Norman Rockwell–esque existence to a much more sophisticated, cosmopolitan life. In a way, it's like SATURDAY EVENING POST or READER'S DIGEST versus VANITY FAIR or HARPER'S BAZAAR. Everybody now is in tune with what is glamorous; everybody knows what's hip. Instead of going to play bingo in church, you may just as easily be heading off to some video-awards ceremony. Switch on MTV and you'll see hip-hop kids and punk rockers of every color, all wearing the same funky shoes. Hang out in Miami Beach and see Rollerbladers zipping down Ocean Drive past outdoor cafés filled with stylish people. It's a fashion exposition 24 hours a day. A lot of these fashions have a pedigree. Look at the kids in Seattle wearing flannel shirts to rock shows—they're the same kind of shirts that people have worn to go camping and hunting in New England for years. Go out to a club in New York and there are guys that look like they came out of a midwestern country club in the early sixties or dropped in straight from a California beach. All of this is now American style.

American fashion designers are forever going off to Europe, all over the world for that matter, but European fashion has been the leading source of inspiration for American designers. Not so long ago, however, we began to see European designers turning out the classic all-American look—khakis, varsity jackets, hiking boots, and the like—but with a uniquely European interpretation. Then we brought it back and did it another way. And now they're all copying our urban hip-hop street looks, but with a different flavor. This is how fashion works: we'll take ideas from them, and they'll take them back, like one big game of ping-pong.

When I started to travel the world, I saw the fruits of American labor everywhere I went, the products and logos that are the trademarks of our industry and our culture. In the most exotic places in the world, you will see people wearing Levi's and drinking Coca-Cola, obsessing over fifties cars, and sporting cowboy shirts and boots, or wearing the rugged clothes we make for the great outdoors. No matter how different the customs, the world is tuned in to the signature emblems of the American lifestyle.

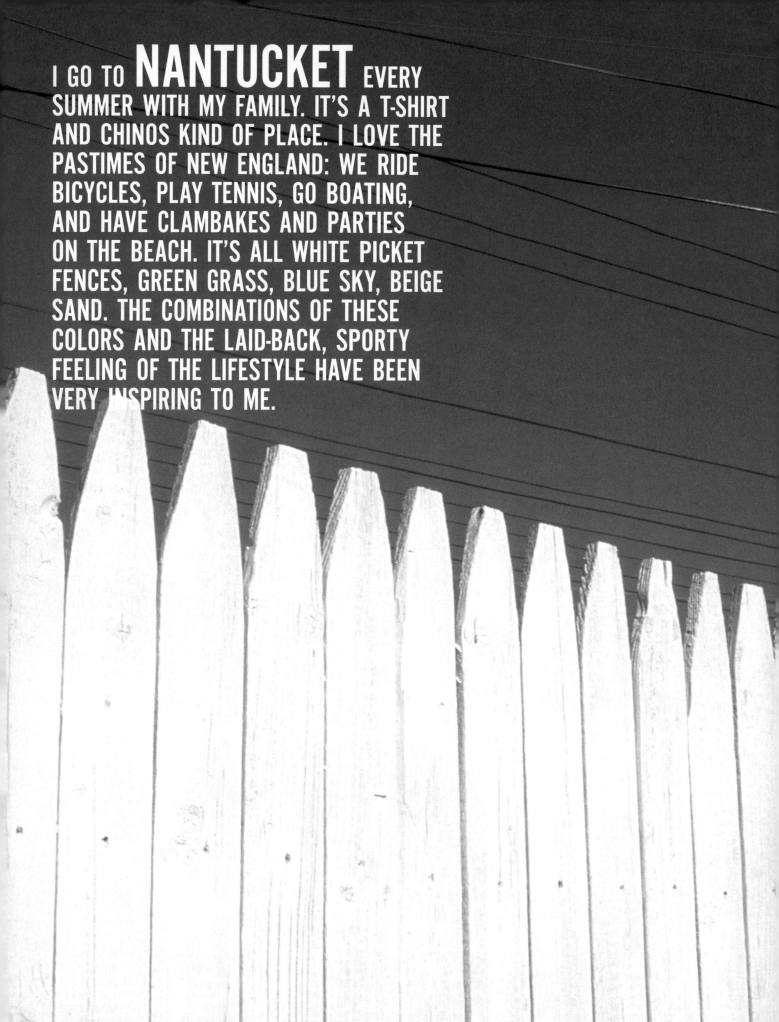

I GO TO **NANTUCKET** EVERY SUMMER WITH MY FAMILY. IT'S A T-SHIRT AND CHINOS KIND OF PLACE. I LOVE THE PASTIMES OF NEW ENGLAND: WE RIDE BICYCLES, PLAY TENNIS, GO BOATING, AND HAVE CLAMBAKES AND PARTIES ON THE BEACH. IT'S ALL WHITE PICKET FENCES, GREEN GRASS, BLUE SKY, BEIGE SAND. THE COMBINATIONS OF THESE COLORS AND THE LAID-BACK, SPORTY FEELING OF THE LIFESTYLE HAVE BEEN VERY INSPIRING TO ME.

IS VERY GENUINE, BUT ALSO HAS A REAL SENSE OF HUMOR.

ND ZIPPER—BUT NOT EVERYTHING YOU SEE IS PERFECT.

MY DAD ACTUALLY DROVE ONE OF THOSE STATION WAGONS. IF

Going and Coming, *Norman Rockwell*
Saturday Evening Post, *August 30, 1947*

AMERICA IS A **CAR** CULTURE. WE'RE IN LOVE WITH TRAVEL AND ALL OF ITS TRAPPINGS, FROM TRUCK-STOP DINERS TO CAR COATS. AS SOON AS I GOT MY LICENSE, I WAS READY TO HIT THE ROAD.

Route 66, Photograph by Andreas Feininger, 1953

The Car Coat

An American classic comes of age

The car has always influenced fashion. It's considered a fait accompli that JFK's bare head was solely responsible for the plunge in hat sales in the sixties, but in fact it was the lowering of the automobile's roofline in the late fifties that lowered the book on the hat industry—there just wasn't enough headroom to wear a hat in the newly streamlined car.

Driving has had an effect on hemlines too. The full-length motoring coat, known as the duster, was needed at the turn of the century to shield the driver from dirt and detritus spewed up around the open-carriage Ford Model-T. The shorter-length car coat, virtually a uniform for the station-wagon set of the fifties, was a hip- to three-quarter-length sport or utility coat made in a variety of fabrics (wool, cotton, corduroy) with a fly-front buttoning and a fur or pile spread collar that simply afforded greater ease in sliding in and out of the vehicle (and made for a more comfortable ride). The term "car coat" has come to mean any coat of shorter length. The duster was briefly revived as a fashion item in the new-wave eighties. Matt Dillon wore a variation in DRUGSTORE COWBOY. His, of course, was leather.

ties car coat. Photograph by Bill Steele

In the fifties, everything was aerodynamic, from Elvis Presley's hair to the fins of a Cadillac. The jazzy styling of old cars is pure Americana, and the shapes and colors continue to exert their influence on fashion.

Tailfins, *Westchester County, New York. Photograph by Elliott Erwitt, 195*

The Tailfin

Design classics for the auto-motivated

BUICK CENTURY   year: 1955   original cost: $2,601

CADILLAC ELDORADO BROUGHAM   year: 1957   original cost: $5,048

CHEVROLET IMPALA   year: 1958   original cost: $2,693

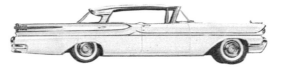

MERCURY MONTCLAIR   year: 1958   original cost: $3,248

CADILLAC FLEETWOOD   year: 1960   original cost: $9,533

FORD FAIRLANE VICTORIA   year: 1956   original cost: $2,294

CHRYSLER NEWPORT   year: 1962   original cost: $3,027

DE SOTO FIREDOME CONVERTIBLE   year: 1956   original cost: $3,052

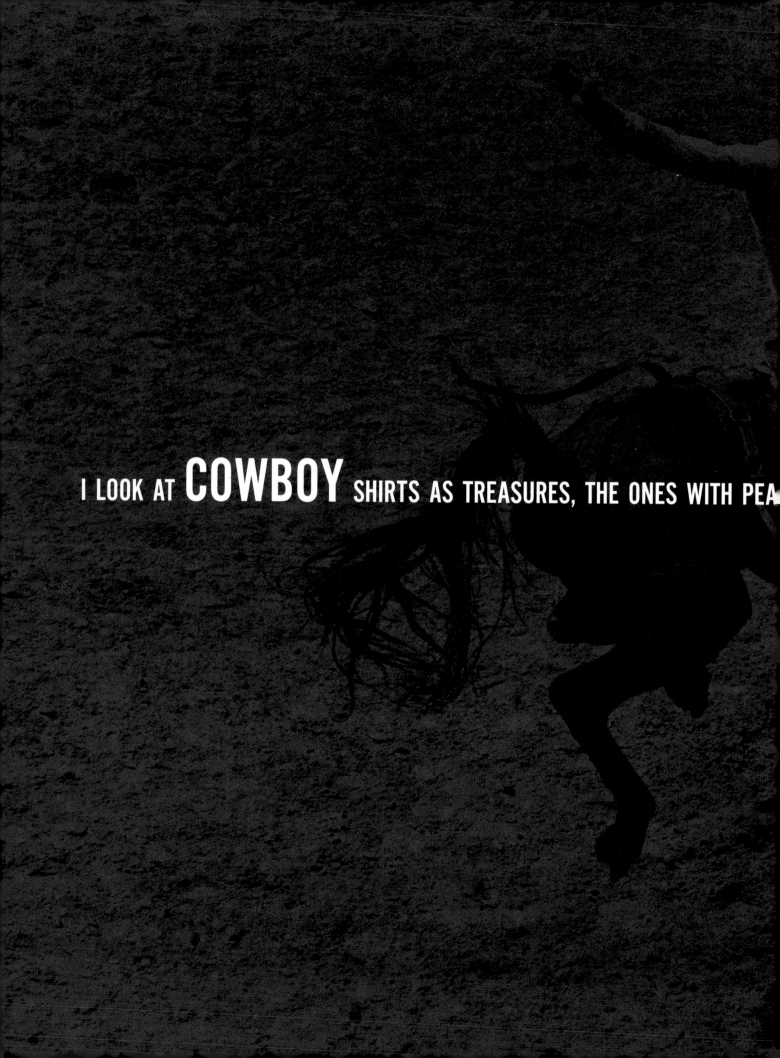

I LOOK AT **COWBOY** SHIRTS AS TREASURES, THE ONES WITH PEA

APS AND FRINGE, EMBROIDERY AND PIPING, THE REAL RODEO SHIRTS.

Yuma, Arizona. Photograph by Norman Mauskopf

ZX Ranch, Paisley, Oregon. *Photograph by Kurt Markus, 1981*

Roy Rogers

Jon Voight in Midnight Cowboy, 1969

Western clothes have their own sense of style. Sometimes they're rough and rugged; sometimes they're dressy and all duded up. The way cowboy shirts look best is with either completely unwashed denims or terribly beat-up jeans.

Gloria Winters and Kirby Grant from the TV show Sky King

John Travolta in Urban Cowboy, 1980

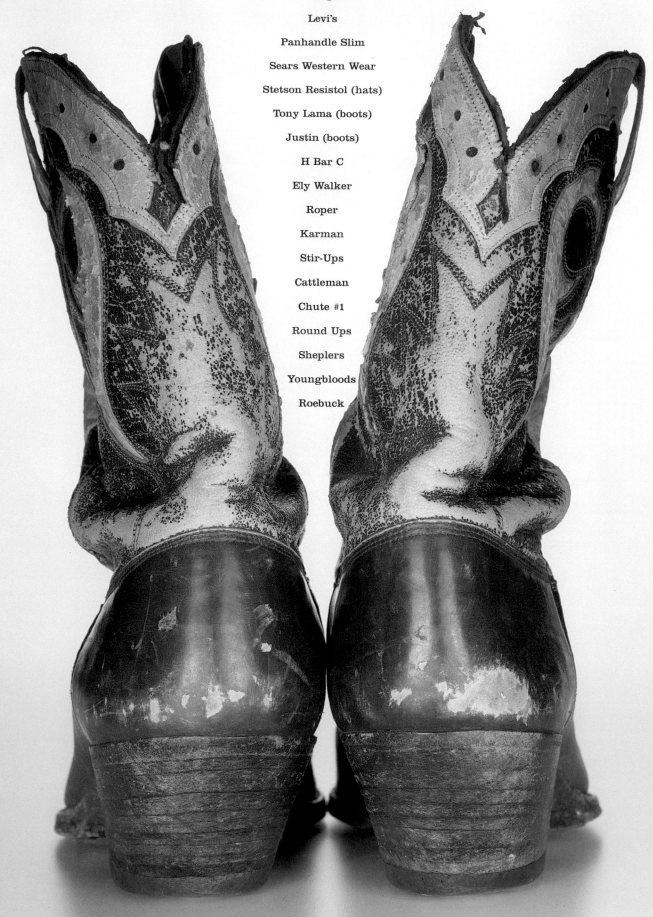

AUTHENTIC WESTERN

The brands buckaroos wear

Wrangler

Levi's

Panhandle Slim

Sears Western Wear

Stetson Resistol (hats)

Tony Lama (boots)

Justin (boots)

H Bar C

Ely Walker

Roper

Karman

Stir-Ups

Cattleman

Chute #1

Round Ups

Sheplers

Youngbloods

Roebuck

Vintage cowboy boots and shirt. Photographs by Bill Steele

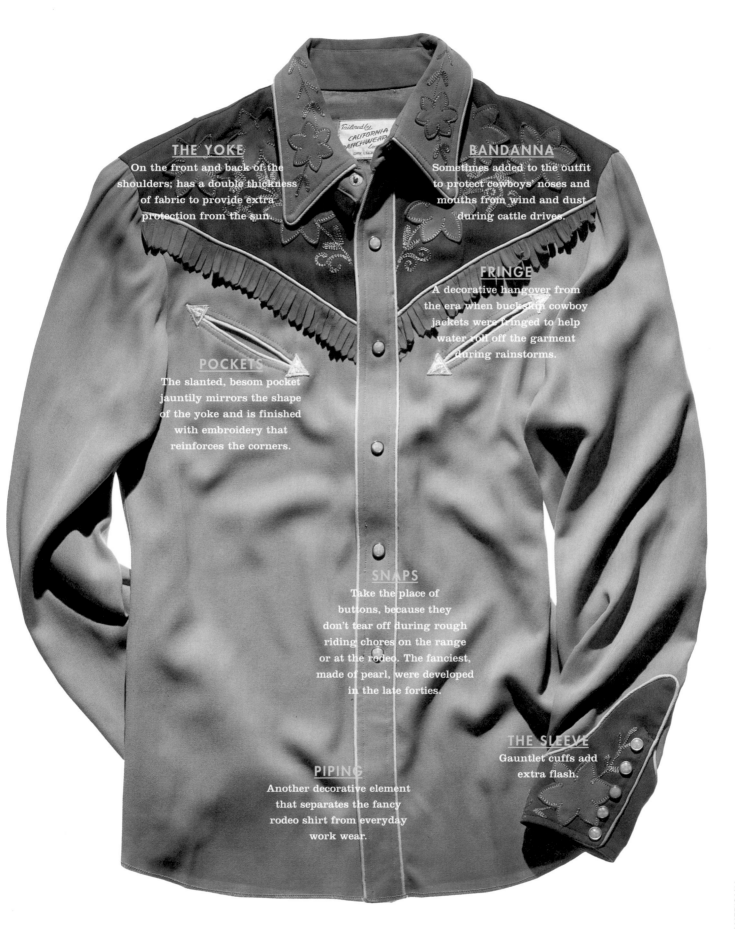

THE YOKE
On the front and back of the shoulders; has a double thickness of fabric to provide extra protection from the sun.

BANDANNA
Sometimes added to the outfit to protect cowboys' noses and mouths from wind and dust during cattle drives.

FRINGE
A decorative hangover from the era when buckskin cowboy jackets were fringed to help water roll off the garment during rainstorms.

POCKETS
The slanted, besom pocket jauntily mirrors the shape of the yoke and is finished with embroidery that reinforces the corners.

SNAPS
Take the place of buttons, because they don't tear off during rough riding chores on the range or at the rodeo. The fanciest, made of pearl, were developed in the late forties.

THE SLEEVE
Gauntlet cuffs add extra flash.

PIPING
Another decorative element that separates the fancy rodeo shirt from everyday work wear.

THERE'S NOTHING AS
INVIGORATINGLY AMERICAN AS A DAY IN
THE GREAT OUTDOORS.
WHEN I WAS A CHILD, WE WOULD
GO ON PICNICS TO THE FINGER LAKES.
ALL THE KIDS WOULD BE RUNNING AROUND,
SWIMMING, OUT IN ROWBOATS AND
MAHOGANY CANOES.

Lake Placid, Adirondack Mountains

GROMMETS
Provide ventilation at the neckline.

SHOULDER
Quilted appliqué provides an extra layer of protection when shooting.

COLLAR
Corduroy for warmth and water repellency.

PLACKET
Covered to avoid buttons getting caught in the brush.

POCKETS
Provide utility and storage, including two-flapped, segmented pockets for storing shotgun cartridges.

Canvas hunting jacket. Photograph by Bill Steele

Backing Up

For as long as people have had something to carry, they've needed something to carry it in. In the past, animal hides were used in Europe, while in Asia, baskets with straps served the purpose. American children used to carry their schoolbooks bound together with a single leather strap. The modern backpack probably originated in the Alpine countries, where it was necessary to have both hands free for hiking through the mountains. In the first half of the 20th century, these rucksacks (from the German word for backpack) were considered quaint and rustic, but their basic design would serve as the pattern for today's most popular unisex bag. In the late sixties, when all things army-navy were in vogue, the olive army pack served as a carryall, while the rise of affordable European travel saw an increase in carrying all worldly goods in one giant bag, in the lifestyle we came to know as backpacking. The crossover from hiking gear to everyday wear began at the University of Washington, where students used camping day packs by JanSport to protect their books from Seattle's constant rainfall. By the early eighties, other day-pack and duffel-bag manufacturers, notably Eastpak, got in on the action, and high-end black leather versions of the backpack appeared. Backpacks with a bootlegged Louis Vuitton logo popped up in urban centers in the early nineties (the company released its own official version, the Montsouris, in 1996), as did high-tech nylon models by athletic companies like Adidas and Nike, surf companies like Quiksilver and O'Neill, luggage manufacturers like Tumi (which produces the popular Kipling line), and sportswear designers like Tommy Hilfiger, DKNY, and Polo Sport.

Flannel shirts are always appropriate for being outdoors in the city or the country. They can be worn as overshirts over a turtleneck or a henley, but they look the most authentic with corduroys or jeans and boots.

A Shirt for Everyman

The humble flannel shirt, a descendant of the wool CPO overshirt, was originally designed to keep hunters warm. Before the mid-sixties, they were largely worn for their intended purpose: outdoor activities. In the late sixties, their sturdy construction, low price, and blue-collar authenticity made them instant campus classics. In the seventies, gay men wore them as part of the macho-man wardrobe, often with the sleeves cut off. Worn around the waist by hard-core punk bands and their followers in the early eighties, the flannel shirt (and, later, shorts) became a staple of the Seattle-based grunge look. While most American sportswear manufacturers offer a version of the plaid flannel shirt, the signature brands are L. L. Bean, Woolrich, Pendleton, Eddie Bauer, Orvis, and Patagonia.

WHY BUFFALO?

A distinctively American look (not a Scottish tartan), buffalo shirts are so named because, in the 1850s, the man who created the oversized two-color checks (black with red, blue, white, yellow, or green) also raised buffalo.

EVERY FOURTH OF JULY, WE'D HAVE A **COOKOUT** AT MY AUNT MARIAN'S, WITH HER FIVE KIDS AND MY EIGHT BROTHERS AND SISTERS RUNNING AROUND, PLAYING SOFTBALL AND BADMINTON, EATING HOT DOGS WITH KETCHUP AND MUSTARD, POTATO SALAD, AND CHERRY PIE—THE AMERICAN FAVORITES.

DOING THE BARBECUE RIGHT hot dogs, hamburgers, chicken, shish kebob, mustard, ketchup, bread-and-butter pickles, chips and salsa, Ruffles potato chips and Lipton soup dip, corn on the cob, potato salad, baked beans, cole slaw, lemonade, Coca-Cola, beer, blender drinks, "s'mores," ice cream, Tiki torches, Hawaiian shirts, Bermuda shorts, chef's apron, chef's hat, Weber kettle grills, butterfly chairs, picnic tables

My mother wore a gingham dress, and my sisters wore blue gingham. Our tablecloths were red gingham. Even the western shirt on my back was red gingham.

Lucille Ball and Desi Arnaz in
The Long Long Trailer, 1954

THE GINGHAM SHIRT

Gingham (from the Malaysian GINGGANG, meaning checked cloth), in its most traditional form, is a woven pattern, a white ground with colored checks that measure 1/4 inch. Best known for the red and white tablecloths found in Italian restaurants, gingham has a homespun charm and is a popular fabric for home decoration as well as clothing. Famous gingham wearers include Raggedy Ann, film critic Rex Reed, Mary Anne (from Gilligan's Island), and hamburger-chain mascot Bob's Big Boy.

GAMES PEOPLE PLAY

Outdoor activities for the not necessarily athletic

Badminton

Capture the flag

Croquet

Dodge ball

Flag football

Hackysack

Hopscotch

Horseshoes

Lawn darts

Mother may I?

Rain on the roof

Red rover

Shuffleboard

Slip 'n' slide

Sprinkler tag

Tetherball

Touch football

Tug-of-war

Ultimate Frisbee

Volleyball

Frankie Lymon and the Teenagers, 1961

CLASSICS

When I was growing up, clothes intrigued me. They were a barometer of my self-esteem and my status at school.

Like most other teenagers, I was a fashion conformist. I wore chinos, five-pocket stretch jeans, Clarke's desert boots, button-down shirts, madras jackets, navy blazers, and crew-neck sweaters. Very Ivy League. As a teenager in the sixties, I was in on the first wave of army-navy fashion. The hippies were wearing military-surplus items because they were inexpensive and anti-establishment. It was a deliberately ironic statement for peace protesters to be turned out in army uniforms. The military great-coat, a big navy blue wool coat with brass buttons, was one of my favorites. I also wore sailor's bell bottoms and midi shirts with a sailor collar, or a blue-and-white striped boat-neck sweater.

These days I like to keep things simple, especially when I get up in the morning with a lot on my mind. I exercise, read the papers, scrub up, give myself the marching orders for the day. I always wear a white or blue shirt. In the summer I

wear chinos, and in the winter, gray flannel trousers. On the weekends I usually wear casual athletic clothes, and at night I often wear darker colors—maybe a turtleneck or velvet jeans or a jacket. But I always dress preppy during the week—it's simple and easy—that's my uniform.

Sometimes I am a bit of a chameleon. Some days I feel like playing the rock-star role, or wearing a motorcycle jacket and a pair of jeans and boots. As a designer, I'm really into luxurious fabrics. I appreciate finely combed broadcloth shirts, pajamas, boxers, and cashmere socks, as well as cashmere blazers by Hermès and many items by Gucci or Prada. But just as much I like a pair of corduroys or a pair of beat-up army twill pants.

Clothes are costumes. Every day people put on what they want to be. They create their own reality. We never stop playing dress-up. As kids, we do it outlandishly to imitate our parents; as adults, we do t to please ourselves and others. If you wear a very erious business suit, that says one thing, and if you wear something baggy and logoed, or maybe straight nd crisp, all tucked-in and preppy, it says another. And then there are those who can wear a suit all week nd dress in drag on the weekend. Whatever.

Fashion is a language. I speak to people all the ime through style, silhouette, attitude, and color. Color is emotion. I like blues, I like Day-Glos and neu-ral tones. I love the colors of nature: sand, water, rees, and sky. If I'm someplace sunny, I might choose astels; for colder climates, I'll go with deeper, richer ones. I love the colors of jelly beans, sherbets, and icorice. I couldn't live without basic black.

Fashion is also an art—of making sure that the ippers work well, the wash and shade are right, and ll the ingredients are exact. It's very much like cook-ng; you have to have the right blend of spices and alt and pepper. I don't believe in pretentious fashion, in clothes that are exorbitantly priced, unwearable, or created as artwork for a museum but never available or accessible on the street.

In my view, fashion is for the moment, but style is an enduring frame of mind. People with good taste never have to try too hard because they know that if you spend too much time looking in the mirror, you'll only end up confused, and they understand that con-fidence is the ultimate fashion accessory. Self-assured people can wear anything.

The key to style is comfort. Clothes should feel lived in, not just put on. If your clothes make you feel out of place, simplify. If you're not sure what to wear, there are a wealth of classic American styles that look good on everyone.

THE GREAT THING ABOUT **JEANS** IS THAT
THEY LOOK RIGHT NO MATTER HOW YOU CHOOSE
TO WEAR THEM. WHETHER BAGGY OR TIGHT, JEANS
SHOULD LOOK LIKE THEY'VE BEEN YOURS FOR
100 YEARS.

James Dean in Giant, 1956

I LIKE TO SEE JEANS WORN WITH A THICK, HEAVY-DUTY LEATHER BELT OR WEBBED FABRIC BELT, AS WORN IN THE MILITARY. THE BUCKLE SHOULD BE SOLID, LIKE DOUBLE D-RINGS OR OLD WESTERN BUCKLES. REMEMBER THE DOUBLE-PRONG BELT BUCKLE ON THE COVER OF THE ROLLING STONES' *STICKY FINGERS?* THAT WAS THE COOLEST.

Custom Jeans and Jeans Customs

Tough and independent, denim is more than just an American way of dressing; it's a billboard for individuality. For the past 50 years, denim has achieved an ever-changing uniqueness by being the canvas through which youth expresses itself.

In the fifties, purism reigned. The newer and bluer your jeans looked, the better. Rolled cuffs revealing the reverse weave of the fabric provided contrast.

Old denim became popular in the sixties. The frayed look was in. Colorful patchwork made jeans a living quilt, and triangular inserts were sewn into straight-legged jeans to transform them into groovy bell bottoms. Some folks even split their jeans at the leg seam, added grommets, and laced them back together.

In the seventies, flares were worn with flair. It was a sign of coolness to have the bottoms of your unhemmed jeans torn from walking on them. Gay men sandpapered the crotches of their jeans to make them more eye-catching. By the end of the decade, punk rockers safety-pinned the legs of their jeans for the tightest fit ever.

Designer jeans ruled the eighties—the tighter the better. People would wear their jeans in the tub and sit out in the sun to dry in order to achieve the perfect fit. Jeans were sold stone-washed, acid-washed, and overdyed in acid colors, but that still didn't stop people from bleaching, ripping, and shredding their jeans or from adding beads, jewels, and sequins.

In the nineties, purity is the trend. People like their jeans honest, whether they're faded relics or starched and dry-cleaned to preserve their color and shape.

Denim: The Rebel Kind

Dateline Anytown, U.S.A. "Alert! Scientists discover denim pants cause juvenile delinquency in teenagers!"

A decade of dishing out denim was kicked off in 1951 when Bing Crosby, America's favorite crooner, was refused a room in a Canadian hotel by a desk clerk who was not allowed to admit anyone into the high-toned resort wearing low-class denim.

In 1957 the venerable Levi Strauss company ran an ad depicting a clean-cut young boy wearing Levi's jeans with the slogan "right for our school." It attracted attention, all right—the wrong kind. One outraged parent wrote that perhaps wearing Levi's was right for school in the west, but not for Peoria. A move to ban Levi's as school wear was launched.

But to no avail. By the end of the fifties, Levi's jeans had become the rage of leisure-loving teenage boys and their older college-age brothers. Though the mere sight of a pair would cause conniption fits in most adults of the day, the majority of America's youth—90 percent according to a newspaper report—wore their blue denims everywhere except in bed and to church.

Jeans became the unisex uniform of the sixties Woodstock generation. Painted, patched, appliquéd, covered in leather and suede, they became the ultimate symbol of individuality and homegrown rebellion.

Andy Warhol made jeans go POP on the cover of the Rolling Stones' STICKY FINGERS album in 1971 by featuring a life-sized depiction of Joe Dallesandro's crotch. This was denim as erogenous zone, a precursor to the ultra-tight designer-jeans era of the late seventies. Throughout the seventies, denim was flared, belled, and turned into outfits of vests, pants, and matching "poor-boy" caps. Three-piece suits of chemically faded blue denim were added to the Levi's line, along with patchwork denim pants-and-vest combos.

The world was informed in a 1982 TV commercial that "nothing" came between Brooke Shields and her Calvins. From that moment on, nothing could be sold to the American public quicker than another pair of designer jeans. Designers such as Sergio Valente, Joujou, and Diane Von Furstenberg all made their mark, but by the end of the decade, Levi's were still the most popular and sought-after jeans worldwide.

The nineties brought denim shirts even into the office, jeans jackets refashioned in leather, satin, and corduroy, as well as jeans in every which way, including loose. It was the era of casual clothing, and the "relaxed fit" worked for everyone from aging baby boomers to hip-hop fans.

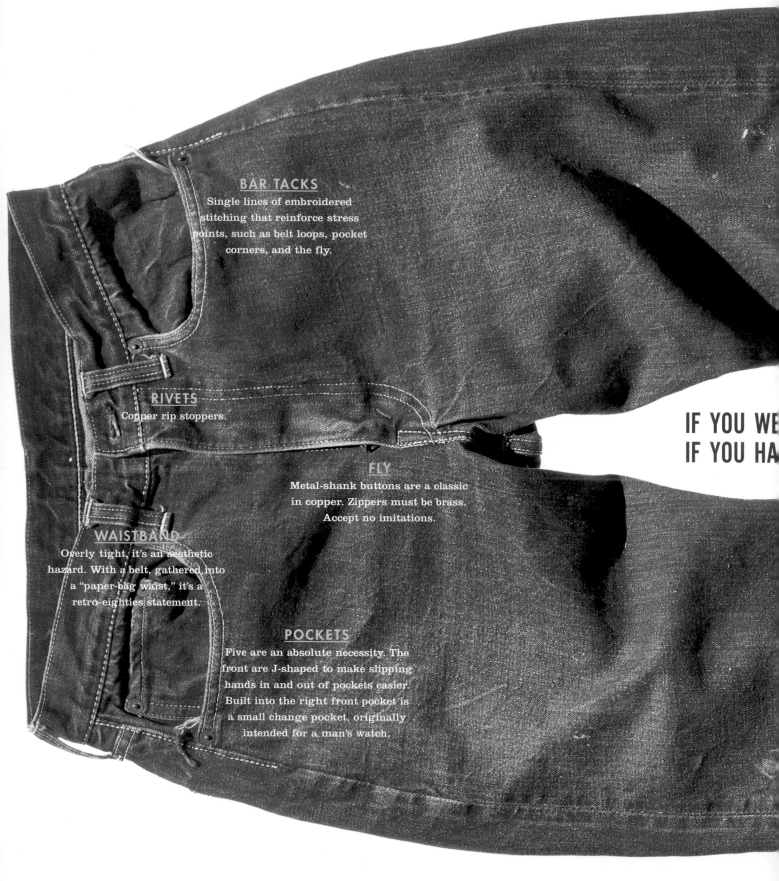

BAR TACKS
Single lines of embroidered stitching that reinforce stress points, such as belt loops, pocket corners, and the fly.

RIVETS
Copper rip stoppers.

FLY
Metal-shank buttons are a classic in copper. Zippers must be brass. Accept no imitations.

WAISTBAND
Overly tight, it's an aesthetic hazard. With a belt, gathered into a "paper-bag waist," it's a retro-eighties statement.

POCKETS
Five are an absolute necessity. The front are J-shaped to make slipping hands in and out of pockets easier. Built into the right front pocket is a small change pocket, originally intended for a man's watch.

IF YOU WE
IF YOU HA

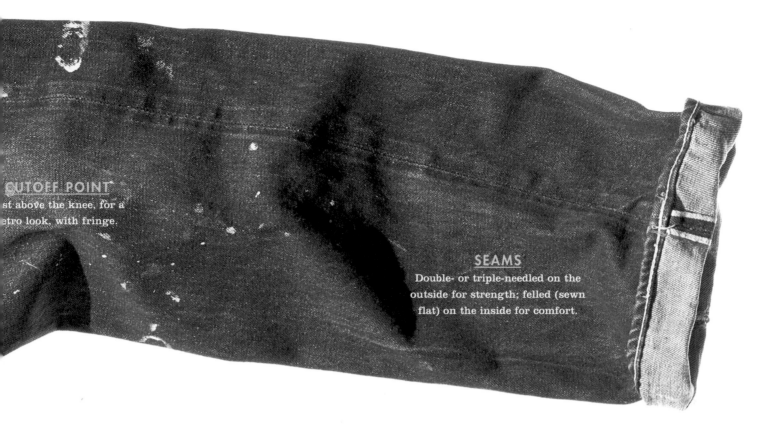

CUTOFF POINT
st above the knee, for a
etro look, with fringe.

SEAMS
Double- or triple-needled on the
outside for strength; felled (sewn
flat) on the inside for comfort.

NS TIGHT, HAVE A CLEAN DOUBLE-STITCHED HEM THAT COVERS YOUR ANKLES.
SE, JUST ROLL THEM UP TWO AND A HALF INCHES.

Vintage Levi's (courtesy of Starstruck, New York). Photograph by Bill Steele

BELT LOOPS
Either five or six; a loop centered on the back seam (as here) gives more definition to the seat and crotch.

CUTOFF POINT
As close to the cheek line as you dare, an homage to Daisy Duke on The Dukes of Hazzard.

TAG
Always on the right. A capital E in "Levi's" indicates an old collectible; an orange tag signifies a zip fly.

YOKE
Helps determine the fit on the hips and rear; the pointier the yoke, the more fitted the jean.

POCKETS
Straight across the top, pointed at the bottom, the original Levi's way.

ARCUATE
The stitching on the back pocket; often imitated, but in this style a registered trademark of Levi's.

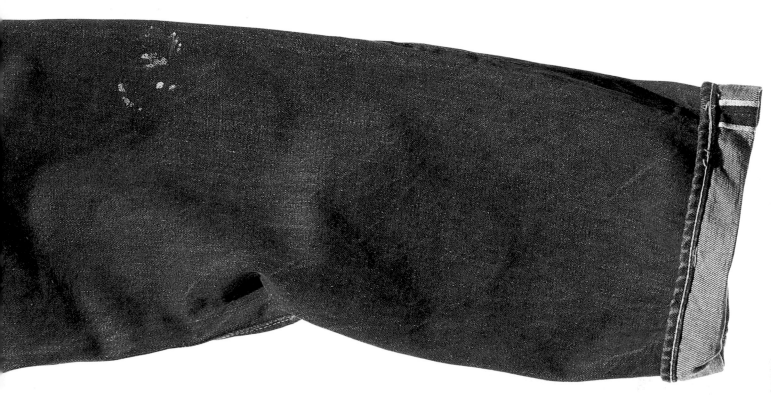

EANS SHOULD LOOK AND FEEL FADED AND COMFORTABLE, AND BE SOMEWHAT
REVERENT, LIKE YOU DON'T HAVE A REGULAR JOB AND YOU DON'T CARE.

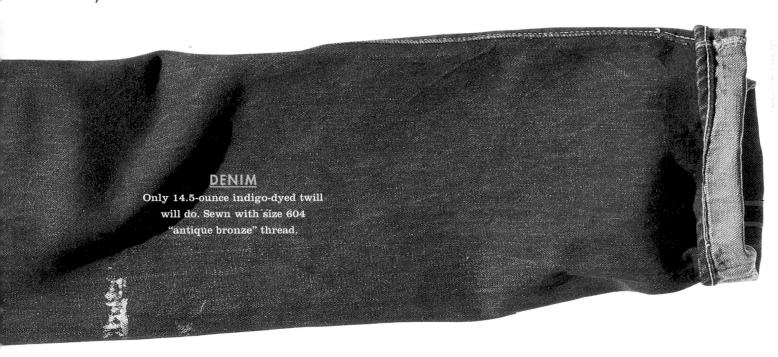

DENIM
Only 14.5-ounce indigo-dyed twill
will do. Sewn with size 604
"antique bronze" thread.

Vintage Levi's (courtesy of Starstruck, New York). Photograph by Bill Steele

The Big Three

LEVI STRAUSS & CO.

The patch on the back of the jeans says that the company was established on May 20, 1873, but the first pair of Levi's jeans was produced in 1872. In that year, Jacob Davis, a tailor in Reno, Nevada, wrote to Levi Strauss, who'd provided canvas and denim clothing for the gold-rush miners and who'd had a wholesale dry-goods business in San Francisco since 1853. Davis offered to come up with a way to rivet the corners of pockets and suggested they take out a patent on the process.

The copper-riveted jeans were known officially as "waist overalls" (and were until 1960); they had only one back pocket, a watch pocket, a cinch, and suspender buttons. In 1886 the leather patch that shows two horses trying vainly to pull the product apart was introduced onto the back of the pants. Around 1890, lot numbers were first employed, and the number 501 was assigned to the signature waist overalls. By 1900 there were two back pockets. Fast-forward to 1967, when lot number 501Z (Z for zipper) became 502-0117 and 501 was used exclusively for the button-fly.

501s are the original, classic, Shrink-to-Fit Levi's: the standard against which all other denim jeans are measured and compared. The Red Tab Device on the back pocket, indicating that the pants are the original, top-of-the-line product, was created in 1936 to identify 501s from a distance. Silver Tab is the Levi Strauss fashion line (with silverish tab and rivets) and comes in a spectrum of colors, including walnut brown, cardinal red, maize, stone, and copper.

The double-bow pattern stitched onto the back pockets of all Levi's is called the Arcuate Design and is the oldest clothing trademark still in use. The durable brown patch that is sewn onto the waistband and embossed with waist and inseam measurements was originally leather, then linen, and is now a special compound identified as "leatherlike—a special family recipe."

LEE APPAREL CO., INC.

Vermont-born Henry David Lee moved west to Ohio at age 13, saved $1,200 working for three years as a hotel clerk, invested in real estate and livery, and eventually purchased Central Oil Company. A sickly man, Lee was forced to sell his business to John D. Rockefeller's Standard Oil Company in 1886, and he relocated to Salina, Kansas, where he established the H. D. Lee Mercantile Company, a wholesale grocery business, and expanded into clothing. Unable to keep enough overalls and dungarees in stock due to unreliable deliveries from eastern suppliers, he decided to start building his own garment factories.

In 1913, Lee's chauffeur is rumored to have come up with an idea. He suggested that the firm develop a one-piece work-wear garment that could be slipped on over his chauffeur's uniform, for when he was underneath the automobile or changing a tire, but that would also serve as an ideal outfit for farm and factory workers wanting to keep debris from getting between their clothes and their skin. Lee employees sewed a jacket and a pair of dungarees together, and the Lee Union-All was born.

The Union-All became the U.S. Army's official doughboy fatigue during World War I. The twenties saw Lee making railroad uniforms and cowboy outfits, and introducing the "denim cowboy pant." In 1926, Lee introduced "buttonless" jeans with zippers, work clothes with slide fasteners, and the U-shaped saddle crotch and tailored sizing, in which rise and seat proportions were based on waist and inseam measurements. Lee went on to outfit James Arness in Gunsmoke, the cast of The Beverly Hillbillies, and Hollywood's Ronald Reagan. In 1964, Lee introduced "no-iron" permanent-press slacks under its Lee-Prest label. In 1972, Lee introduced the leisure suit, "a sporty interpretation of the business suit," followed a year later by Ms. Lee, a new label for women.

WRANGLER, INC.

"Real cowboys don't wear Levi's" is a kind of mantra in Greensboro, North Carolina, where the original Wrangler western-wear product, the 13MWZ, was designed and manufactured in 1947. So it is fitting that 12,000 pairs of cowboy-cut jeans and other Wrangler products were ordered by Robert Redford for the cast of THE HORSE WHISPERER, filmed in New York and Montana in 1997. The code 13MWZ stands for the 13th prototype of the Men's Western Zipper style—cowboys call 'em "13s."

Ben Liechtenstein, a.k.a. "Rodeo Ben," a Philadelphia tailor, who specialized in making outfits for rodeo performers and cowboy-movie stars like Roy Rogers and Gene Autry, was the designer of the first Wrangler western jeans. To research what men needed in the jeans they wore on the trail or at home on the range, Ben traveled west and canvassed a posse of cowpokes. Their advice: (1) More belt loops to accommodate wide leather belts with big buckles. A mere five loops had been the standard. (2) Rear pockets higher up so the buckaroos wouldn't have to sit on the lumps made by their wallets while in the saddle. (3) Smooth rivets around the pockets that wouldn't scratch their beloved saddles. (4) A watch pocket snug enough to prevent loss of watches and coins. (5) A long inseam so the jeans wouldn't ride up to the top of the boot when sitting tall in the saddle. (6) A heavy-duty zipper, maneuverable while wearing riding gloves. Prior to this, buttons had been standard issue.

So Rodeo Ben went to work filling this tall order. When finished, he capped off his sartorial achievement by designing a patch for the back of the jeans, with the name Wrangler scripted in a rope motif. The patch was made of Neolite, a sturdy material used in shoe soles, which, unlike leather, didn't shrink and wrinkle when washed. Today the patch graces the backsides of over 98 percent of the Professional Rodeo Cowboys Association membership.

Denim shirts and jackets say traditional American work wear, but at the same time they have a relaxed, Saturday flavor. The acceptance of the jeans shirt as a casual alternative for the office is proof that, in today's world, denim has become an established way of life.

Steve McQueen

ORIGINAL DENIM

The word "denim" derives from SERGE DE NIMES, Nimes being the city in southern France where the soft, durable fabric was invented in the 1500s. Levi Strauss imported the material from Nimes in 1873 and added a twist by dyeing it indigo. The classic Levi's jacket has no side pockets.

Jackson Pollock. Photograph by Hans Namuth, 1952

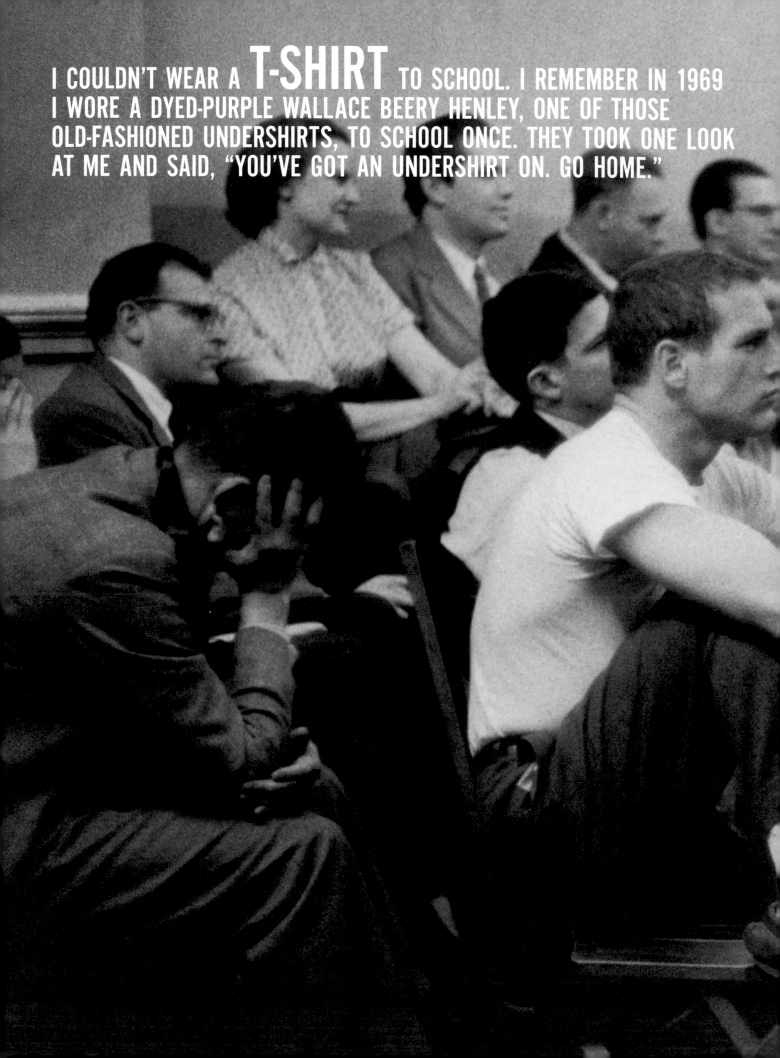

I COULDN'T WEAR A **T-SHIRT** TO SCHOOL. I REMEMBER IN 1969 I WORE A DYED-PURPLE WALLACE BEERY HENLEY, ONE OF THOSE OLD-FASHIONED UNDERSHIRTS, TO SCHOOL ONCE. THEY TOOK ONE LOOK AT ME AND SAID, "YOU'VE GOT AN UNDERSHIRT ON. GO HOME."

Paul Newman at the Actors Studio. Photograph by Eve Arnold, 1955

Paul Newman in Hud, 1963

Photograph by Cornell Capa, 1958

There was a time when wearing a T-shirt was a rebellious statement, a way of saying you were a no-nonsense, hardworking guy. Today it is every bit as athletic and sexy, but also the height of casual style.

T-Times

In the beginning, T-shirts were meant to be worn loosely underneath shirts to keep you warm and keep them dry. For those who didn't want the top of the T-shirt to show underneath an unbuttoned collar (a look that has become a preppy staple), there were V-necks and sleeveless undershirts. Once the T-shirt became acceptable outerwear, its size, shape, cut, and decoration became a reliable badge of the wearer's identity. The greasers were the first to adopt the tight white T-shirt as a uniform, usually with a pack of filterless smokes rolled up in one sleeve. Sans cigarettes, the tight white T-shirt has been a macho symbol for men of every lifestyle and sexual orientation.

In the sixties, T-shirts took on color: bright horizontal stripes on baggy shirts for surfers, rainbow-colored tie-dyed and batik shirts for hippies (and now Deadheads and hackysack players). In the seventies, T-shirts shrank.

Sleeves were capped at the shoulder (often with a colored hem), and hems cropped to midriff length; decorations often included big silver stars and words spelled out in metallic studs.

In the new-wave era, the T-shirt went XXL. British designer Katharine Hamnett scored big with oversized messages on oversized T-shirts (popularized by the pop group Frankie Goes to Hollywood), and some girls wore belted huge T-shirts as dresses. In the nineties, there is something for everyone: body-fitting T-shirts in stretchy, sheer, and luxury fabrics for the athletic and high-fashion types, extra-roomy T-shirts with logos and futuristic graphics that fit hip-hop kids and the rave generation, even T-shirts under button-down shirts—like on the guys in the television show Friends.

Tony Curtis

WHEN I WAS YOUNG, BOXER SHORTS WERE FOR OLD MEN. FOR JUST ABOUT EVERYONE ELSE, **UNDERWEAR** CAME IN ONE COLOR AND STYLE. TIGHTY WHITIES. NOWADAYS, THERE ARE SO MANY OPTIONS. BOXERS LOOK GOOD ON EVERYONE, ESPECIALLY IF YOU HAVE A BELLY. IF YOU'RE THIN, BRIEFS LOOK GOOD; FOR THE MID-THIGH STYLE, YOU SHOULD BE FIT SINCE IT DRAWS ATTENTION TO THE LEGS; FOR A BIKINI, YOU HAVE TO BE IN INCREDIBLE SHAPE; AND FOR A THONG, YOU HAVE TO BE A MODEL IN A GUCCI AD.

Jockey advertisements, 1953

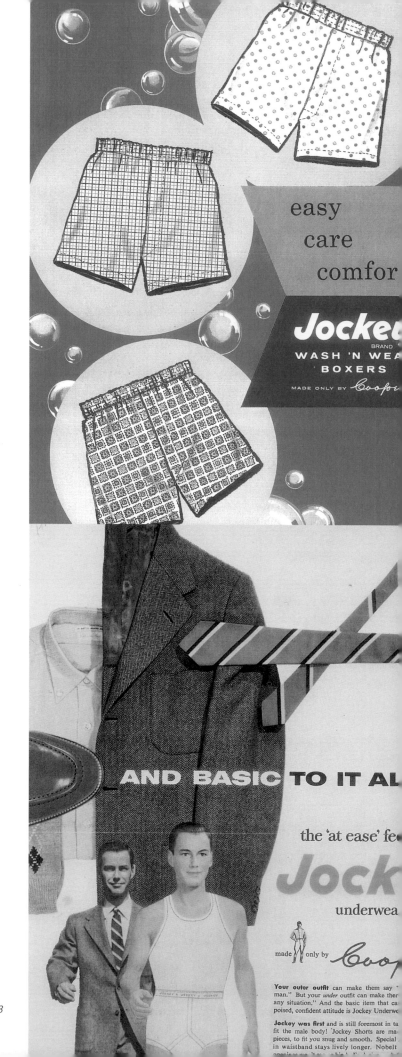

Underwear:
A Brief History

Tom Cruise in Risky
Business, *1983*

1934 is a year to remember: that year, in IT
HAPPENED ONE NIGHT, Clark Gable took off his
shirt to reveal a bare chest, and the market for
undershirts took a bath. That was also the year
an executive from Jockey International, Inc.,
inspired by a postcard of a bikini-clad man on
the Riviera, redesigned men's knit underwear.
The following year, Jockey International introduced the Y-front brief (a configuration of fabric
panels and seams that make up the buttonless
fly opening). Soldiers wore newfangled army-
issue briefs in World War II, and thereafter, once
they returned home, they preferred their briefs.

For a while, briefs separated the boys from
the men. In the nineties, bikini cuts (said to offer
the greatest enhancement of God's gifts to you)
created another generation gap.

In the late eighties, everything got mixed
up: guys started wearing colorful boxer shorts
to hang out in or hit the beach (and girls liked
them for the same reasons), or sticking out from
under a pair of baggy jeans. The fitness movement, particularly the craze for bike shorts, led
to elongated briefs (which fit better than boxers
under jeans and lean trousers) and even uni-
tards. And for the fearless or flawlessly shaped,
the thong arrived from Brazil.

*(Y-front is a trademark of and used with permission of Jockey
International, Inc.)*

CHINOS AND KHAKIS ARE A MUST FOR ANY WARDROBE.
I THINK EVERYONE SHOULD WEAR THEM TO THE OFFICE.

Photograph by Cornell Capa, 1958

THE KHAKI DRILL

Khakis come from the Urdu word KHAK, which means dust or earth. Originally they were the warm-weather military trousers worn by the English. They picked up their nickname, chinos, because, until American sportswear manufacturers began making them, they were largely made in China.

These days, there are a lot of styles of chinos. You can wear them with short hems, like they used to do in the sixties, when preppies called them highwaters or floods, or you can wear them loose and baggy, like they do today on Cape Cod. You can toss them in the washing machine and then throw them on or send them to the dry cleaners and get them back with a sharp crease down the leg. They look good with a T-shirt, blazer, or black cashmere sweater.

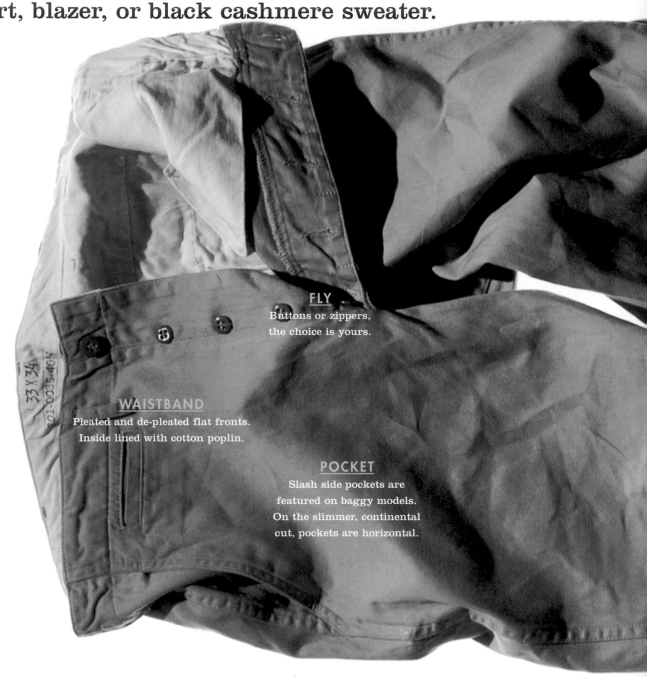

FLY
Buttons or zippers, the choice is yours.

WAISTBAND
Pleated and de-pleated flat fronts. Inside lined with cotton poplin.

POCKET
Slash side pockets are featured on baggy models. On the slimmer, continental cut, pockets are horizontal.

FABRIC
Army-issue khakis are heavier than chinos in cotton twill; newer styles are more formfitting with stretch fabrics.

Fifties chinos (courtesy of Fools and Horses, Brooklyn, New York). Photograph by Bill Steele

I DIDN'T GO TO COLLEGE; I WAS LEARNING A LOT ANYWAY BY RUNNING MY OWN BUSINESS. BUT I LIVED NEAR CORNELL, ITHACA, COLGATE, HAMILTON, AND AN ALL-WOMEN'S SCHOOL IN ELMIRA, AND WE USED TO DRIVE TO THE CAMPUSES AND HANG OUT. THERE WERE PARTIES, CONCERTS, SPORTS, DANCES—ALL THESE KIDS JUST HAVING FUN. AND THE WAY EVERYBODY DRESSED WAS IRREVERENT

IVY LEAGUE.

Sweating It Out

In the beginning, college athletes wore wool sweaters during competition, usually with the letter of their school appliquéd in felt on the front; later the letters were interwoven. (The letter sweater, which became popular after World War II as a cardigan, was more for show than for play.) In the twenties, the Knickerbocker Knitting Company, the first company to sell sweatshirts with academic logos (the first being Wentworth Military Academy in Lexington, Kentucky), changed its name to Champion because so much of the business was with the university sports teams. From 1919 to 1938, logoed, fleeced cotton sweatshirts were used for warm-up practices. Responding to complaints from athletes that the all-cotton sweatshirt shrank in the wash, Champion employee Sam Friedland patented the reverse-weave process in 1938. In the late eighties, the hooded sweatshirt became a universal fashion statement, whether worn by suburban sports fans, hip-hop kids, or gay activists.

Polo coats

Stadium boxy blazers

Tweed jackets with suede elbow patches

Navy blazers with crests

Madras shirts

Flannel shirts

Oxford shirts

Rep striped ties

Crew-neck sweaters

Cardigans and letter sweaters

Argyle sweaters

Sweater vests

Corduroys

Khakis

Gray flannel slacks

White socks

Argyle socks

Penny loafers

Flat caps

Wing tips

NOW

Down jackets

Hooded sweatshirts

Jeans

Chinos

Track pants

V-neck sweaters

Vintage sports jackets

Plaid flannel shirts

Jams

Cargo pants

Carpenter pants

Camouflage pants

Anoraks

University T-shirts and sweats

Doc Martens

Birkenstocks

Running shoes

Baseball caps

Photograph by Elliott Erwitt

CLASSICS

71

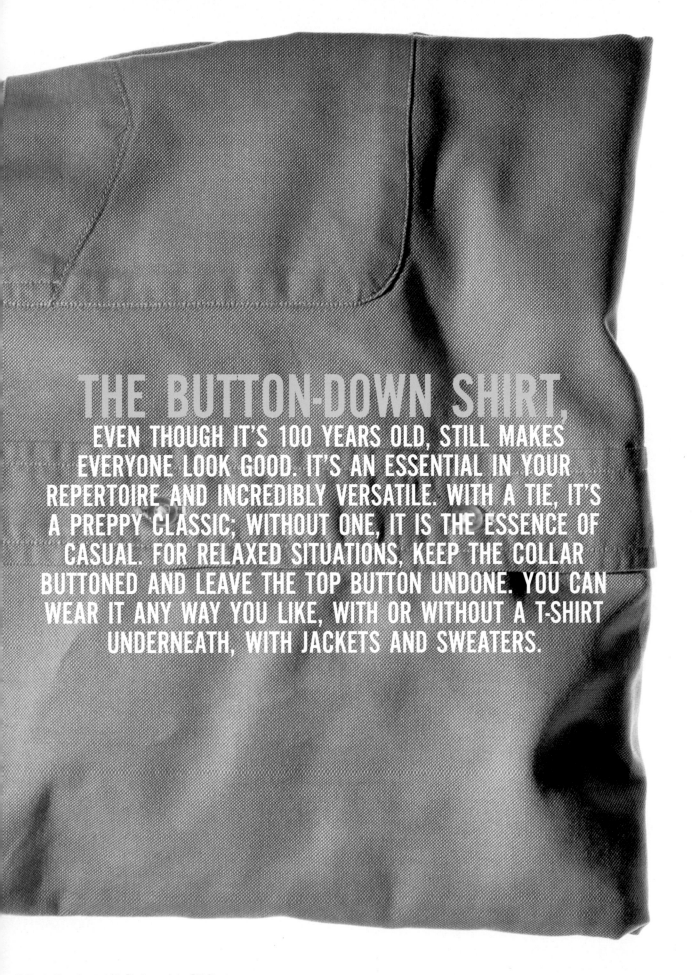

THE BUTTON-DOWN SHIRT,

EVEN THOUGH IT'S 100 YEARS OLD, STILL MAKES EVERYONE LOOK GOOD. IT'S AN ESSENTIAL IN YOUR REPERTOIRE AND INCREDIBLY VERSATILE. WITH A TIE, IT'S A PREPPY CLASSIC; WITHOUT ONE, IT IS THE ESSENCE OF CASUAL. FOR RELAXED SITUATIONS, KEEP THE COLLAR BUTTONED AND LEAVE THE TOP BUTTON UNDONE. YOU CAN WEAR IT ANY WAY YOU LIKE, WITH OR WITHOUT A T-SHIRT UNDERNEATH, WITH JACKETS AND SWEATERS.

Sixties button-down shirt. Photograph by Bill Steele

HOW TO BUY
A COTTON SHIRT

All shirts are not created equal. For the finest quality, feel the fabric. Egyptian and Sea Island cottons have the smoothest surface, with a high thread count (the number of threads per square inch). Pima cotton, introduced in 1925, is an exceptionally strong and firm hybrid of Egyptian cottons developed in Pima County, Arizona. Most shirts, however, are made from oxford cloth, a soft, durable cotton that takes starch like nobody's business, in a plain or basket weave (the latter is most typically found on button-down shirts), or broadcloth, a soft, somewhat glossy cotton that tends to wrinkle easily. For the coolest summer cotton, try end-on-end, a loose, breathable weave in which colored threads are interwoven with white, lending a subtle iridescence.

WHY BUTTON DOWN?

The button-down shirt was originally designed to keep collars from flapping into the faces of polo players as they rode at high speed across the field.

Anthony Perkins

All About Collars

The tab collar is mod and meticulous, with a fabric that buttons or snaps underneath a tie, pushing the knot (which should be small) front and center. The tab fits any face and is extremely flattering to heavier-set jawlines.

The round or club collar, a favorite of British schoolboys, has no points, and has holes for a tie bar which serve the same function as a tab collar.

The button-down was created by Brooks Brothers in 1900 and suits a wide variety of faces, with collars generally measuring between 3 1/8 to 3 1/4 inches long.

The straight or turndown collar varies in length according to the styles of the time, and is the most versatile, elongating short or round faces.

The wing collar is found on a formal shirt. Worn with tuxedos, it gives any face an air of elegance.

The spread collar requires a large tie knot and adds weight to a thin or finely featured face. It is not recommended for the jowly.

The contrast collar sets off a colored or patterned shirt with a pristine white collar. It's an eighties yuppie classic, adopted by CEOs, lawyers, investment bankers, and people with British tailors.

Tab Hunter

P4231-4

DEPENDING ON HOW YOU WEAR THEM, **SWEATERS** CAN MAKE YOU FEEL SOPHISTICATED AND SHARP OR COMFORTABLE AND COZY.

Pure Cashmere

The wool comes from the cashmere goat, which lives in Mongolia. It takes 16 goats to supply enough fiber to make a plush four-ply sweater.

Scottish cashmere is the finest in the world. Look for the Ballantyne, Scotch House, and Pringle labels.

Unlike mohair and angora, cashmere doesn't shed and is nearly wrinkle-proof. Cashmere blended with wool, nylon, and silk lends durability to hard-wearing garments like trousers and socks. Properly cared for, cashmere has a life span of 20 years.

Warren Beatty

SWEATER CLASSICS

Wools to pull over your eyes

Cardigan

Fisherman's sweater

Crew-neck Shetland

Ribbed turtleneck

Knit waistcoat

Varsity sweater

Letter sweater

Shawl-collar pullover

Suede-front cardigan

Scoop-neck poor-boy

Belted Guatemalan sweater

Punk mohair sweater

Long-sleeve polo sweater

Navajo sweater

Icelandic ski sweater

Lamb's-wool V-necks

Nautical sweaters (navy and
    white stripes or solid navy
    with buttons on the shoulder)

Argyle sweater vests

Ski sweaters

Fair Isles sweaters

Striped racing sweaters

Cashmere sweaters

Mister Rogers

HAND-SEWN IN NEW ENGLAND, **WEEJUNS** ARE THE OLD IVY LEAGUE CLASSICS. LIKE MOCCASINS, YOU CAN WEAR THEM WITH ANYTHING. YOU CAN WEAR THEM WITHOUT SOCKS, AND THE MORE BEAT UP THEY GET, THE BETTER THEY LOOK.

WHY A PENNY?

G. H. Bass & Co. introduced loafers in the U.S.
in the thirties, based on a design for Norwegian
peasant shoes, hence the nickname "Weejuns." They
were an instant hit for loafing around (therefore
becoming known as "loafers") on college campuses.
They had a leather "saddle" across the front, which
some bright fellow discovered could hold a penny,
which brings us to the familiar name
"penny loafers." Over the years,
this casual shoe has been streamlined and
refashioned in everything from shiny vinyl to red
suede, but the original—cordovan leather with beefy,
rolled stitching connecting the apron to each side
of the shoe—is still the greatest.

Fifties loafers. Photograph by Bill Steele

NO ONE LIKES TO
BE LABELED,
BUT YOU CAN TELL
A GOOD DEAL
ABOUT PEOPLE
BY THE
LABELS
THEY CHOOSE
TO WEAR
AND HOW THEY
WEAR THEM:
ON THE
SLEEVE
OR CLOSE
TO THE
CHEST.

Vintage labels. Thomas Oatman Collection

Closet Classics

The elements of the civil wardrobe

High tops
Loafers, sneakers, wing tips
Tank tops
Chesterfield coat
Leather gloves, mittens
Bomber jacket
Cotton socks and wool socks
Wool, cotton, cashmere, and
    fisherman's knit sweaters
Cargo pants
Anorak
Chinos, jeans, gray flannel and
    gray tropical-wool trousers
Carpenter pants
Western shirts
Tartan and regimental scarves
Barbour jacket
Stadium coat
Ski jacket, ski pants
Cardigans
Tuxedo
Jeans jacket
Pin-stripe, herringbone, solid
    gray or navy suit
Military shirts
Tennis gear, white
Ray-Ban aviators and Wayfarers
Ribbed turtleneck
Double D-ring, double-prong, and
    webbed belts
Golf sweater, pants, and shirts
Hawaiian shirts
Boxers and briefs
Button-down and tab-collar shirts
Wellies
Black grosgrain tie, black socks,
    and patent-leather shoes
Baseball cap, ski caps
Flannel, denim, corduroy, and
    chambray shirts
Sandals
Doc Martens
Military jacket
Riding pants and boots
Camel double-breasted polo coat
Rep striped tie
Peacoat
Bowling shirts
Topsiders
Basketball shorts
Jams
Square-cut bathing suit
Speedos

ANYTHING HAVING TO DO WITH **NAVY** IS AN EMOTIONAL TURN-ON. IT IS MY FAVORITE COLOR. I LOVE AIRCRAFT CARRIERS, SAILORS LINED UP, AND AMERICAN FLAGS BILLOWING IN THE WIND. I LOVE THE UNIFORMS OF NAVAL OFFICERS AND SWABBIES, THEIR STURDY CONSTRUCTION, CRISP FABRICS, AND ARCHITECTURAL SHAPES.

SAIL ON
Presenting sea legs and arms

Peacoats with anchor buttons

Chambray deck shirts

Square-collared midi top

Navy wool bell bottoms with 13 buttons

Navy-and-white striped boat-neck sweaters

Slickers

White cotton deck pants with two slit pockets

Fabric belts

Sailors in high wind. Photograph by Wayne Miller

SAILOR PANTS

The original navy sailor pants laced up in the back and had 13 decorative buttons in the front, representing the original colonies of the United States. The back-lacing trousers made for a tight fit, which helped sailors climb around the ship and kept them from getting caught up in the rigging. The famous bell bottom hem of sailor pants was designed to make rolling up the pants easier for those who were assigned to swab the deck.

PEOPLE LOVE GREAT QUALITY.
THEY LOVE RUGGEDNESS AND
A GREAT SOLID DESIGN. THAT'S
WHY FASHION DESIGNERS
CONTINUE TO PRODUCE FASHION
STATEMENTS FROM BASIC
SERVICE UNIFORMS FROM ALL
BRANCHES OF

THE MILITARY.

A LOT OF DETAIL HAS GONE
INTO THE MAKING OF THOSE
ITEMS: DOUBLE-STITCH SEAMS,
REINFORCED BAR TACKS, DEEP
REINFORCED POCKETS, HEAVY-
DUTY TWILLS MADE TO
WITHSTAND THE WEAR AND
TEAR OF SERVICE. AND
MILITARY UNIFORMS ARE
LIKE GREAT WINES, THEY
GET BETTER WITH AGE.

Private Elvis Presley, Fort Chaffee, Arkansas

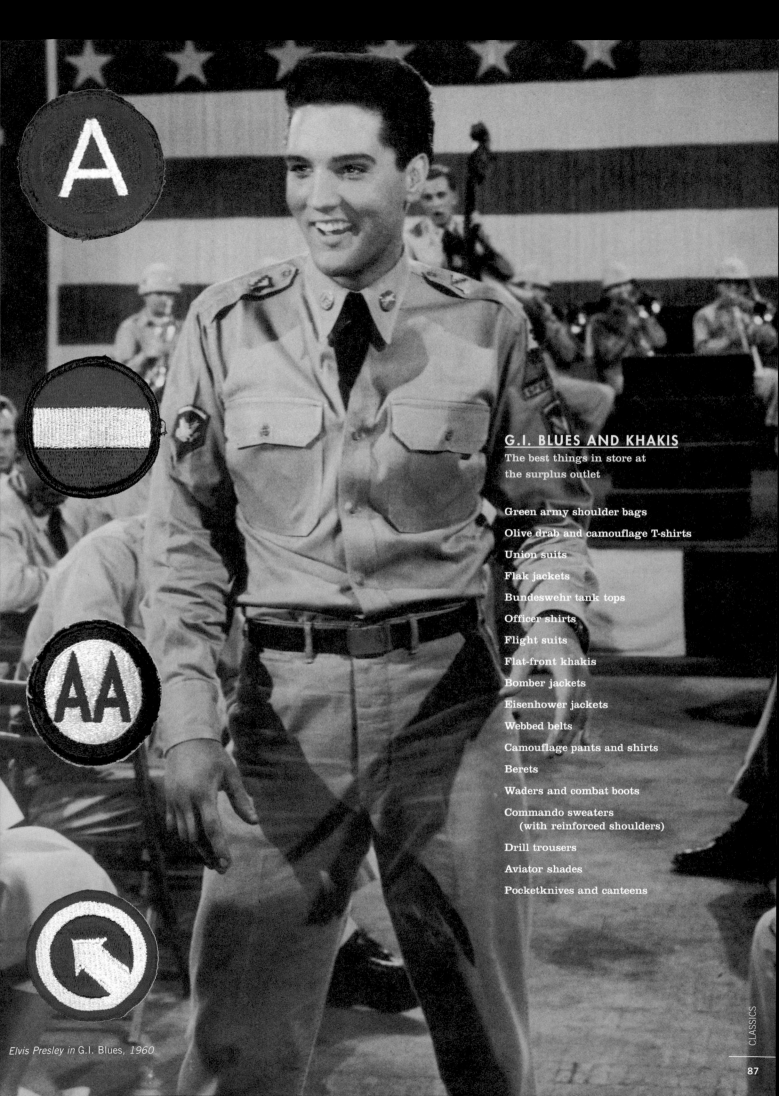

G.I. BLUES AND KHAKIS
The best things in store at
the surplus outlet

Green army shoulder bags

Olive drab and camouflage T-shirts

Union suits

Flak jackets

Bundeswehr tank tops

Officer shirts

Flight suits

Flat-front khakis

Bomber jackets

Eisenhower jackets

Webbed belts

Camouflage pants and shirts

Berets

Waders and combat boots

Commando sweaters
(with reinforced shoulders)

Drill trousers

Aviator shades

Pocketknives and canteens

Elvis Presley in G.I. Blues, *1960*

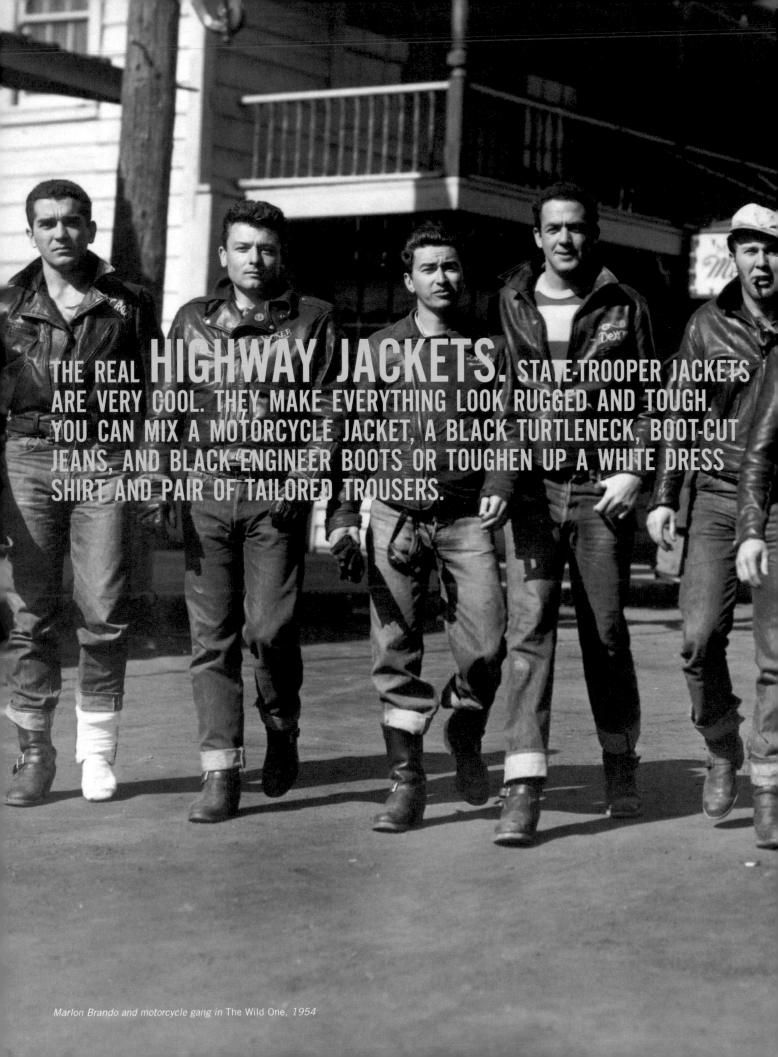

THE REAL **HIGHWAY JACKETS.** STATE-TROOPER JACKETS ARE VERY COOL. THEY MAKE EVERYTHING LOOK RUGGED AND TOUGH. YOU CAN MIX A MOTORCYCLE JACKET, A BLACK TURTLENECK, BOOT-CUT JEANS, AND BLACK ENGINEER BOOTS OR TOUGHEN UP A WHITE DRESS SHIRT AND PAIR OF TAILORED TROUSERS.

Marlon Brando and motorcycle gang in The Wild One, *1954*

THE PERFECTO

Irving Schott devised the leather motorcycle jacket in 1928, three years after he revolutionized outdoor sportswear by introducing the zipper into his jackets. Beginning in 1915, Schott's jackets were given the name Perfecto, after his favorite cigar. The Perfecto motorcycle jacket is worn for protection against both injury and the elements. It was a Harley-Davidson distributor who first approached Schott and suggested his jackets be used aboard motorcycles. In 1954, the Perfecto motorcycle jacket was featured in THE WILD ONE.

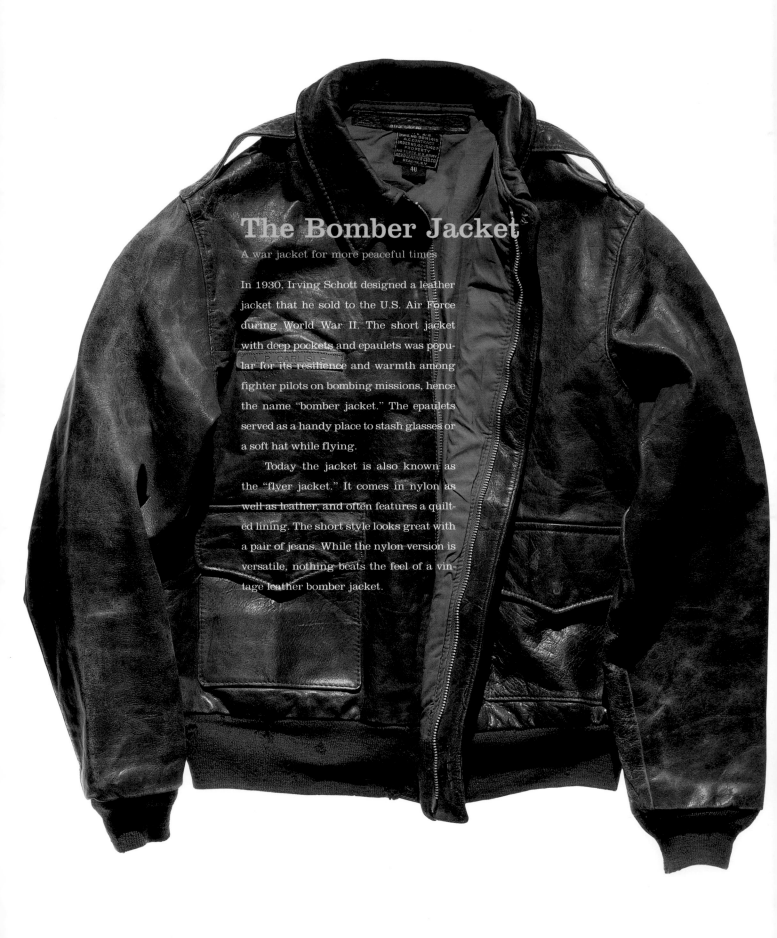

The Bomber Jacket

A war jacket for more peaceful times

In 1930, Irving Schott designed a leather jacket that he sold to the U.S. Air Force during World War II. The short jacket with deep pockets and epaulets was popular for its resilience and warmth among fighter pilots on bombing missions, hence the name "bomber jacket." The epaulets served as a handy place to stash glasses or a soft hat while flying.

Today the jacket is also known as the "flyer jacket." It comes in nylon as well as leather, and often features a quilted lining. The short style looks great with a pair of jeans. While the nylon version is versatile, nothing beats the feel of a vintage leather bomber jacket.

Vintage A-240 airman's jacket. Photograph by Bill Steele

HOW TO SHOP FOR A VINTAGE LEATHER JACKET

Motorcycle jackets are the all-time favorite leather jackets. The most popular vintage ones are from the fifties—very old Schott, early Harley, and the Brand labels. But when looking for a vintage leather jacket, remember that a motorcycle jacket is not your only option. Bomber jackets, the real ones from World War II, are very durable and still available, some even with their original mink collars. Some actually have the original owner's airplane name inked onto the sleeve, which increases the jacket's worth. Note: Real bomber jackets are always brown. Always.

The feel of leather is as important as its appearance. Ideally, the best vintage motorcycle jackets are soft and fairly lightweight. When examining an old leather jacket, look for peel-ing or signs of dryness. You'll recognize the problem the moment you touch it. The earliest motorcycle jackets often featured wombat-fur lining. Today linings of older jackets are usual-ly pretty beat up, but that is no gauge of the jacket's real worth. You can always replace the lining with a cotton-blend material made for that purpose.

It's usually pretty easy to tell if you are buying a real bomber jacket—look for an air-force insignia where the zipper is sewn in at the inside bottom of the jacket. One clue in sizing up a motorcycle jacket is that the more collectible ones from the forties and fifties never have as many zippers as jackets from the sixties.

THE MINUTE A MAN PUTS ON A **SUIT**, THERE'S A CHANGE IN HIS BEHAVIOR. IT'S THE BUSINESSMAN'S UNIFORM, HIS COAT OF ARMOR. THE STYLE, THE CUT, THE FABRIC, AND THE FIT ARE THE SIGNIFIERS OF HIS RANK AND INDIVIDUALITY.

Gregory Peck in The Man in the Gray Flannel Suit, *1967*

1940s

GANGSTERS AND HEROES

Although that extreme exaggeration of a suit, the Zoot, was popularized by bandleader Cab Calloway and worn with menacing enthusiasm by the "hep" and gangster crowds of the day, its street life was extremely brief. In 1942, three years after its introduction (allegedly inspired by the dress-up taste of Al Capp's cartoon character Li'l Abner), it was outlawed in the U.S. due to its flagrantly excessive use of cloth during wartime rationing. The War Production Board also saw to it that such wasteful details as cuffs, patch pockets, pleats, yokes, full or double anything, and vests were eliminated from men's suits in general. Finally, at war's (and wit's) end, the look we associate with the forties reared its rugged head—the hard silhouette of the full-cut double-breasted suit. Shoulders were padded, jacket buttons set lower, and lapels cut longer to accentuate height. The look was tall and slim, to be worn with spread-collar shirts and wide, Windsor-knotted ties. Gary Cooper, Cary Grant, and Clark Kent were the guys to reckon with. Recommended for the broad-shouldered or those who like to look it.

1950s

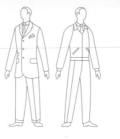

LEAN AND MODERN

The sack suit, popularized by Brooks Brothers and J. Press, blew into town with the Cold War. Nondescript, formless, and forgiving, it was natural-shouldered, with a thin silhouette—worn with thin lapels, thin tie, button-down shirt. It was part of conscripting the trim, conservative, conformist salary man into the daily work-force sea of olive drab and charcoal gray. Ivy League. Madison Avenue. Rock Hudson. Tony Randall. The Button-Down Mind of Bob Newhart. Gregory Peck in THE MAN IN THE GRAY FLANNEL SUIT, and of course the young JFK and RFK. For those who appreciate the sleek, slim, and slenderizing.

1960s

MODS AND CONTINENTALS

The skinny, shiny, center-vented version the sack suit, worn by the Rat Pack early the decade, evolved into the Continental from the pioneering menswear design Pierre Cardin and Yves Saint Laurent. tight-fitting suit featured strong pad shoulders, movement-restricting high armholes, and a nipped-in waist. The jac was side-vented and the trousers w tapered and cuffless. (By the end of decade, the pants began to flare sligh Johnny Carson epitomized the Contine look, which later evolved further into Edwardian dandy/mod/Carnaby Street s that came over with the British music i sion. A look for a decade of overpower variety.

Cary Grant

Rock Hudson

Dean Martin

1970s

YESTER LEISURE

blown Continental. Wide lapels. 747 collars. Represented by Roger Moore 07, it was a kind of modified safari suit abardine, featuring a fitted jacket with ed chest pockets, and wide-flare bell oms. Worn with long-pointed collar , open at the neck. John Travolta, Peter da, Peter Sellers. Although it brought us polyester leisure suit, the decade also menswear designers finally get some ct, most notably those who created an o-American look by combining English try dressing with Hollywood glamour. dulge, it helps to be rail thin, synthet-endly, and aesthetically liberal.

1980s

DESIGNER TAILORING

A return to the elegance of the thirties and forties—with a slouchy, unconstructed Italian attitude. Kevin Costner and co-stars arresting in Giorgio Armani in THE UNTOUCHABLES. Richard Gere filing and cross-referencing his G.A. in A.G. (Giorgio Armani in AMERICAN GIGOLO). A little stiffer was Michael Douglas wearing Allan Flusser in WALL STREET—even the shirts seemed to have shoulder pads. And then came the Japanese garçons in the form of Comme des Garçons and Yohji Yamamoto; it was like going from Armani to origami. Dark, sophisticated suits for nighttime; some were so complicated in construction that they really needed operating instructions. A decade of classics and oddities, all worth a second look.

1990s

REDEFINED ELEGANCE

Take your choice: one button, two, three, four, or six buttons. With an eye for detail and classic construction, suits shaped up. In the early part of the decade, the theatrical ruled: long, high-buttoned frock coats teamed up with flat-front trousers for a dandy look. Tuxedo dressing took a rock-star turn, pairing dinner jackets with leather pants and poetic shirts (sans tie). By the end of the decade, classic Savile Row tailoring was updated for a new generation, and a sleek new silhouette emerged, based on the streamlined look of the early sixties, with emphasis on clean lines and lustrous fabrics, to be worn with solid-colored shirts and ties.

n Travolta

Richard Gere

John Faureau and Vince Vaughn

THE APPEAL OF AMERICAN WORK CLOTHES IS THE UTILITARIAN THOUGHT BEHIND THEM. THEY'RE INEXPENSIVE, FUNCTIONAL, TOUGH, AND DURABLE, AND YOU DON'T HAVE TO IRON THEM. KHAKI OR FOREST GREEN PANTS WORN WITH A WORK SHIRT CREATE A REALLY CLEAN AND CRISP IMPRESSION. A **SERVICE-STATION** ATTENDANT WEARING NAVY PANTS AND A LIGHT-BLUE SHIRT STITCHED WITH HIS NAME CONVEYS AN HONEST MASCULINITY.

Working at the Hess station in Elmira, I had a shirt with a big logo on the back. To me, it meant I was capable of performing this grown-up duty in life. As long as I can remember, wearing logos has been an essential American style. People are proud to wear a name that associates them with an organization. In fact, it can help separate them from the crowd, giving them a sense of security and authority.

Vintage garage-mechanic's uniform. Photograph by Bill Steele

Steve Martin in The Jerk, 1979

WHEN I WAS A KID,
BATHING SUITS
WERE NOT SEXY. THEY WERE
CALLED TRUNKS; THEY LOOKED
LIKE A SHORTER PAIR OF WALKING
SHORTS. MINE WERE PLAID
MADRAS WITH A LITTLE CLIP
ON THE FRONT AND A
CHANGE POCKET. THEY TOOK
HOURS TO DRY.

Burt Lancaster and Deborah Kerr in From Here to Eternity, *1953*

I'd recommend the basic boxer shape for everybody; the longer surf trunks that have been going in and out of style since the sixties beach movies continue to make statements on and off the sand.

Sean Connery and Margaret Nolan in Goldfinger, 1964

Annette Funicello and Frankie Avalon in Beach Blanket Bingo, *1965*

all guys are great in **Jantzen**

swim trunks
sunclothes

Mark Spitz, about 1968

EIGHT-POUND SUIT

The Jantzen Company, formerly the Portland
Knitting Company, made its first bathing suit
for members of the Portland Rowing Club.
It was a stretchy, ribbed knit wool body suit
that looked like a combination of today's tank
top and bike shorts. It weighed a
whopping eight pounds when wet.
By contrast, the men's racing suit that
originated in Australia in the twenties, now
known generically as the Speedo, weighs less
than eight ounces. The medal sweep of the
1956 Australian Olympic swimming team
brought the Speedo brand worldwide
attention.

SHADES MAKE EVERYONE LOOK COOLER, BUT THE ONLY REAS

Fifties aviator sunglasses. Photograph by Bill Steele

YOU SHOULD WEAR THEM AT NIGHT IS IF YOUR EYES LOOK REALLY TIRED.

Cruise Control

According to Bausch & Lomb, the manufacturer of Ray-Ban sunglasses, its two biggest-selling sunglass styles had their biggest sales years when Tom Cruise wore them in his films. The humble Wayfarer, which had been languishing since its introduction in 1952, became instantly famous in Cruise's RISKY BUSINESS (and went on to define new-wave style on the faces of the Blues Brothers, Madonna, Corey "Sunglasses at Night" Hart, Huey Lewis, and countless others, and to get a name check in Don Henley's song "The Boys of Summer").

The aviator frame (the original Ray-Ban product) was developed for the army air corps, which needed anti-glare goggles for pilots. The aviators were released to the public in 1937, and became Tom Cruise's signature gear in TOP GUN. In JERRY MAGUIRE, Cruise selected a pair of the already hip Arnett, another product by Bausch & Lomb. To launch its newest sunglasses, the Predator 2, Bausch & Lomb outfitted Tommy Lee Jones and Will Smith with shades for their 1997 film MEN IN BLACK.

Rebecca De Mornay and Tom Cruise in Risky Business, *1983 (top); Tom Cruise in* Top Gun, *1986.*

SHADES

In ancient China, judges wore smoky
quartz lenses to hide their facial expressions.
In 1430, when eyeglasses were invented,
some were also darkened. Protective glasses
were developed in the latter half of the
19th century, using mica and amber.
Sunglasses as we now know them were first
created in 1885. In addition to providing
protection from the sun, they have been
widely adopted as fashion statements since
their popularization by Hollywood movie stars
in the thirties and forties.

Dan Aykroyd and John Belushi in The Blues Brothers, *1980*

WHEN IT COMES TO SPECS, HORN RIMS HAVE THE UNIQUE ABILITY TO MAKE A NERD LOOK LIKE A SWINGER AND VICE VERSA.

A Short History of Horn Rims

In the 1700s, the shells of tortoises were carved to hold lenses; today the practice is rare, but the color still survives: the horns of certain animals have been carved into frames known as horn rims. For a pretty penny, you get water-buffalo horn rims—without cruelty, too: water buffalo shed their horns every year. The alternatives are mold-injected plastic or optical-quality frames made from acetate zylonite.

Cary Grant

Woody Allen

Clint Eastwood

Clark Kent

Allen Ginsberg

Jerry Lewis

Buddy Holly

Arthur Ashe

The Specs

How to make them fit your face

You want to make an impression. You want to look strong, hand-some, and rich. Like Ari Onassis or Marcello Mastroianni. Or you want to look vulnerable but brainy, nerdy but chic. Like Woody Allen or Elvis Costello.

If you have delicate features, stick with wire rims. Otherwise, remember this: The squarer the frame, the sharper it looks: think Peter Sellers, Arthur Ashe. The rounder, the nerdier: think Jerry Lewis, Harold Lloyd.

If your face is square, try rounder frames. If your face is long, choose a frame that has more depth (the distance from the top to the bottom) than width (the distance from the bridge to the temple). If your face is short, choose a rectangular frame that has more width than depth.

HORN RIMS

Nerd glasses

National Health specs (British)

Buddy Hollies

Clark Kents

Blues Brothers

Engineers' glasses

Sears specials

ATHLETICS

Energy, speed, thrust, the burning desire to win—to me, that's what sports are all about. Athletics bring extreme excitement to American life.

Like most American boys, I had a dream that one day I would be a pro ball player; it didn't really matter which game. I played pitcher, second base, and shortstop in the local Little League, and I started out as safety and ended up becoming quarterback in small-fry football. I collected baseball cards and football cards. I followed our hometown baseball team, the Elmira Pioneers, a farm team for the Orioles. I liked the Orioles, but I liked the Yankees better. I was a fan of Syracuse, Notre Dame, the Cleveland Browns, the Green Bay Packers, and the 49ers, and my heroes were Ernie Davis—the Elmira Express—Jim Brown, Jim Taylor, Mickey Mantle, and Wilt Chamberlain. The rougher sports were very interesting to me; all the grunts and groans, the pushing and shoving. But it came as a rude awakening when I turned 13 and still weighed in at only 90 pounds.

As a teenager, I went on to learn a great deal about sports attire and equipment from my employment in a sporting-goods store, an experience that would eventually inspire much of what I do in all aspects of my collections today. Things weren't so high-tech back then. Tennis rackets were still made of wood, and jerseys were made of wool; college football players wore leather helmets, and a coach could typically be seen running around the field in a long overcoat and wing-tip shoes.

It's interesting how, until recently, sports equipment had been considered so much for its utility alone. That has changed dramatically, especially after urban kids put their stamp of approval on athletic clothes by wearing them off the fields and courts and on the streets. It began with hero worship—the desire to emulate one's favorite athlete or as a pure expression of support for a team—and ended up as one of the most significant fashion statements of the nineties.

Meanwhile, the traditions of the English gentleman's sports, polo, cricket, and hunting, the country life pursuits, continue to exert their big attraction. Polo matches are thrilling to watch—the clumping noise and awesome power of the horses running across the field. There's a certain aura around the sport; the spectators are so interesting in the way they dress, putting on their own exclusive fashion show. The world of antique sports equipment and art is inspiring as well—the old wool baseball jerseys which have evolved into casual American sportswear, and the cricket uniforms of the past, which gave us today's tennis sweater. Mixing these with elements of the high-tech uniforms of today brings me something totally different.

When I was a kid, there were no Rollerblades or snowboards, and windsurfing was unheard of. I learned to ski with leather boots and wooden skis on the icy slopes of a local resort in upstate New York. Today's modern-miracle materials let you achieve peak performance no matter what level you're at: boots that hold your feet in the best position for downhill, underwear that wicks away perspiration, Ultrex jackets that are windproof but breathable. In my sports clothing, I first aim for authentic details and then I make sure it's functional. After that, I care about the style. Whether it's a logoed sailing jacket or a hockey or a rugby jersey, authenticity is what matters most to people. As opposed to regular clothes, this look says you're a player on the team, even if you aren't.

AS KIDS, WE THOUGHT IT WAS NEAT TO SNEAK OUT OF BOWLING ALLEYS WITH A PAIR OF BOWLING SHOES TO WEAR WITH OUR JEANS. BUT THE EMBROIDERED SHIRTS ARE THE THING THAT REALLY SIGNIFY THAT IT'S A GOOD-TIME SPORT.

COLLARS
Are often in contrasting colors to the body of the shirt. On some shirts, the figure of a bowler is embroidered on the collar.

SLEEVE HEMS
Usually come in contrasting colors.

EMBROIDERED NAME
Always goes above the pocket; team logo goes on back.

BUTTONS
Often match the color of the collar. On some old shirts, buttons are shaped like bowling pins.

CLASSIC CUT
Is boxy, to allow for a full swing. Some shirt bodies have contrasting front panels; others have a different colored yoke across the front and back shoulders.

CUSTOMIZE YOUR BOWLING SHIRT

You can buy bowling shirts from most pro shops and bowling-supply stores, as well as from some sporting-goods outlets. Both the American Bowling Congress and the Professional Bowling Association have their own lines, most of which can be custom screen-printed or embroidered with your name and logo.

You can also have your pro shop order basic shirts from Hilton Active Apparel (847-675-1010). For classics, try placing an order with King Louie (816-765-5212), who feature three cotton-poly shirt styles: The Kramer (a basic body with contrasting collars and buttons in five color combos and an embroidered bowler on the collar); The Turbo (blue, red, or black with matching epaulets and collar on a white front and back yoke); and The Blackburn (with a square shirttail and

contrasting front panels; derived from an English soccer team's uniform).

To order your own shirt direct, call Classic Products (219-484-2695), which does hand embroidery and silkscreen printing of names and logos (as long as they're not trademarked) on a variety of shirt styles (no minimums, but two weeks' processing time).

Memory Lanes

The most striking bowling sites in America

BILTMORE HOUSE
Asheville, North Carolina. Built in 1895 in the basement rec room of railroad millionaire Cornelius Vanderbilt's house. For strolling, not rolling.

HOLLER HOUSE
Milwaukee, Wisconsin. Two lanes, human pinsetters, and a chalkboard for scoring. Built in 1910.

PIONEER BOWL
Yucca Valley, California. Built in 1947 in Pioneertown, a famous setting for Hollywood westerns. Vintage equipment.

FIESTA BOWL
Highway 27, Lady Lake, Florida. This alley, built in 1990, is styled to look like the Spanish-Mexican mission in San Antonio.

COUNTRY MART LANES
Leon, West Virginia. Four lanes in a minimart/hardware store.

SHOWBOAT HOTEL AND CASINO
Las Vegas, Nevada. Want to roll a few frames Christmas Day? No problem here. 106 lanes. Never closed.

NATIONAL BOWLING HALL OF FAME AND MUSEUM
St. Louis, Missouri. Houses a collection of over 750 bowling shirts.

ROBERT LEE KNIGHT'S BOWLING HALL OF FAME
Colorado Springs, Colorado. One of the biggest private collections of memorabilia. Free tours.

ROSSI LANES
Washington Avenue, Elmira, New York. Where I learned how to bowl.

DIXIE LANES
Caton Avenue, Elmira, New York. Where my dad bowled on Schreibman Jewelers' teams.

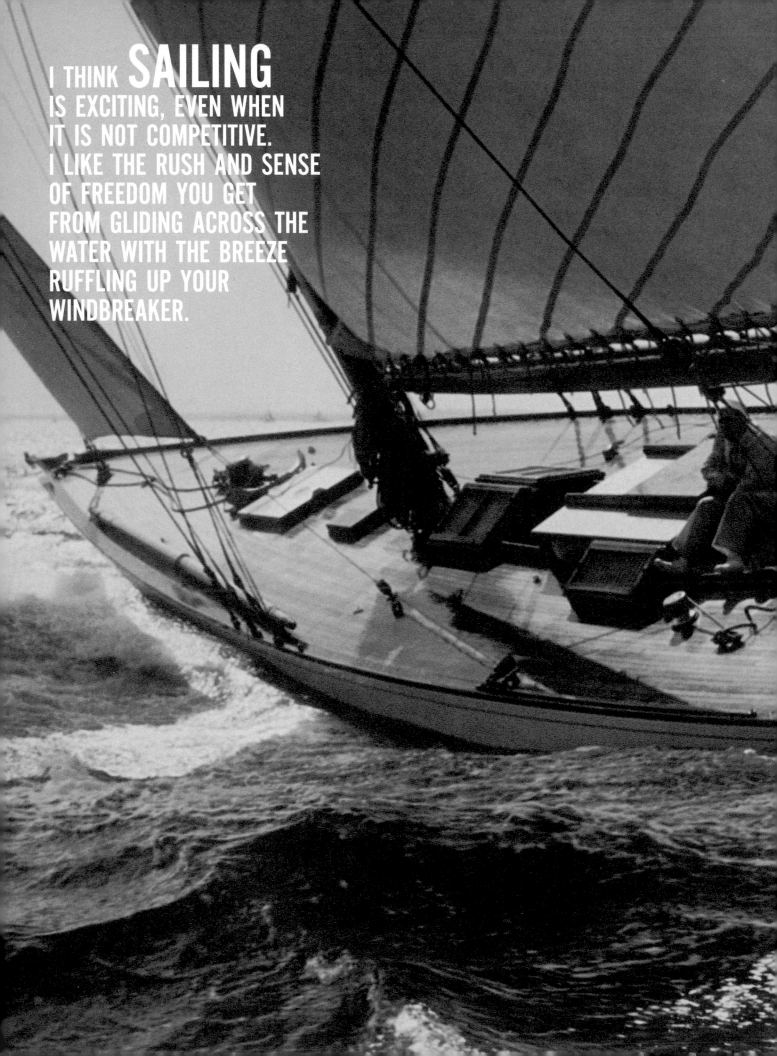

I THINK **SAILING** IS EXCITING, EVEN WHEN IT IS NOT COMPETITIVE. I LIKE THE RUSH AND SENSE OF FREEDOM YOU GET FROM GLIDING ACROSS THE WATER WITH THE BREEZE RUFFLING UP YOUR WINDBREAKER.

SAILING GEAR

The Sperry Topsider was inspired by a dog. In 1935, yachtsman Paul Sperry was trying to design a rubber-soled shoe that would provide good traction on wet, slippery boat decks. One winter morning, while walking his cocker spaniel Prince, he noticed that the dog didn't slip on the ice. He examined his pooch's paw and saw a deep wavy pattern, which he copied onto a piece of rubber—and the boat shoe was born.

The anorak was invented in 1924 by a 22-year-old tailor named Jakob Anorak. Initially, the large overgarment was favored by Prohibition-era bootleggers, who could hold up to 30 bottles of whiskey in the inner pockets. In the thirties, Anorak restyled the garment with a thicker lining, and soon it became the official uniform of policemen. In the fifties, the classic anorak with a detachable hood was introduced in nylon and other water-resistant fabrics. It quickly became a favorite among the sailing set.

President John F. Kennedy

Oilskins (water-resistant, foul-weather gear, also known as oilies)   Hooded anorak (pullover or zip-front styles)   Windproof and waterproof, breathable jacket with Velcro closures   Nylon overalls or pull-on pants   Polar-fleece sweaters or vests   Deck shoes   Helly Hanson jacket

VELCRO

Velcro was invented in 1948 by a Swiss mountaineer named George de Mestral, who returned from an alpine walk covered in cockleburs. While picking them off his socks and pants, he discovered that they were covered with thousands of tiny hooks that clung to the fibers of his clothing. He then designed a fastening system based on his discovery and took its name from the French "velour crochet," which means "velvet hook."

The Nautical Flag Lexicon

Graphics that really say something

Keep Well Clear
at Low Speed

I Am Carrying
Dangerous Goods

Yes (Affirmative)

I Am Maneuvering
With Difficulty

I Am Directing My
Course to Starboard

I Am Disabled;
Communicate With Me

I Require a Pilot

I Have a Pilot
On Board

I Am Directing My
Course to Port

I Am on Fire;
Keep Clear of Me

I Have Something
to Communicate

You Should Stop
Your Vessel

My Vessel Is
Stopped

No (Negative)

Man Overboard

All Persons to
Report on Board

I Request Free
Pratique

No Meaning

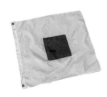

My Engines Are Going
Full Speed Astern

You Are Running
Into Danger

I Require
Assistance

I Require Medical
Assistance

Stop Carrying Out
Your Intentions

I Require a Tug

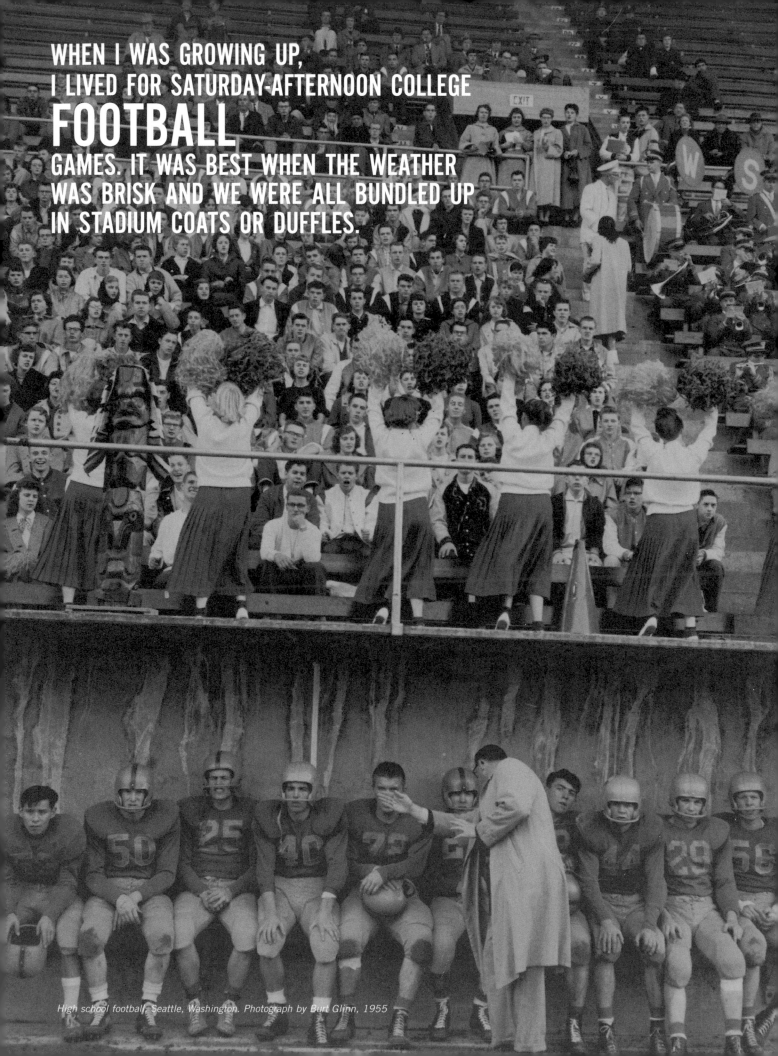

WHEN I WAS GROWING UP,
I LIVED FOR SATURDAY-AFTERNOON COLLEGE
FOOTBALL
GAMES. IT WAS BEST WHEN THE WEATHER
WAS BRISK AND WE WERE ALL BUNDLED UP
IN STADIUM COATS OR DUFFLES.

High school football, Seattle, Washington. Photograph by Burt Glinn, 1955

Post-game embrace. Photograph by Burt Glinn, 1955

Michigan Wolverines North Carolina (Chapel Hill) Tar Heels Akron Zips Montana Grizzlies Kentucky Wildcats Florida Gators Pennsylvania State Nittany Lions Nebraska Cornhuskers Tennessee State Tigers University of Tennessee Volunteers Minnesota Golden Gophers Hawaii Rainbow Warriors University of Wisconsin Badgers Auburn Tigers University of Arkansas Razorbacks Georgia Bulldogs Purdue Boilermakers Virginia Tech Gobblers Duke Blue Devils Kansas State Wildcats University of Connecticut Huskies North Texas Mean Green Virginia Cavaliers Arizona Wildcats Arizona State Sun Devils Texas Christian Horned Frogs Cincinnati Bearcats South Carolina Fighting Gamecocks Clemson Tigers Maryland Terrapins Kent State Golden Flashes Georgia Tech Yellow Jackets Mississippi State Bulldogs North Carolina State Wolfpack New Mexico Lobos Oklahoma State Cowboys Mississippi Ole Miss Rebels Pittsburgh Panthers Boston College Eagles

What most distinguishes team logos and mascots is the strong, solid typography, a venerated component in American athletic clothing.

Cleveland Brown Jim Brown. Photograph by Robert Riger, 1958 (courtesy of James Danziger Gallery)

Green Bay Packer Forrest Gregg. Photograph by Robert Riger, 1960 (courtesy of James Danziger Gallery)

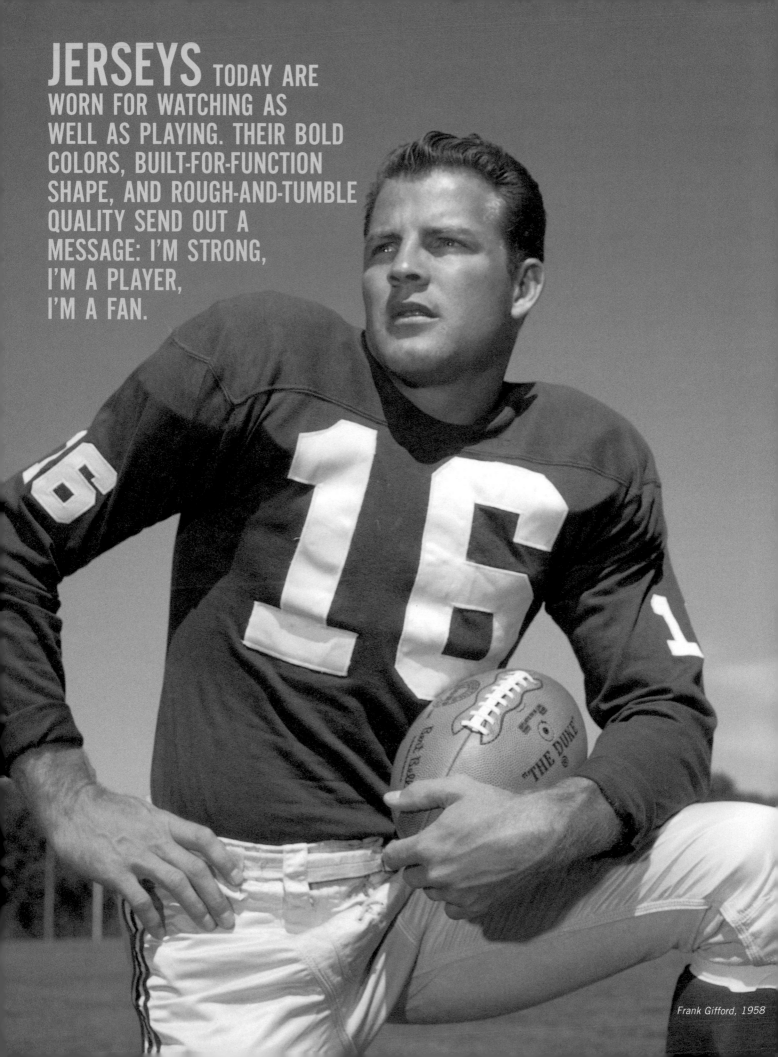

JERSEYS TODAY ARE WORN FOR WATCHING AS WELL AS PLAYING. THEIR BOLD COLORS, BUILT-FOR-FUNCTION SHAPE, AND ROUGH-AND-TUMBLE QUALITY SEND OUT A MESSAGE: I'M STRONG, I'M A PLAYER, I'M A FAN.

Frank Gifford, 1958

Mick Jagger, 1981

The Jerseys: American Style

HOCKEY

Oversized (to fit over padding)
V-neck
Contrast-colored yokes
Team number on the back
Embroidered team name and logo
on the front
Quick-drying nylon
Square hem

FOOTBALL

Perforated cotton or nylon
High V-neck (formerly crew necks)
Stripes on the sleeve
Player number on the back
Team name on the front
Square hem

BASKETBALL

Sleeveless (to allow maximum
shoulder movement)
Double rows of piping
Team name on the front
Player name and number
on the back
Baggy shorts (thanks to
Michael Jordan)
Side-vented hem

BASEBALL

Pajama-type front
Ribbing or piping
Collarless
Pin stripes
Baseball cap
Stockings
Short, wide sleeves
Rounded shirttails

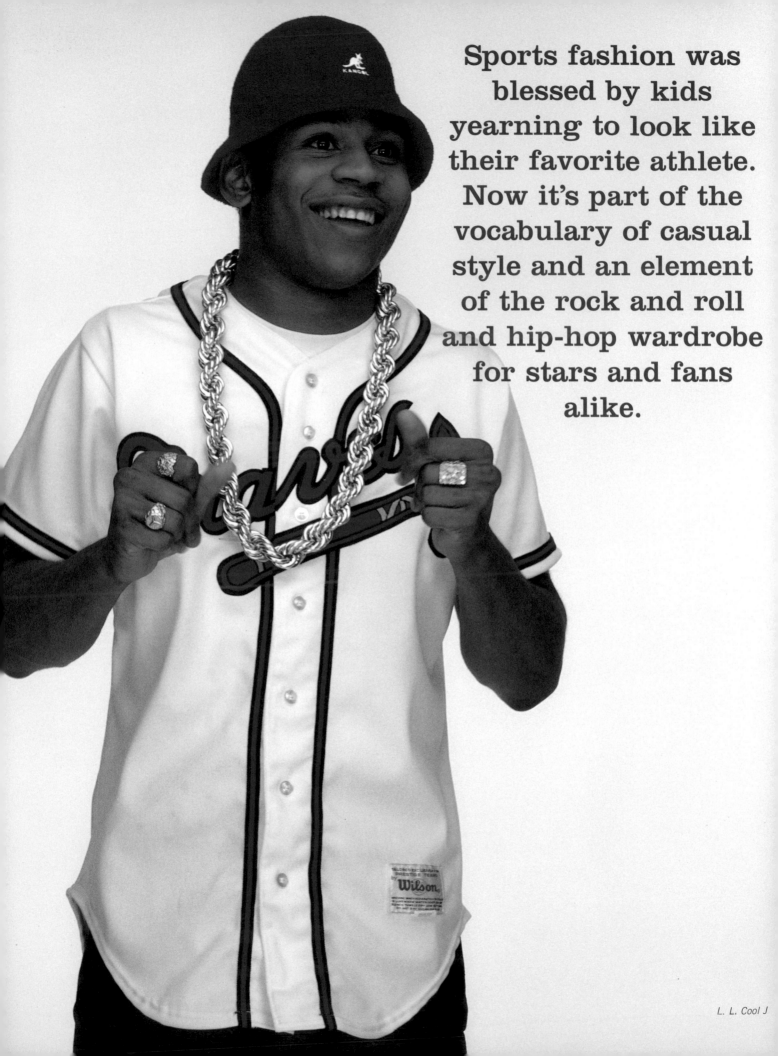

Sports fashion was blessed by kids yearning to look like their favorite athlete. Now it's part of the vocabulary of casual style and an element of the rock and roll and hip-hop wardrobe for stars and fans alike.

L. L. Cool J

MICKEY SHIRT

In 1991 a privately owned flannel jersey that was originally worn by Mickey Mantle was put up for auction at $50,000; it sold for $71,500.

New York Yankee Mickey Mantle, 1955

GOLFERS ARE AS CONCERNED WITH WHAT THEY WEAR AS WITH THEIR GAME. IF THEY CAN'T PLAY, AT LEAST THEY MUST LOOK GOOD.

GOLF SHIRTS

ARE VERY CLASSIC, BUT THEY ALSO DECLARE, "LOOK AT ME, I'M A LITTLE BIT MORE COLORFUL THAN THE OTHER GOLFERS." A GOLF COURSE IS THE ONLY PLACE WHERE A PINK SWEATER WITH PLAID PANTS DOES NOT GET A SECOND LOOK.

SLEEVE
Hemmed, not banded, to allow maximum freedom while swinging.

Fifties golf shirt with specialized tee pocket. Photograph by Bill Steele

BUTTON LOOP
Rarely used, it
provides a clean line
between the collar
and placket.

LOOPS
Hold golf tees in place.

POCKET
Holds scorecards;
button keeps them from
falling out when
bending over.

SIDE VENT
Allows for twisting
motion when swinging
woods and irons.

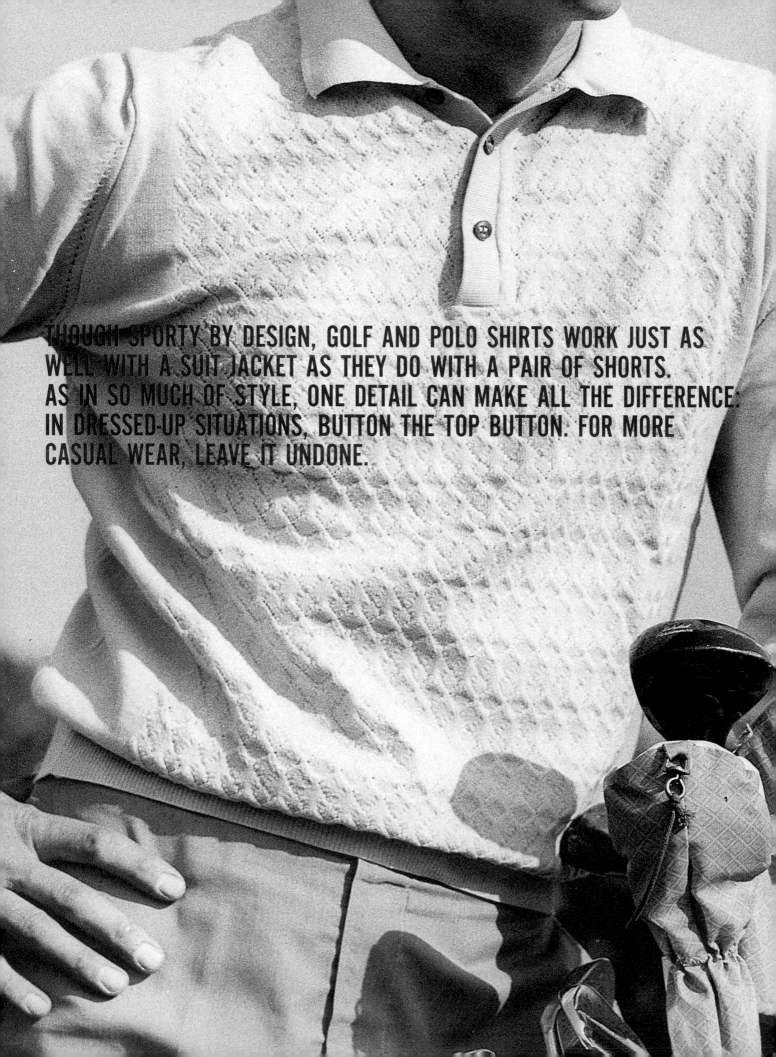

THOUGH SPORTY BY DESIGN, GOLF AND POLO SHIRTS WORK JUST AS WELL WITH A SUIT JACKET AS THEY DO WITH A PAIR OF SHORTS. AS IN SO MUCH OF STYLE, ONE DETAIL CAN MAKE ALL THE DIFFERENCE: IN DRESSED-UP SITUATIONS, BUTTON THE TOP BUTTON. FOR MORE CASUAL WEAR, LEAVE IT UNDONE.

LOGO HALL OF FAME

Choose your badges of honor

Lacoste—Crocodile

Munsingwear—Penguin

Brooks Brothers—Golden fleece

Tommy Hilfiger—Crest

Ralph Lauren—Polo player

Ashworth—Golfer

Greg Norman—Shark

Nautica—Sailboat

Sahara—Camel

Slazenger—Panther

Cobra—Snake

Pine Valley Golf Club—Shield

Augusta National—U.S. map

Merion Golf Club—Wicker basket

Quaker Ridge—Quaker

Kapalua Resort—Butterfly

Ko-Olina Resort—Ladybug

THE GOOD-SPORT SHIRT

The original shirt that polo players wore was a lightweight, long-sleeve woolen jersey. The difference between today's short-sleeve polo shirt (derived from tennis shirts of the early 1900s) and a golf shirt is simple. The polo has a banded sleeve hem, which hugs the arm, while the golf shirt has a loose sleeve, a slightly fuller cut, and a pocket.

WHEN I WAS GROWING UP, TENNIS CLOTHES COULD BE SUMMED UP IN TWO WORDS: WHITE AND TIGHT.

At Your Service

In the beginning, tennis players wore jerseys with knickers. During the first U.S. nationals in 1881, men wore white flannel pants. Nearer the end of the century, they adopted single-breasted jackets and white or blue striped flannel trousers, as well as rubber-soled canvas shoes. In 1926, René Lacoste, known as "le Crocodile," scandalized the tennis world by wearing a short-sleeved knit tennis shirt (looking very much like today's polos) at the 1926 Davis Cup championship. It had a long tail in the back, which ensured that the shirt would stay tucked in when serving or going for a lob. The first person to wear tennis shorts during competition was H. W. "Bunny" Austin in 1932 at Forest Hills. After World War II, tennis clothes consisted of white cotton shorts and tennis shirts and sweaters. Today, tennis attire has stepped away from traditional whites to splashy colors on high-tech fabrics, while classic whites remain a staple of the preppy wardrobe.

René Lacoste

TENNIS DRESS

The tennis sweater originally had stripes in order to distinguish between members of different tennis clubs or university teams. (The tennis sweater was derived from cricket, another sport traditionally played in white clothing and with team or school colors on the neck and cuffs.) In the twenties, Broadway plays frequently featured a young leading man who would burst onto stage wearing a striped V-neck sweater, saying "Tennis, anyone?" but it was the dandy Prince of Wales, later Edward VIII, who popularized tennis sweaters off the courts.

Tennis star Bill Tilden in the forties

DURING GRAND PRIX SEASON, I WOULD GO TO WATKINS GLEN TO WATCH THE

RACING.

ALL THE DRIVERS LOOKED HEROIC IN THEIR UNIFORMS—COVERED IN PATCHES AND WITH THEIR CARS EMBLAZONED WITH LOGOS. EVEN THE PIT CREW LOOKED SHARP. ONCE, AFTER A RACE, I WENT INTO THE PIT AND BOUGHT A CREW MEMBER'S UNIFORM RIGHT OFF HIS BACK. I PUT IT ON IMMEDIATELY. IT WAS STILL DAMP WITH MOTOR OIL AND HIS PERSPIRATION— I WOULDN'T HAVE EVEN CONSIDERED WASHING IT . . . IT WAS THE BEST $20 I EVER SPENT.

Leather motocross pants. Photograph by Bill Steele

The bold colors, shapes, and graphics of racing gear have left the track and become part of our street style. The wearer's message is the most powerful brew of function, fashion, and speed.

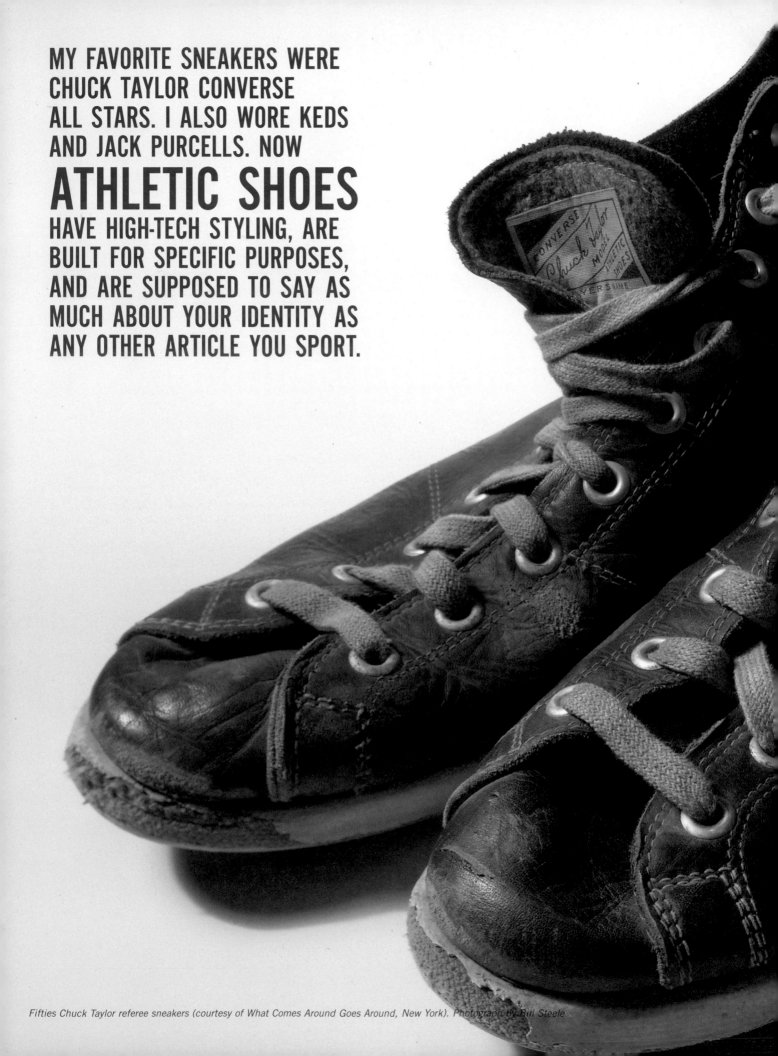

MY FAVORITE SNEAKERS WERE CHUCK TAYLOR CONVERSE ALL STARS. I ALSO WORE KEDS AND JACK PURCELLS. NOW **ATHLETIC SHOES** HAVE HIGH-TECH STYLING, ARE BUILT FOR SPECIFIC PURPOSES, AND ARE SUPPOSED TO SAY AS MUCH ABOUT YOUR IDENTITY AS ANY OTHER ARTICLE YOU SPORT.

Fifties Chuck Taylor referee sneakers (courtesy of What Comes Around Goes Around, New York). Photograph by Bill Steele

MAGIC FEET

In the collection of the Basketball Hall of Fame,
Springfield, Massachusetts

Forties Converse All Stars

Wilt Chamberlain's size 15 Converse (worn 1971–72)

Magic Johnson's size 15 Converse (worn 1985–86)

Larry Bird's size 14 Converse (worn 1985–86)

Isiah Thomas's size 12 1/2 Asics (worn 1993–94)

Michael Jordan's size 13 Nikes (worn 1995–96)

Scottie Pippen's size 16 Nikes (worn 1995–96)

Charles Barkley's size 16 Nikes (worn 1995–96)

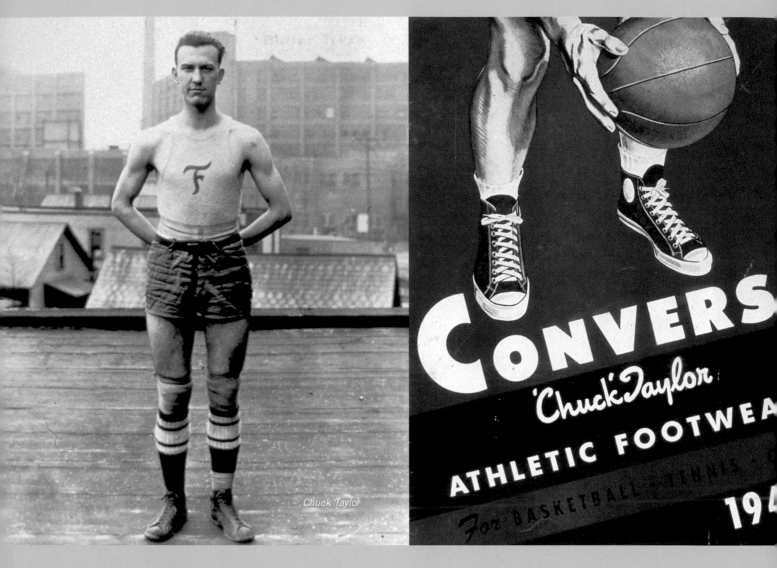

Chuck Taylor

CONVERS

'Chuck'Taylor

ATHLETIC FOOTWEA

For BASKETBALL TENNIS

194

ALL-TIME BEST   Adidas Finalist Adidas Formula 1 Adidas Nite Jogger Adidas Stan Smith Adidas Super Star
Converse All Star Converse Chris Evert Etonic Street Fighter Fila Grant Hills New Balance 320 Nike Air Jordans Nike
Elite Nike Huarache Nike LD-100 Nike Pippens Pro-Keds Royal Puma Easy Rider Reebok Aerobic Reebok DMX

SNEAKERS 101

How to shop for athletic shoes

Take your old ones in with you and tell the salesman what you like and don't like about them. Wear the socks you'll actually be wearing with them. Describe to the salesman the activities you'll be pursuing in the shoes. Make sure that the shoe feels good from the moment you put it on. Check that there is adequate room in the toe box, that the shoe does not pinch your arch, and that your ankle feels well supported. Stand up, walk around, jump around. Shop late; feet swell up during the day.

How to care for athletic shoes

While most people routinely throw canvas sneakers into the washing machine, this is not recommended. It is far better to stuff them with paper or cloth so they maintain their shape, handwash them with a mild detergent (adding bleach for whites) and a soft brush, rinse, and restuff the shoes and allow them to air-dry. You can also buy commercial shoe shampoos, available from such manufacturers as Kiwi. For leather shoes, there are a multitude of cleaners, conditioners, and polishes, but since many of today's sports shoes are made of multiple fabrics and colors, the best solution is to have them professionally cleaned.

Michael Jordan, 1997

CATCHERS ALWAYS WORE THEIR
BASEBALL CAPS
BACKWARDS, BUT I DON'T THINK
THAT'S WHY KIDS STARTED
DOING IT. I THINK IT WAS BOTH
PRACTICAL AND STYLISH.
IF THEY WERE PLAYING
BASKETBALL, IT HELPED
THEM SEE THE HOOP;
IF THEY WERE OUT WITH
GIRLS, IT MADE THEIR
FACES EASIER TO SEE,
BUT I THINK MAINLY IT'S
BECAUSE THEY WANTED TO
LOOK IRREVERENT, LIKE
THEY DIDN'T PLAY BY
THE RULES.

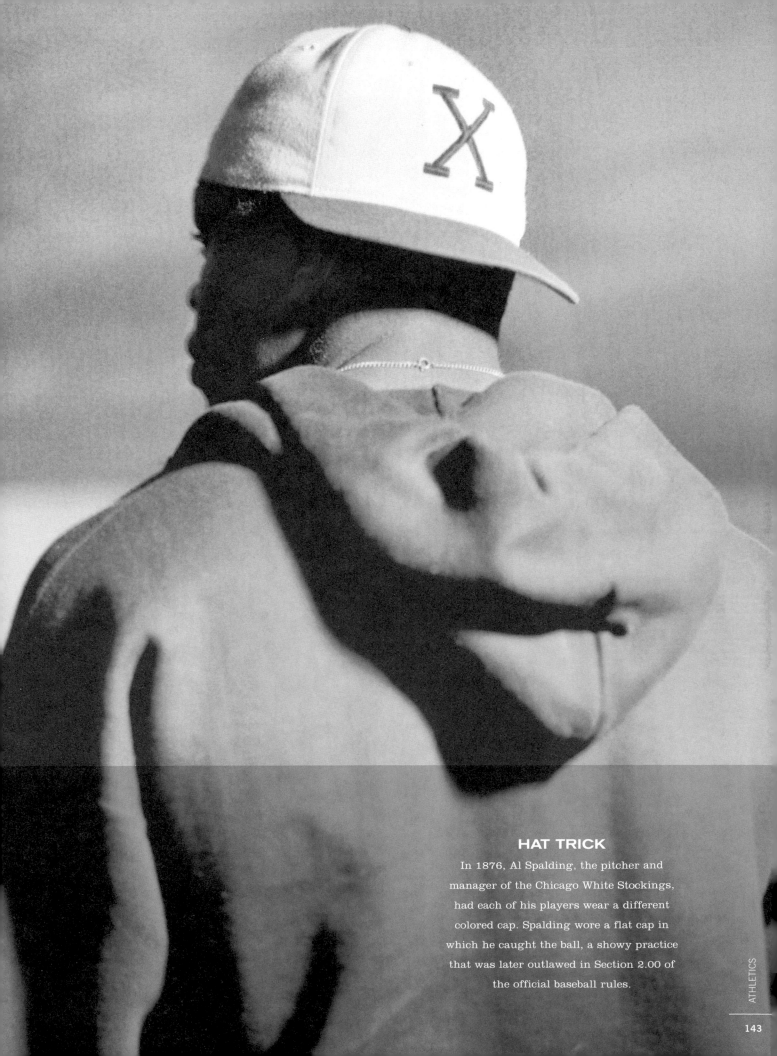

HAT TRICK

In 1876, Al Spalding, the pitcher and manager of the Chicago White Stockings, had each of his players wear a different colored cap. Spalding wore a flat cap in which he caught the ball, a showy practice that was later outlawed in Section 2.00 of the official baseball rules.

SKIING

IS EXHILARATING. YOU GET SPEED, ACTION, VIBRANCY, AND FRESH COLD AIR ALL DAY. APRÈS-SKI IS ANOTHER THING ALTOGETHER: PART RELAXING, PART WARMING UP, AND PART WORKING ON YOUR MOVES.

SKIWEAR STAPLES

Clothes we were inclined to wear

Stocking caps

Puffy parkas

Dmitri sweaters

   (as worn by Spyder Sabitch)

Reindeer sweaters

Snowflake-pattern sweaters

Spider-brand ski sweaters

   (with padding on the

     shoulders and arms)

Turtlenecks

Racing-stripe sweaters

Snowboarding shorts

Long johns

Wool ski pants

Topping It Off

In the beginning, ski caps served one purpose: to keep your head and ears warm. Ever since skiing became a popular middle-class sport in the U.S., the ski cap has shifted sizes and shapes from long stocking (now made in polar fleece) to pompomed wool (like the one Michael Nesmith wore in every episode of The Monkees), to the standard blunt-top watch cap, which began as a nighttime warmer-upper for seamen and became a favorite among rappers and slackers alike.

Above: Michael Nesmith of the Monkees

Peter Fonda in Easy Rider, *1969*

SOUND+VISION

I see everything through the pop-culture lens.

It all started innocently enough, with Disney movies, family TV shows like Dennis the Menace and My Three Sons. I liked watching westerns and sports as well as suspense shows like The Twilight Zone—Rod Serling always looked so perfectly put together. I was very impressed with Sean Connery in the early James Bond films, and the clothes in THE SOUND OF MUSIC have been an inspiration for my winter collections. But when the Beatles arrived, they changed my life. I wanted to grow my hair long and to be in a band. I saw A HARD DAY'S NIGHT and was forever captivated.

English rock has influenced me totally. It's something I grew up with—I think I was the first kid to discover it in my high school—and it has been with me ever since. By the mid-sixties, I was getting into a real mod headset; all the rock and roll bands were my influence and I wanted to look like them. The more showy they were, the more interesting they were to me. I wasn't into looking at bands in jeans and T-shirts; even if I liked their music, there was a lack of appeal. I liked a band with an eclectic look, like the Stones: Mick had his unique sexiness; Brian Jones was wearing smocks and frocks; Charlie Watts was always crisply tailored. Even the Beatles, though they dressed

alike, had their signature items: John Lennon's Greek fisherman's cap, Ringo's rings. I went for the dandy look of the Kinks. And I worshiped the Who, Blind Faith, and Traffic; they were much more irreverent than the American groups.

It took a while, but by the late sixties American rock groups started showing signs of style. Jefferson Airplane and the Doors looked and sounded fantastic. Musicians were beginning to embrace fashion in a way they never had before. Hendrix was an innovator. Still, the British bands were continually breaking new ground. I found Deep Purple, the Small Faces, Spooky Tooth, and Jethro Tull inspired me. Rod Stewart took things to a higher level. The Who were operatic, and Led Zeppelin, as they sang, paved a stairway to heaven. But then Bowie and T-Rex came along and the whole look changed. Androgyny was in; glitter rocked. By that time I had moved to New York and was going to shops like Jumpin' Jack Flash, Granny Takes a Trip, and Limbo, which were the places to go for real serious rock and roll clothes. I was wearing snakeskin high-heeled platforms, velvet bell bottoms that were low-cut, very tight at the hips, and flared out at the bottom. I wore midriff tops so you could see my stomach. One of my tops had a star on it; I wore another that was ribbed, together with a jacket that had round lapels, just like Rod Stewart used to wear.

A few years later, when punk started happening in the underground, I got a spiky haircut and got into the Ramones, the Police, the Cars, and the whole new-wave scene. But I didn't love that as much as I loved the Studio 54 disco era. And then I started hearing rap: music and poetry, filled with pride and anger and adventure. Like the Motown artists, like Jimi Hendrix, like the outrageous funk bands of the seventies. The sense of style that rappers exhibited was terrific. It was, and is, a combination of designer goods and athletic clothes that were functional and accessible, and that transformed street kids into sporty superheroes—Run DMC and their Adidas, the Beastie Boys wearing Volkswagen hood ornaments as medallions, and then all the rappers wearing designer and sports logos, from Louis Vuitton to Nike.

Today, American music and arts are one big glorious mix of iconography. Everybody borrows from one another, and everybody wants to get in on the act. It's easy to see why rappers and kids like to dress like sports heroes, and why sports stars like to make movies and records and design their own clothes. Pop culture feeds on change. These are some of the moments I've been through, the styles that now seem classic and that continue to inform me.

WHEN ROCK AND ROLL

BEGAN, LEGENDS LIKE JOHN LEE HOOKER, CHUCK BERRY, BO DIDDLEY, AND B. B. KING DRESSED TO KILL. THE R&B STARS WANTED SHINE, SEQUINS, GLAM; THEY WANTED POINTY-TOED SHOES. JUST PICTURE LITTLE RICHARD IN THE SEQUINED SUITS; THAT WAS FASHION WAY BEFORE GLAM CAME ON THE SCENE.

Chuck Berry

Bo Diddley

B. B. King

John Lee Hooker

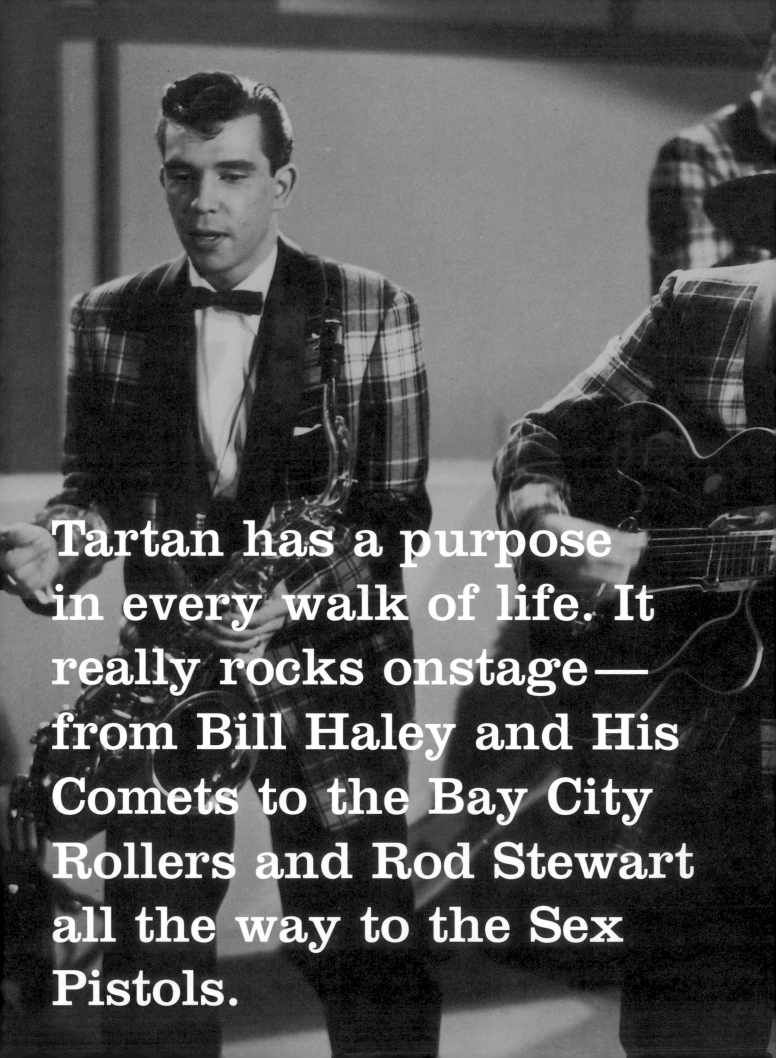

Tartan has a purpose in every walk of life. It really rocks onstage—from Bill Haley and His Comets to the Bay City Rollers and Rod Stewart all the way to the Sex Pistols.

Bill Haley and His Comets

Chubby Checker

James Brown

SO MUCH OF ROCK STYLE AS A CONCEPT COMES FROM MOTOWN. EACH ARTIST HAD A SLEEK SIGNATURE SOUND AND AN IMAGE POLISHED TO A HIGH GLOSS. IN ITS GLORY DAYS, THE MOTOWN LOOK WAS SUITABLE FOR ROUNDS ON THE GOLF COURSE, COUNTRY-CLUB DANCING, AND NIGHTS AT THE COPA—ALL PARTY DRESSES AND SHARP SUITS.

Stevie Wonder

Temptations

Smokey Robinson and the Miracles

THE MOTOWN SOUND

They looked as good as they sang

The Supremes

Smokey Robinson and the Miracles

The Temptations

Stevie Wonder

The Four Tops

Marvin Gaye

Martha and the Vandellas

Mary Wells

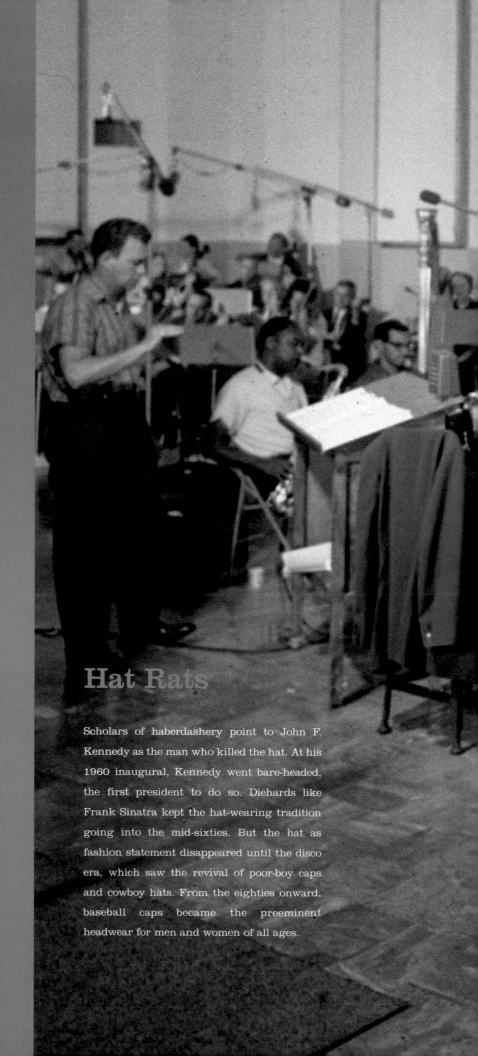

THE RAT PACK
GAVE ELEGANCE
A NEW DEFINITION:
SHINY SHARKSKIN
SUITS,
SKINNY LAPELS,
THIN TIES, SLIM
PANTS, AND THE
KIND OF HATS MEN
WOULD WEAR TO
THE RACETRACK.

Hat Rats

Scholars of haberdashery point to John F. Kennedy as the man who killed the hat. At his 1960 inaugural, Kennedy went bare-headed, the first president to do so. Diehards like Frank Sinatra kept the hat-wearing tradition going into the mid-sixties. But the hat as fashion statement disappeared until the disco era, which saw the revival of poor-boy caps and cowboy hats. From the eighties onward, baseball caps became the preeminent headwear for men and women of all ages.

Sammy Davis, Jr.

SHARP DRESSERS

You could do worse than to look like them

Cast of The Man From Uncle

Cast of Mission Impossible

Cast of Reservoir Dogs

Sammy Davis, Jr.

Sean Connery

Dean Martin

Frank Sinatra

Peter Lawford

Fred Astaire

Rod Serling

Jerry Lewis

Tom Jones

Serling

Sean Connery in Thunderball, 1965

Reservoir Dogs. 1992

SOUND-VISION

THE BEATLES AND THE ROLLING STONES WERE AT THE FOREFRONT OF THE MOD REVOLUTION. BOTH GROUPS REDEFINED WHAT MEN COULD WEAR AND CREATE A KALEIDOSCOPIC ROCK STYLE THROUGH THEIR ROCK STARDOM.

The Beatles

Dressed to Thrill
Fashion trends popularized by the Fab Four

Mop-top haircuts (a long variation of the Caesar)

Big smiles

Collarless jackets

Jackets without lapels

Beatle boots (also known as Chelsea boots)

Greek fisherman's caps (John Lennon)

Flashy rings (Ringo Starr)

Suede jackets (RUBBER SOUL era)

Band uniforms and mustaches (SGT. PEPPER'S)

Wire-rim glasses (John and Yoko Ono)

Beards (LET IT BE)

Rolling Stones

Dressed to Kill
Stones style

Shaggy hair and Prince Valiant cuts

Big lips

Tight jeans

Turtlenecks and tab-collar shirts

Velvet jackets

Edwardian shirts

Pin-stripe suits and polka dots (Brian Jones)

Skull rings (Keith Richards)

Army uniforms

Capezios

Long scarves

Funky corduroys

Paisleys and foulards

Jumpsuits

Athletic wear

They seek him here, they seek him there,
His clothes are loud, but never square.
It will make or break him so he's got to buy the best,
'Cos he's a dedicated follower of fashion. . . .
And when he does his little rounds
'Round the boutiques of London Town,
Eagerly pursuing all the latest fads and trends,
'Cause he's a dedicated follower of fashion.

—*The Kinks, "Dedicated Follower of Fashion," 1966*

The Temptations

Prince

Paul Revere and the Raiders

The Ruffled Shirt

WHO

Ray Davies, Paul Revere and the Raiders, Beau Brummel, Albert Finney (as Tom Jones), Tom Jones (as Tom Jones), Prince.

WHAT

A shirt so formal it requires only a bow tie, now frequently worn without for a decadent rock and roll look. Comes with wing or straight collar, buttons or buttonholes for studs, French cuffs. Worn underneath a jacket, the shirt fronts command center stage whether they are decorated with plain cotton bibs, vertical pleats, flattened horizontal loops, or fanciful ruffles.

WHEN

After noon at a formal wedding, after six at a black-tie event, after hours at a club (ditch the tie and undo a few buttons).

WHERE

In a Vegas lounge, in a rock video, at a party, at the altar.

HOW

Tucked into leather pants, hanging out with jeans, under a black jacket, with a tux.

WHY

To conform to formality, to confound normality.

IN 1974, WHEN MY **HAIR** WAS AT ITS LONGEST EVER, I WENT TO THE PAUL MCGREGOR SALON ON ST. MARKS PLACE, WHICH IS NOW A CLUB CALLED CONEY ISLAND HIGH. IT WAS A ROCK AND ROLL HAIR FACTORY. EVERYBODY WOULD WALK IN WITH REALLY LONG HAIR AND WALK OUT WITH A COIF. I GOT A SHAG AND IT WAS LITERALLY STANDING UP ON TOP.

David Cassidy

THE HAIR KING

When Elvis dyed his hair
blue-black and slicked it down with Royal
Crown pomade, TIME magazine called it "five
inches of buttered yak wool." It was reduced to
a flattop on March 25, 1958, when he joined the
military, and did not regain its theatrical
magnificence until the late sixties when the
King made a TV special in which he appeared in
black leather and rakish sideburns.

HAIRCUTS WE REMEMBER

Robert De Niro's mohawk in TAXI DRIVER

David Bowie's Ziggy cut

Mick Jagger in PERFORMANCE

Dirk Bogarde in VICTIM, and blond in MODESTY BLAISE

Johnny Rotten's punk cut

Brad Pitt's vertical 'do in JOHNNY SUEDE

Ed "Kookie" Byrnes on 77 Sunset Strip

Troy Donoghue in PARRISH

Michael Jackson's Jheri curls
      (inspired by Little Richard)

James Brown's pompadour

Tina Turner's PRIVATE DANCER fright wig

Diana Ross's recent extensions

Any Elvis Presley hairstyle

Roger Daltrey's TOMMY mane

Shaun Cassidy's feathered shag

Marc Bolan's ringlets

A Flock of Seagulls

New-wave wedge

Big hair

George Clooney's Caesar

David Lee Roth's shifting hairline
      (a movable feast)

Rod Stewart's Maggie Mae

Jimi Hendrix's Afro

Joey Ramone's bangs

Jethro Tull's (Ian Anderson) thick-as-a-brick mane

Bob Marley's dreads

Janis Joplin's frizz

Keanu Reeves's SPEED buzz cut

Ricky Nelson's waterfall

Yul Brynner's chrome dome

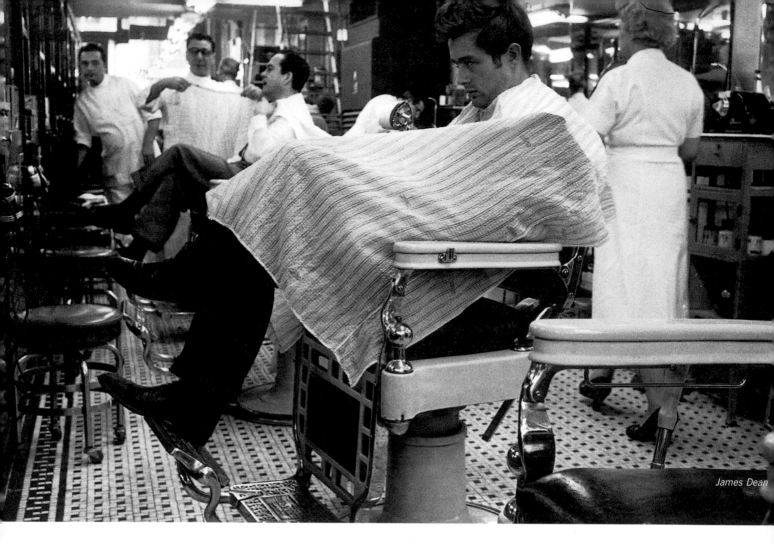

James Dean

Barbershop specials: Crew cut Flattop Brush cut Short back and sides Businessman's cut Cue ball Box and fade Mop top Pudding bowl Prince Valiant Rave mop Pompadour Military buzz Dork knob (smallish ponytail) Ponytail Braid Mohawk Mohican Center-part Suedehead Afro Jheri curl Cornrows Ducktail D.A. Dreadlocks Caesar Shag Rooster cut Spike

Little Richard *Twiggy* *David Crosby* *Sly Stone*

After the Beatles, long hair made you cool. It could be straight, curly, a big Afro, as long as it was long.

When I was in high school, facial hair was absolutely outlawed. In the fifties and sixties, only beatniks, radicals, and Uncle Sam wore goatees.

Thelonious Monk

Don Sullivan in The Rebel Set, *1959*

Malcolm X

WHILE THE BRITISH INVASION WAS TAKING HOLD, THE CALIFORNIA **SURF SCENE** EMERGED AS A TRULY AMERICAN PHENOMENON, WITH ITS OWN LANGUAGE IN MUSIC AND FASHION. TO ME THIS WAS EXOTIC AND HOMEGROWN AT THE SAME TIME.

Jan and Dean

Surfin' Safaris

The Beach Boys—brothers Carl, Dennis, and Brian Wilson—began playing in high school with their cousin Mike Love and school friend Alan Jardine. In the beginning they were known as the Pendletons, a name they took from their favorite plaid shirts. Later they adopted striped T-shirts and surfer shirts (solid-colored, short-sleeved shirts with white piping around the neck and placket), the predominant style of the surfin' sixties. Despite their name, only one Beach Boy, Dennis, was a serious surfer; tragically, he drowned in 1983 and was buried at sea.

THE OLD-WAVE SURF BANDS: Jan and Dean Dave Myers and the Surftones The Bel-Airs The Rumblers The Chantays The Pyramids The Surfaris The Rhythm Rockers Jim Waller and the Deltas The Lively Ones The Surf Stompers The Impacts The Challengers The Astronauts The Ventures The Impacts The Crossfires (later became the Turtles) The Tornadoes Bob Vaught and the Renegades The Vulcanes Eddie and the Snowmen

Surf Life

Phil Edwards, Wind & Sea, Hang Ten, Greg Noll, and Bing surfboards

Pontiac GTOs, woody station wagons, Ford Mustangs

Fender guitars and amps—Leo Fender, a manufacturer from Fullerton, California, provided and sponsored many local musicians with equipment and consequently became responsible for the popular surf sound

Made-in-Hawaii Hawaiian shirts

Katin Jams and Bermuda shorts in copper brown, light blue, turquoise, red, usually with floral designs and piping

Hang Ten shirts—broad-striped T-shirts with embroidered feet logos

Revell model kits—created by hot-rod artist Ed "Big Daddy" Roth, these cartoonish car kits included the Weird-Ohs, Rat-Fink, and Freaky-Rider series

Coppertone suntan lotion

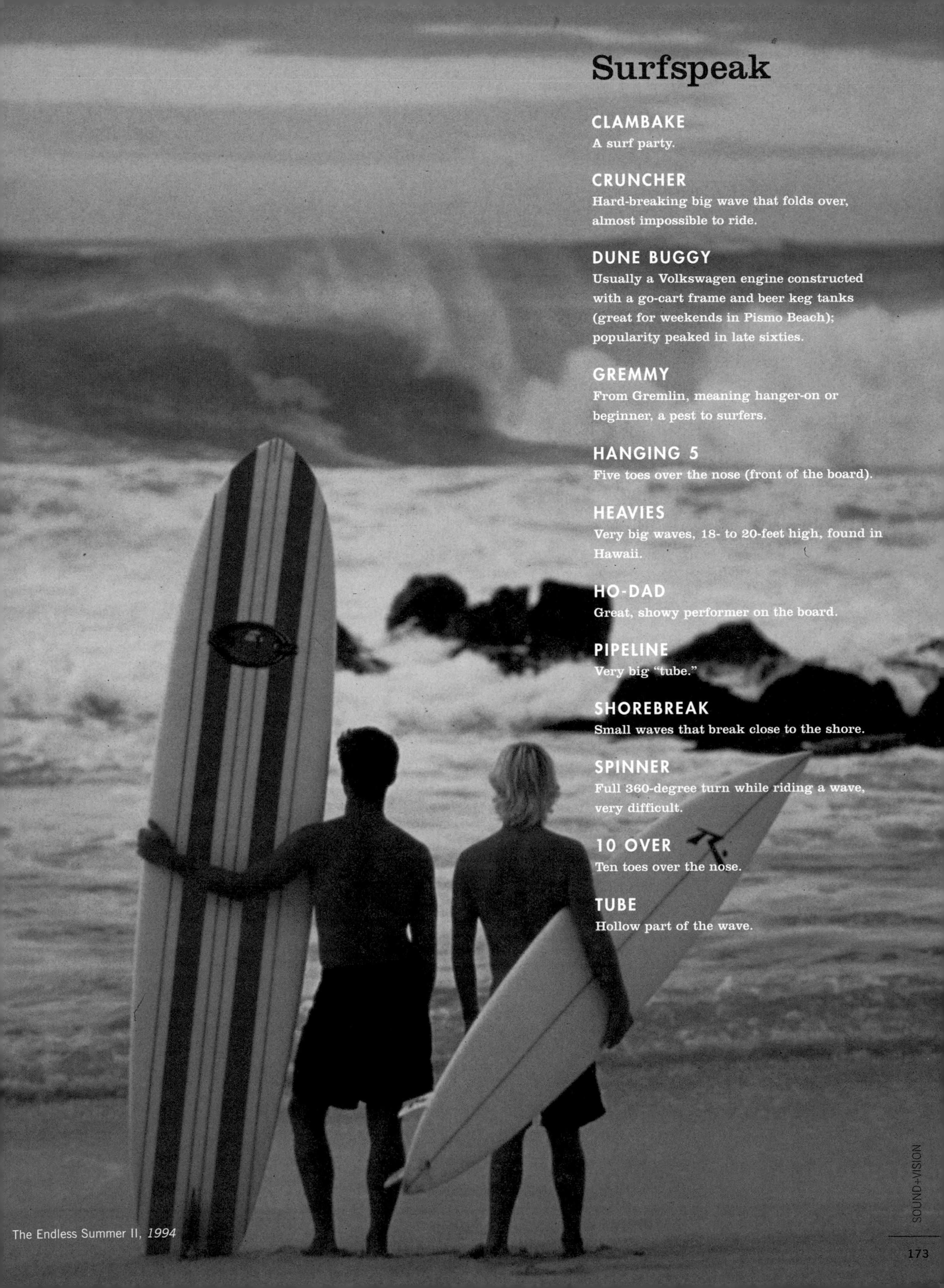

Surfspeak

CLAMBAKE
A surf party.

CRUNCHER
Hard-breaking big wave that folds over, almost impossible to ride.

DUNE BUGGY
Usually a Volkswagen engine constructed with a go-cart frame and beer keg tanks (great for weekends in Pismo Beach); popularity peaked in late sixties.

GREMMY
From Gremlin, meaning hanger-on or beginner, a pest to surfers.

HANGING 5
Five toes over the nose (front of the board).

HEAVIES
Very big waves, 18- to 20-feet high, found in Hawaii.

HO-DAD
Great, showy performer on the board.

PIPELINE
Very big "tube."

SHOREBREAK
Small waves that break close to the shore.

SPINNER
Full 360-degree turn while riding a wave, very difficult.

10 OVER
Ten toes over the nose.

TUBE
Hollow part of the wave.

The Endless Summer II, *1994*

IN THE SIXTIES, THE **PREPPY** LOOK WAS EVERYWHERE—MY THREE SONS HAD IT; SO DID DUSTIN HOFFMAN IN *THE GRADUATE*. IT WAS A REFINED, EDUCATED LOOK, THE LOOK OF OLD MONEY, AND YET IT WAS COMFORTABLE. EVEN TODAY, IT'S FOR THE PERSON WHO REALLY DOESN'T HAVE TO WEAR ANYTHING FASHIONABLE OR SHOWY TO BE SMART. IT WORKS IN EVERY CORNER OF THE WORLD, BUT WE'VE TURNED IT INTO AN AMERICAN CLASSIC.

Robert Redford

Three Sons TV show

Dick Van Dyke and Mary Tyler Moore

Dustin Hoffman in The Graduate, 1967

WOODSTOCK

WAS THE SECOND CIVIL WAR, A WAR BETWEEN THE ESTABLISHMENT AND THE COUNTERCULTURE. IT WAS REALLY THE UNVEILING OF A NEW, FREE WORLD: ALL OF THESE REVOLUTIONARY INDIVIDUAL FASHION STATEMENTS TOGETHER IN ONE PLACE AT ONE TIME. I WISH I COULD'VE BEEN THERE.

WOODSTOCK MUSIC and ART FAIR
SUNDAY
AUGUST 17, 1969
10:00 A. M.
Good For One Admission Only
$7.00
M 02950
NO REFUNDS   GLOBE TICKET COMPANY

Eddie Floyd

'57 vintage Strat

Eric Clapton

Buddy Guy

Bonnie Raitt

Jeff Beck

Yngwie Malmsteen

Richie Sambora

The Fender Stratocaster

Rock's shapeliest accessory

In 1954, the Fender Guitar Company of Fullerton, California, created the first Stratocaster. It was designed by Leo Fender, Freddie Tavares, and Bill Curson to fill a growing demand for an easy-to-play guitar, one that allowed for a freer range of movement onstage than the earlier, boxy electric guitars. The Stratocaster's biggest advantage was its body—shaved in back to contour to the player's body, with well-balanced "twin horns," and good neck-to-body ratio. It was also the first electric guitar to have three pickups, a tone-control switch, and a tremolo, or vibrato, bar. The original Stratocaster was dark sunburst, off-white, or blond with a maple neck (future versions had a neck of rosewood). Since its creation, it has been the most popular electric guitar ever made. Eric Clapton has said, "It's about as close to perfect as a guitar can be."

STARS WHO SWEAR (OR SWORE)
BY THE STRATOCASTER

Buddy Holly and the Crickets

Dick Dale and the Deltones

Gene Vincent and the Blue Caps

The Beach Boys

Bill Haley and His Comets

Ritchie Valens

George Harrison

Keith Richards

Jimi Hendrix

Ry Cooder

Stevie Ray Vaughan

Ritchie Blackmore

Albert Lee

Robert Cray

Richie Sambora

Jeff Beck

Eric Clapton

Bonnie Raitt

Mark Knopfler

Nile Rodgers

Jeff Lynne

Steve Miller

Dweezil Zappa

Jimi Hendrix

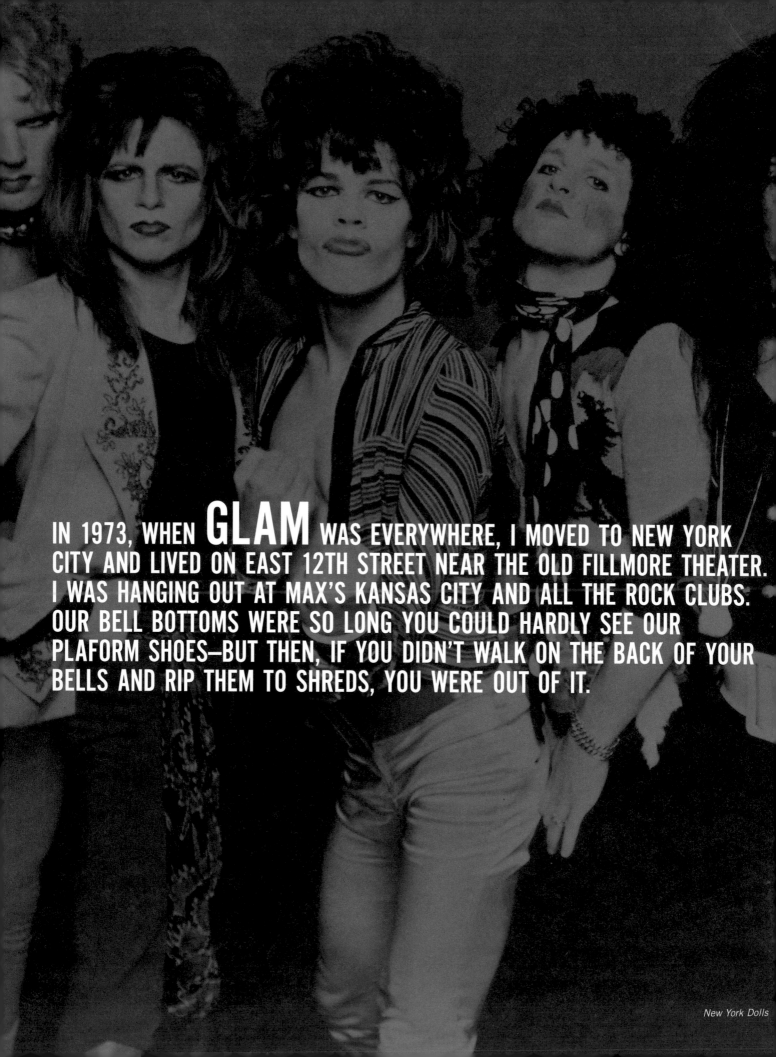

IN 1973, WHEN **GLAM** WAS EVERYWHERE, I MOVED TO NEW YORK CITY AND LIVED ON EAST 12TH STREET NEAR THE OLD FILLMORE THEATER. I WAS HANGING OUT AT MAX'S KANSAS CITY AND ALL THE ROCK CLUBS. OUR BELL BOTTOMS WERE SO LONG YOU COULD HARDLY SEE OUR PLAFORM SHOES—BUT THEN, IF YOU DIDN'T WALK ON THE BACK OF YOUR BELLS AND RIP THEM TO SHREDS, YOU WERE OUT OF IT.

New York Dolls

d Bowie

Marc Bolan

Sweet

UNDONE TO THE NAVEL

Putting the sex into unisex

Earrings

Spandex

Feather boas

Striped poor-boy shirts

Thigh-high boots

Velvet bell bottoms

Anything in Lurex and lamé

Silver leather

Gold leather

Eye shadow

Hennaed hair

Girls' blouses

Opera gloves

Snakeskin boots

Bump-toe and platform shoes

Costume jewelry

Studded T-shirts

Lightning bolts and stars

Enormous belts

Chain belts

Silk scarves

Hip-huggers

Satin anything

Sequins

Glitter

LIKE EVERY PREPPY KID, THE **SHOES** I GREW UP WEARING WERE WHITE BUCKS WITH BRICK RED SOLES, JUST LIKE THE KIND PAT BOONE WORE, AND I WEAR THEM TO THIS DAY. BUT WHEN IT CAME TO GLAMOUR, NOTHING FIT BETTER THAN A PAIR OF HIGH-HEELED SNAKESKIN BOOTS.

Seventies snakeskin boots.
Photograph by Bill Steele

Pat Boone and his white bucks

Nancy Sinatra and her boots

Carl Perkins without his blue suede shoes

Shoe Biz

In the beginning, rock and roll made a point. So did rock and roll shoes, from R&B's shiny black oxfords to Carl Perkins's blue suede shoes. When rock went "white bread," Pat Boone made white bucks and round-toed saddle shoes popular. Then came the Beatles, who refashioned ankle-high Chelsea boots into pointy-toed boots with stacked Cuban heels. In the late sixties and seventies, rock shoes made big news with platform soles and bulbous "bump toes," and boots went thigh-high. Mick Jagger, who had been hanging out with ballet greats Nureyev and Baryshnikov, wore Capezio jazz oxfords onstage in 1975, starting a trend that was revived in the eighties by such British New Romantics as Duran Duran. Punk revitalized the fifties crepe-sole suede shoe (also known as a "brothel creeper") and introduced Doc Martens to the world. In the nineties, Docs still rule, while rappers and latter-day punks have embraced classic sneakers and high-tech high tops as their footwear of choice.

WHEN **STUDIO** OPENED, IT WAS A REAL BUZZ. HALSTON, GUCCI, FIORUGI, SATIN SHIRTS AND DESIGNER JEANS. WE WENT EVERY NIGHT BECAUSE WE NEVER KNEW WHAT TO EXPECT AND WE DIDN'T WANT TO MISS ANYTHING. IT'S HARD TO IMAGINE NOW THAT PEOPLE ACTUALLY PARTIED LIKE THAT AND WERE ABLE TO FUNCTION THE NEXT DAY.

Now everybody can get into Studio 54

Jeans advertisement. Photograph by Gordon Munro

Minnelli, Halston, and
e Rubell

David Geffen and Joni Mitchell

LaToya and Michael Jackson

Andy Warhol, Debbie Harry, and
Grace Jones

Polyester

In England, just after World War II, J. T. Dickson and J. R. Whinfield of
the Calico Printers Association devised a way to spin molten polymers—
giant molecules created by combining elements from coal and petro-
leum—into threads, creating the first polyester fiber. DuPont purchased
the patents in 1950 and 1952, coining the term "wash and wear" to
describe a blend of cotton and acrylic. Polyester was first produced in
mass quantities in 1953.

Early polyesters were called modacrylic, Acrilan, Dynel, Orlon, and
Chromspun. Nice, but spongy and impenetrable, with problems holding
dyes. As technology advanced, polyester became refined enough to imitate wool, down, suede, silk, or rubber, depending on how the chemicals
were processed. Polyester seemed a miracle fabric, holding its color and
shape in perpetuity and requiring virtually no care.

In the early seventies, to compete with the "natural" backlash, the
evil synthetic fiber took on such trade names as Kodel, Fortel, Crepesoft,
and Golden Touch. And by 1974 double-knit polyester ruled the world:
leisure suits, pantsuits, slacks, and shirts in fab textures, boffo colors
like powder blue and terra-cotta red, fluorescent flares, and eye-poking
patterns like paisley and peace symbols.

In 1977, John Travolta made polyester history in his white SATURDAY
NIGHT FEVER suit. By the eighties, however, polyester was deemed
gauche; synthetic microfibers were in. But that was just gilding the lily.
By the end of the nineties, tight, wildly patterned polyester clothes—or
polyester mixed with cotton and Lycra in athletic clothes—became the
most fashionable clothes on the club scene.

Disco Duds

DAY	NIGHT
A. Smile	Fiorucci
Bonhomme	Gucci
Pierre Cardin	Halston
Faded Glory	Charles Jourdan
Gentleman John	Kenzo
Huk-A-Poo	Nik Nik
Landlubber	Pucci
Michael Millea	Gloria Vanderbilt
Flo Toronto	Diane Von Furstenberg
Truth & Soul	Claude Montana
Viceroy	Jordache
Billy Whiskers	Sasson
	Bonjour
	Willi Wear
	Thierry Mugler

A GROUP OF YOUNG PEOPLE DECIDED TO PUT OUT MESSAGES OF LIFE IN A RHYTHMIC WAY. NOW A LEGITIMATE FORM OF EXPRESSION,

HIP-HOP

CONTINUES TO MAKE HISTORY. IT ALL BEGAN AS A RESULT OF THE YOUTH CULTURE EMBRACING AND WEARING STATUS SYMBOLS, DESIGNER LABELS, AND ATHLETIC NAMES AND WEAVING THEM INTO THEIR TESTIMONY. THE COMMUNITY HAS BEEN AND CONTINUES TO BE AN INSPIRATION TO ME—HOW I LOOK AT FASHION AND DESIGN FOR THE YOUNG PEOPLE.

The Fugees. Photographed by Matthew Rolston

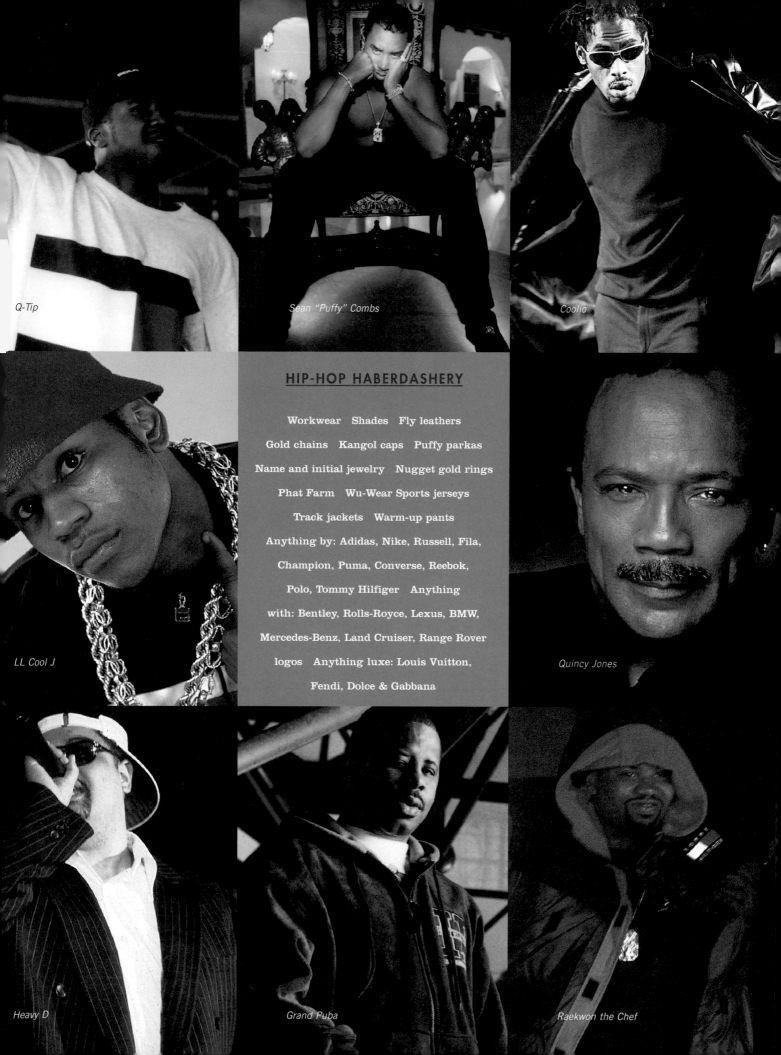

Q-Tip

Sean "Puffy" Combs

Coolio

LL Cool J

Quincy Jones

Heavy D

Grand Puba

Raekwon the Chef

HIP-HOP HABERDASHERY

Workwear   Shades   Fly leathers

Gold chains   Kangol caps   Puffy parkas

Name and initial jewelry   Nugget gold rings

Phat Farm   Wu-Wear Sports jerseys

Track jackets   Warm-up pants

Anything by: Adidas, Nike, Russell, Fila,

Champion, Puma, Converse, Reebok,

Polo, Tommy Hilfiger   Anything

with: Bentley, Rolls-Royce, Lexus, BMW,

Mercedes-Benz, Land Cruiser, Range Rover

logos   Anything luxe: Louis Vuitton,

Fendi, Dolce & Gabbana

THE **ALTERNATIVE** LOOK IS A COMBINATION OF MUSICAL AND VISUAL STYLES INFLUENCED BY SKATEBOARDING, PUNK ROCK, HEAVY METAL, AND RAP. IT'S AN ANTI-FASHION STATEMENT THAT HAS DEVELOPED INTO ITS OWN FORM OF CHIC BY DRAGGING WELL-WORN AMERICAN CLASSICS OUT OF THE CLOSETS AND THRIFT SHOPS AND ONTO THE ROCK AND ROLL STAGE.

Kurt Cobain

THE ALTERNATIVE ESSENTIALS

Essential alternatives from A to X

Adidas

Airwalk

Baby-doll dresses

Backpacks

Baggy butt jeans

Baseball caps

Ben Sherman shirts

Black Flys

Body piercing

Boxer shorts

Carolina boots

Caterpillar boots

Converse One Stars

Dee Cee

Dickies

Doc Martens

Earrings

Flannel

Georgia Giants boots

Goatees

Heavy-metal T-shirts

Jams

Milkfed clothes

Mohair sweaters

Muscle cars

Nail polish

Oakleys

Pocket watches

Red Wing boots

Tattoos

Thermal (waffle-weave) underwear

Too-big and too-small shirts

Underground comics

Vans

Watch caps

Wallets with chains

X-Girl

X-Large

EVERYONE WANTS TO BE IDENTIFIED AS PART OF A CERTAIN GROUP OR **TRIBE.** I THINK PEOPLE PERCEIVE THEMSELVES AS BEING A CERTAIN TYPE AND THEN FOLLOW THAT TO THE ABSOLUTE. THEY BECOME FANATICAL ABOUT HOW THEY LOOK AND HOW THEY DRESS AND GO TO GREAT LENGTHS TO BECOME THIS PARTICULAR PERSON. SO THEIR CHOICE OF CLOTHING, HAIRCUTS, SHOES, GLASSES, JEWELRY, CASUAL WEAR, UNDERWEAR, AS WELL AS WHERE THEY GO AND HOW THEY GET THERE, IS ALL WRAPPED UP INTO THEIR PSYCHOLOGICAL BEING.

West Side Story, *1961*

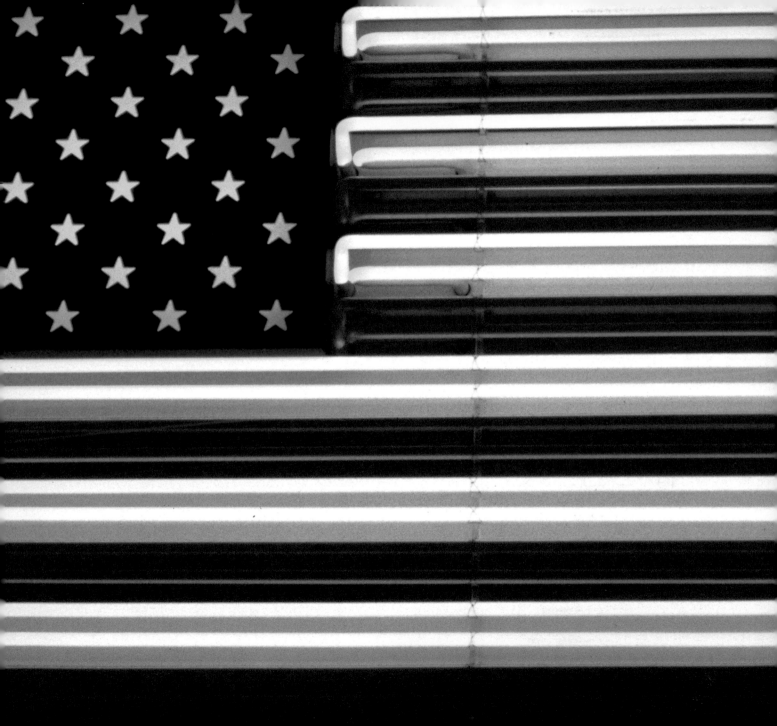

Putting this book together, compiling my memories of growing up, my thoughts about America, my ideas about the way we live, has made me realize that style is nothing less than the way we carve out our existence. It is what we like and what we don't, the things that make our hearts beat faster and make us feel comfortable. It is our individual eccentricities and our common interests.

Today we live in a society composed of different tribes and customs. Pop culture is our common denominator. It comprises people, places, ideas, and objects that constantly influence each other, causing new hybrids in style. There is music-inspired fashion and pop songs about shopping and runway models. There are products designed to look like Warhol paintings and TV commercials that push the frontiers of filmmaking in 60 seconds or less. Hip-hop fans adopt preppy fashions while suburban kids borrow looks and ideas from urban kids. Appropriation has become an art form in itself. We work and speak in a language that is derived from many cultural sources. We are equal-opportunity employers of a vast, ever changing world of personal styles.

I see this trade-off taking place, and it motivates me to do new, innovative things. I can take ideas from the past or from the future and put them together in a meaningful way for tomorrow. Anything is possible. After all, I have been through 40 years of cultural change, from Ozzie and Harriet to Nirvana and the Notorious B.I.G. I have experienced the excitement of being young and reckless and all the contentment of becoming a successful businessman and a happy, loving family man. I still get a rush every time I hear Pete Townshend strike a chord or listen to Run DMC rap about their Adidas. And, in my own way, I believe I am as much a producer of pop culture as I am a product of it.

I wouldn't have it any other way. The way Americans dress and work and play has become a standard for the rest of the world. And with technology opening new doors every day, the world is getting smaller every day. Style is still a highly personal quality, but it is one that causes ripples throughout the world. With the World Wide Web, e-mail, and digital TV, it is only natural that we will develop new cultural icons that will expand our understanding of style and our expression of it. As the culture changes, I've found that fashion is just one means of communication, so it's time to explore the world of style from the inside out with TV, video, books like this, music, and the Internet. As a man of pop culture, I hope to continue to investigate how it works, how ideas and images can be put together, taken apart, and reassembled. I want to learn who sets the styles and how it all comes about. And what it all means.

ADDITIONAL ACKNOWLEDGMENTS Editorial associates: Nadine Hwa, Orville Kiser, Robin Maltz, Samuel Pizarro II, Anne Marie Purdy, Maura Reilly, and Tara Rodgers. Additional research and writing: Charles Cermele, Jeff Indusi, Lance Loud, Seven McDonald, Katy McNerny, Stephen Saban, Rachel Small, and Mike Vague. Additional picture research: John Clarke, Ari Form, and Ana Ossowski.